The Bootstrapper's Guide to the Mobile Web

Practical Plans to Get Your Business Mobile in
Just a Few Days for Just a Few Bucks

by Deltina Hay

Quill
Driver
Books

LIBRARY
Fresno, California

Notice of Copyright

Published by Quill Driver Books,
An imprint of Linden Publishing.
2006 S. Mary, Fresno, California 93721
559-233-6633 / 800-345-4447
QuillDriverBooks.com

Edited by Ric Williams

Cover design by Jason Hranicky

Interior layout by Deltina Hay

ISBN: 978-1-61035-052-5

Printed in the USA on acid-free paper.

Library of Congress Cataloging-in-Publication Data

Hay, Deltina.

The bootstrapper's guide to the mobile web : practical plans to get your business mobile in just a few days for just a few bucks / by Deltina Hay.

p. cm. -- (The bootstrapper's guide)

Includes bibliographical references and index.

ISBN 978-1-61035-052-5 (pbk. : alk. paper)

1. Mobile commerce. 2. Mobile communication systems--Economic aspects. 3. Web site development. I. Title.

HF5548.34.H39 2012

658.8'72--dc23

2012001383

Notice of Liability

For my father—printer, newspaper man, designer, commercial fisherman, restaurateur, bookkeeper, barkeep, architect, drafter, carpenter, plumber, electrician, motel owner, poet—the greatest bootstrapper I ever knew.

Acknowledgments

Thanks

Special thanks to Dragonfly Designs, Milano Cafe, Plumb Web Solutions, Social Media Power, Quill Driver Books, and Comedy Sportz for volunteering their mobile web strategies and mobile sites as examples. And special thanks to Dave Evans and Paul Gillin for permission to use their head shots and books in the Social Media Power examples.

Special thanks to Sue Dyson for her contributions and hard work, and a special thanks to Jason Hranicky for his continued hard work and patience.

A very special thanks to my friend and editor, Ric Williams, who keeps my writing understandable and periods at the end of my bulleted list items. And thanks and love to my mother, who continues to support my bootstrapping nature.

The author is especially grateful to Kent Sorsky and the entire staff of Linden Publishing for their continued confidence.

Permissions Granted

The mobile screen shots used in this book were taken with the "No Root Screen Shot It" app created by Edward Kim.

The author would like to thank the following companies for permission to use their screen shots. The following are trademark holders of the listed services' logos, graphics, designs, page headers, button icons, scripts, and other services. All rights are reserved and used by permission:

© Adobe and PhoneGap are either registered trademarks or trademarks of Adobe Systems incorporated in the United States and/or other countries.

© Afilias Limited and mTLD Top Level Domain Ltd. 2011: goMobi, ready.mobi, dotMobi. The dotMobi and goMobi logos are used by permission of mTLD Top Level Domain Ltd.

© Akmin Technologies Pvt Limited 2011: mobiSiteGalore. All rights reserved.

© Appcelerator, Inc. 2011: Appcelerator Titanium. All rights reserved.

© appMobi 2011: appMobi. All rights reserved.

© Azalea Software, Inc. 2011: Qrdvark. All rights reserved.

© bMobilized 2011: bMobilized. All rights reserved.

© BraveNewCode, Inc. 2011: WPTouch. All rights reserved.

© Cowemo, Inc. 2011: Mobile Phone Emulator. All rights reserved.

Trademark Notice

Boot·strap: to help oneself without the aid of others; use one's own resources. —*Webster's Dictionary*

Table of Contents

2. Mobile Applications   107

3. Mobile Marketing Tactics   185

List of QR Codes

1. Mobile Websites

2. Mobile Applications

3. Mobile Marketing Tactics

Introduction

"Rapid ramp of mobile Internet usage will be a boon to consumers, and some companies will likely win big (potentially very big) while many will wonder what just happened." —Morgan Stanley[1]

Why the Mobile Web, and Why Now?

There is a lot of hype today about how many people own mobile devices and how much time people spend on them. One survey found that "one third of Americans are more willing to give up sex than their mobile phones[2]." While this is a great quote for shock value, all it really tells us is that people are pretty darned fond of their smartphones.

Indeed, look at some overall numbers:

- There are presently 5.3 billion mobile device subscribers[3].
- There will be nearly as many mobile devices as there are people in the world by 2015[4].
- There are 48 million people in the world who have mobile phones, even though they do not have electricity at home[4].
- SMS (text messaging) traffic is expected to break 8 trillion in 2011[5].

So everyone has or will have a mobile device. What's the big deal? Everyone needs a phone, right? What does this matter to our website optimization or online marketing efforts? The following numbers reveal the business impact of an increasingly mobile world more clearly:

- By 2012, almost all mobile devices produced will be able to access the Internet[6].
- There will be 788 million mobile-only Internet users by 2015[4].
- By 2014, mobile Internet browsing will surpass desktop browsing[1].
- Mobile ad revenue will sky rocket to $20.6 billion by 2015[7].
- Shopping on the mobile web will reach $119 billion in 2015[8].

The issue is not that everyone has a mobile device, but that they all have *Internet access* via that device—and that many of them access the web *only* through their mobile device. More importantly, they are taking advantage of that access by searching, purchasing, and clicking through on mobile ads at unprecedented rates.

This is great news for those of us who market on the Internet. But it can be equally *bad* news for those who are not prepared for this mobile opportunity. Imagine that someone visits your conventional website from their mobile device and your site loads so slowly the user just moves on to the next site in their search results. Or perhaps your site eventually loads, but with no images and with a gaping hole where that spiffy piece of Flash you paid so much for is supposed to play. Or worse, the user receives a message from their browser informing them that your site cannot be viewed on their mobile device. These are very possible scenarios for a website that is not mobile-ready.

You have invested a lot of time, effort, and money into creating and optimizing your web presence. Now is not the time to let that go to waste as your customers transition to using their mobile devices to access your company!

Luckily, you have a host of solutions available to get your web presence mobile-ready, with many of them taking very little time, effort, or money to implement. If you have HTML experience, you can use responsive web design to create separate styles sheets without the need to alter your existing website code, or use new web standards found in HTML5 and CSS3 to create your site from scratch.

But don't despair if you do not have web programming experience. There are many tools and services you can use to create a successful mobile web presence. Many of these solutions require very little time or money. There are specific mobile solutions available for those of you who use CMS solutions like WordPress as well.

The Bootstrapper's Guide to the Mobile Web outlines mobile website best practices and explores many possible solutions for your mobile website, providing you with the knowledge to make an informed decision about the options available. You can then use the strategy worksheets and real-world examples featured in the book to help implement your chosen solution. The book also addresses important considerations and decisions you need to make for your mobile website such as creating custom domains, detecting and redirecting mobile traffic to your mobile site, and addressing search engine optimization issues.

We also address the hot topic of mobile apps. Mobile applications can offer you or your business an unencumbered environment in which to engage your audience. A well-planned mobile app can give you a lot of additional exposure, and improve customer interaction and brand loyalty. Mobile apps can also be great outlets for selling products and services.

But mobile apps are not for everyone. Depending on their complexity, mobile apps can be expensive to develop and maintain. Your efforts may best be put into improving your mobile website and making it easy for users to save your website as a shortcut on their mobile device's home screen. This book helps you weigh the pros and cons of mobile apps and helps you decide if they will be a good addition to your overall mobile web strategy.

There are some nice tools and services that can help you create affordable mobile apps easily. If you have some programming experience, you can program apps yourself or utilize user-friendly frameworks to help create your app. Mobile app services range in complexity and price, but offer some nice (and affordable) alternatives to programming or spending a lot of money on development.

The web-app-versus-native-app debate is ongoing in the mobile app development world. This book shows you the difference, as well as alternatives such as creating web apps that can be easily converted to native apps. More important, the book provides you with the knowledge you need to weigh your options and make the decisions that work for you now and will grow with your future plans. Once your decision is made, you can then proceed with your mobile app plan using the worksheets and examples provided in the book.

Still, the mobile web is more than just mobile websites and mobile apps. New technologies often give rise to innovative approaches to marketing. QR codes are one such example. These nifty little bar codes bridge the gap between the digital and physical world in a way that opens up a whole new approach to online marketing. This is made possible by the portable nature of the mobile device.

And let's not forget social media! Not only are social networking sites the second most accessed mobile apps (behind games), but there is a "local" trend to social media that is ever present on mobile devices in the form of location-based services. Local businesses can especially benefit from a location-based marketing plan on sites like Yelp, foursquare, Google Places, and more.

Research has shown that mobile device users click through on ads far more often than desktop users[9]. Mobile web advertising requires a different approach than what you may be used to. If you use Adwords, you need to focus your efforts on ads targeted to mobile devices. And you always want to make sure that your mobile ads send users to mobile-optimized landing pages or websites.

This book helps you take full advantage of these additional mobile web opportunities by providing plans, strategies, resources, and real-world examples. Looking to the future, the book also takes a close look at augmented reality, near field communication, and other mobile trends that are fast becoming mainstream.

If you *really* want to be prepared for the mobile web—the entire mobile web—this book is for you!

Make no mistake: Mobile *is* the future of the Internet, and now *is* the time to act. This book is designed to help you prepare for this imminent future.

What Is the Mobile Web?

Thinking of the mobile web as just a new way of using the same old Internet is a mistake. The mobile web is more than just people using smaller screens to access the Internet. It is also about how people are changing the way they use the Internet, and the new tools that are emerging as a result. The mobile web is also changing the way people search on the Internet, thus having a major impact on search optimization techniques.

As we discover in the first chapter of this book, "Mobile Websites," the way people browse the mobile web is different, as are their expectations of websites and how they take action on those websites. In the second chapter, "Mobile Applications," we discover that people love spending time using mobile apps, but they use mobile browsers equally as much. The final chapter, "Mobile Marketing Tactics," explores emerging tools and current search trends that are equally important to a successful mobile web presence.

Mobile Devices and Markets

A mobile device is defined as a small, hand-held computing device, typically having a display screen with touch input and/or a miniature keyboard. In this book, when we refer to a mobile device, we are referring to feature phones, smartphones, and tablet computers like the iPad.

Predictions show that the mobile phone market will be dominated by Android, iOS (Apple), Windows Phone (which recently merged with Nokia), and Blackberry platforms (in that order)[10]. The examples in this book reflect these predictions by focusing on these top platforms.

Who Should Read This Book

This book is for the bootstrapper: the resourceful business owner, the motivated author, the innovative entrepreneur, the head of your company's IT or marketing department, as well as the student of marketing, media, PR, web design or development, or Internet studies.

The author's previous book is used in countless universities as the basis in courses on social media. This text can be equally as useful as a basis in courses on mobile marketing and mobile web design.

Web designers and developers should use this book to expand their offerings to include mobile web design, mobile marketing, and mobile search trends.

If you maintain your own website, you will benefit from reading this book, especially if you have a stake in the Internet economy.

How to Use This Book

There are three chapters in this book: "Mobile Websites," "Mobile Applications," and "Mobile Marketing Tactics." Each of these chapters is a stand-alone guide to its respective topic. The introduction to each chapter can help you decide whether the contents of the chapter are relevant to your objectives.

The "Mobile Websites" and "Mobile Applications" chapters outline options, planning guides, strategies (along with worksheets), and examples to help you find the best solution for your mobile website or application.

The "Marketing" chapter addresses additional mobile tactics and tools such as QR codes and location-based marketing, complete with strategies and plans for integrating these tools into your existing marketing strategy.

Bootstrapper's Guides

The opening page of each chapter has a summary of what is in the chapter as well as a "Bootstrapper's Guide." This guide can help you navigate to sections that are most relevant to your needs, thus saving you time.

Additionally, each major section of a chapter has its own Bootstrapper's Guide that outlines the contents of the respective section. The reader could, theoretically, just read all of the Bootstrapper's Guides in the book and walk away with a good understanding of how to proceed with their mobile web strategy.

Bootstrapper's Guides are not offered for sections that are strictly instructional, like strategy worksheet sections or specific examples of tools and techniques.

QR Code Enhancements

Throughout the book, you will find QR codes that take you to websites, tutorials, videos, and extensions of the book's contents, such as additional examples, example strategies, or online forms.

QR codes are bar codes that, when scanned by a mobile device, redirect the user to a URL or perform some other function. Read more about QR codes on page 186. You need a QR code scanner to access the QR codes in this book. Many smartphones come with pre-installed scanners, but there are many scanners available in case yours does not[11].

At the end of each chapter are "QR Code Notes" that summarize the destination of each QR code featured in the chapter, and provide a direct link in case you would rather access the QR code destination using the direct URL from a browser. If you have the e-book version of the book, the QR code images link directly to their destination.

Resources

Resources cited within the body of the text are included as endnotes. Additional resources can be found at the book's companion site, TheBootstrappersGuide.com.

This companion site to the book contains linkable resources and suggestions for further reading organized by chapter. The site also contains links to online forms and worksheets to be used in your entire mobile web strategy. You will notice references to the resources, sheets, and forms throughout the book. Each chapter concludes with a section that outlines what can be found on the companion site for that chapter.

Glossary of Terms

The glossary of terms at the end of the book is not meant to be an exhaustive list of terms used in the book. They are terms that may not be defined within the text, or are used prior to being defined.

Conventions

Endnotes: Sources and tools referenced within the body of each chapter are cross-referenced as endnotes at the end of the respective chapter using Chicago Style Guidelines.

Navigation: Navigation on a site or within an application is depicted as "First Level Menu Item/Second Level Menu Item/Third Level Menu Item" and so forth.

Interchangeable Terms

The following sets of terms are used interchangeably throughout the text:

- "Key Term," "Keyword," and "Tag"
- "Widget" and "Badge"
- "URL," "Link," and "Hyperlink"
- "Internet" and "Web"
- "Clickable" and "Tap-able"

Online Support

Visit the book's companion site, TheBootStrappersGuide.com, for links to resources, support, Facebook pages, Twitter accounts, and other ways to reach the author or publisher of this book.

Examples Used in the Book

We discuss many different software and online platforms throughout this book. It is important for you to note that these platforms are constantly changing. However, we have tried to give you a general idea of the capabilities of each one, so that even if the look and feel of a platform changes, you will still have an understanding of its functionality.

Even though we may demonstrate only a few platforms for a given topic, please be aware that there are many other choices available. Our demonstration methods are not meant to be preferential; they are meant to offer the reader the best overall approach to a successful experience in the mobile web.

Endnotes

1. Morgan Stanley. "Internet Trends." http://www.morganstanley.com/institutional/techresearch/pdfs/Internet_Trends_041210.pdf

2. Telenav. "Survey Finds One-Third of Americans More Willing to Give Up Sex Than Their Mobile Phones." http://www.telenav.com/about/pr-summer-travel/report-20110803.html

3. ITU. "ITU estimates two billion people online by end 2010." http://www.itu.int/net/pressoffice/press_releases/2010/39.aspx

4. Cisco. "Cisco Visual Networking Index: Global Mobile Data Traffic Forecast Update." http://www.cisco.com/en/US/solutions/collateral/ns341/ns525/ns537/ns705/ns827/white_paper_c11-520862.html

5. PortioResearch. "Mobile Messaging Futures 2011–2015." http://www.portioresearch.com/MMF11-15.html

6. Gartner. "Gartner Outlines 10 Mobile Technologies to Watch in 2010 and 2011." http://www.gartner.com/it/page.jsp?id=1328113

7. Gartner. "Gartner Says Worldwide Mobile Advertising Revenue Forecast to Reach $3.3 Billion in 2011." http://www.gartner.com/it/page.jsp?id=1726614

8. ABI Research. "Shopping by Mobile Will Grow to $119 Billion in 2015." http://www.abiresearch.com/press/1605-Shopping+by+Mobile+Will+Grow+to+%24119+Billion+in+2015

9. Google Mobile Ads Blog. "Smartphone user study shows mobile movement under way." http://googlemobileads.blogspot.com/2011/04/smartphone-user-study-shows-mobile.html

10. Gartner. "Gartner Says Android to Command Nearly Half of Worldwide Smartphone Operating System Market by Year-End 2012." http://www.gartner.com/it/page.jsp?id=1622614

11. 2d Code. "QR Code and 2d Barcode Readers." http://2d-code.co.uk/qr-code-readers

1 Mobile Websites

"Anything Google creates...will first be placed on the mobile platform and then be worked around for the desktop...I believe that in 3 years desktop computers will be irrelevant." —Google CEO Erik Schmidt, 2010[1]

In This Chapter

How People Use the Mobile Web

Why a Mobile Website?

Planning Your Mobile Website

Mobile Website Best Practices

Options for Creating Your Mobile Website

Preparing Your Strategy, Preparing Your Content, Example Strategies

Step-by-Step Website Examples

Custom Domains, Mobile Traffic Detection and Redirection

Optimization, Testing, Analytics, Promotion

Bootstrapper's Guide

I don't have time for statistics: Skip to page 11

I don't need to be convinced, show me how to start: Skip to page 12

Give me a list of best practices, and I'll be on my way: Skip to page 16

I don't need a strategy, just tell me my options: Skip to page 24

Take me straight to the meat, I'll wing it as I go: Skip to page 34

I have a mobile website, show me how to improve it: Skip to page 79

Mobile Websites

We shared some impressive statistics about general mobile usage in the introduction to this book, but there are some interesting numbers when it comes to the use of mobile *browsers*, too. Initially, many industry thought-leaders predicted mobile apps would put an end to users searching for information and businesses on traditional browsers. The numbers show a different story.

A June 2011 comScore study showed that browsers were used by 40.1 percent of mobile subscribers, while downloaded applications were used by 39.5 percent[2]. Gartner predicts that "By 2013, the combined installed base of smartphones and browser-equipped enhanced phones will exceed 1.82 billion units and will be greater than the installed base for PCs thereafter[3]." They go on to say that "Websites not optimized for the smaller-screen formats will become a market barrier for their owners...."

With most service providers offering 3G or 4G service, browsing the Internet using mobile devices is much easier for users today. And with browser usage surpassing downloaded applications, you can count on your customers looking for you online. The question is whether or not your site is ready for them.

How People Use the Mobile Web: I Want It NOW!

▶ **Bootstrapper's Guide** ◀

√ People don't "surf" the mobile web.
√ They know what they want and act on it.
√ They want location, news, social media, and products.
√ They recommend, buy, and follow up more than desktop users do.

It is important to understand that people browse differently on mobile devices than they do on their desktop computers. Users don't typically "surf" the web using mobile devices. Their motives are intentional and action-based. They know what they are looking for and they are more likely to take action once they find it.

Consumers use mobile search mostly to access local information, stay informed, buy products, and download music and videos.

In a study from Google conducted by Ipsos OTX[4]:

- Search engine websites are the most visited websites, followed by social networking, retail, and video sharing websites.

- Nine out of 10 smartphone searches results in an action (purchasing, visiting a business, etc.).
- 24% recommended a brand or product to others as a result of a smartphone search.
- 95% of smartphone users have looked for local information.
- 88% of these users take action within a day, indicating these are immediate information needs.
- 77% have contacted a business with 61% calling and 59% visiting the local business.
- 79% of smartphone consumers use their phones to help with shopping, from comparing prices and finding more product info to locating a retailer.
- 74% of smartphone shoppers make a purchase, whether online, in-store, or on their phones.

Take these facts into consideration when creating your mobile website. When a potential customer lands on your site, assume they are there for a specific purpose. Your goal is to predict the customer's intentions, and make certain there is a way for them to take action easily without navigating away from your site. If your site loads too slowly, does not clearly present actionable items, or if content and buttons are too small for visitors to access, they will likely move on.

Why a *Mobile* Website: A big deal

> ### ▶ Bootstrapper's Guide ◀
> ✔ Mobile websites need to load fast and be free of Flash.
> ✔ Mobile websites need to adhere to industry standards.
> ✔ If a site is not compliant, it will not be listed in directories.
> ✔ If your site is hard to navigate on mobile devices, folks will move on.

You may think your website displays fine in mobile browsers, even if it is a little small. So what's the big deal? As we will see, just having a mini version of your existing website is not going to cut it. You need a *mobile* version of your website that addresses all of the following issues.

Load Time: Slow Kills

While a website designed for mobile will load in around four or five seconds, a traditional website can take as long as 40 seconds to load on a mobile device. Not only will this lead to much frustration for your site visitors, but it will also keep your site from placing well in mobile searches.

Mobile Searches: You Want In

Even if your site displays properly in mobile browsers, it may not be indexed by mobile search algorithms. When one uses a search engine on a mobile device, the search query accesses a separate index maintained for mobile content. If your website is not optimized for mobile search engines, it will not place well in such search results.

Mobile Browser Standards: Different Strokes

Mobile browsers do not work the same as desktop browsers. They do not render video, Flash, image galleries, and many other software and scripts in the same manner as desktop browsers. Most mobile browsers simply ignore Flash. If your site uses Flash or other proprietary software, it may not load in mobile browsers at all. A mobile version of your website that adheres to mobile standards as set by W3C's mobile web initiative[5] will solve these issues.

User Experience: Convenience Matters

As noted earlier, users have different expectations when browsing with mobile devices. Not only are they seeking specific information when they land on your site, but they also expect an experience that is consistent with the device they are using. If you force users to do the "pinch and pull" (magnify your site) in order to read your content or navigate your site, they will probably move on.

You want to maintain as much control as possible when it comes to how browsers display your content, as well as what content is most accessible to your mobile site visitors. Always keep your users in mind, and present your site and content in a way that is most convenient for them and the device they use.

Planning Your Mobile Website

> ### ▶ Bootstrapper's Guide ◀
>
> ✓ Plan for user expectations: Why are they coming to your site? What are they seeking? What type of actions are they likely to take?
> ✓ Define business objectives: Outline immediate goals and resources.
> ✓ List the must-have features for your site based on the previous steps.

Later in the chapter we explore a number of mobile website solutions, but first you need a plan for determining which solution best suits your overall strategy. You may be tempted to pursue a solution because it seems the most convenient or affordable, only to discover down the line that it does not offer the features you need. Creating a mobile website strategy helps you identify needs such as what content to include on your site and which features can help present that content. Look for specific example strategies later in the chapter, but for now think in broad strokes.

User Expectations

Earlier we discussed how people use the mobile web: In a nutshell, they visit websites on their mobile devices with intentionality and typically take action on those intentions. They spend most of their time seeking contact and local information, visiting social media sites, researching retail products, and downloading music and video. Keep these behaviors in mind as you develop your mobile website strategy.

Specifically, try to answer the following questions about prospective site visitors:

Why are they most likely coming to your site?

If your business is local, visitors are most likely looking for your hours or location. If you sell products, they have probably come to your site to learn more about what you sell.

What information are they most likely seeking?

Again, if you have a local business, chances are they are seeking contact information, a map, or perhaps a menu. If your business is strictly online, they may be researching product or service information.

What type of actions are they most likely to take?

For a local business, they want to click on a map, review a menu, call your business, etc. If you are selling products on your site, they want to click on a product review or a buy-now button.

Or, you could just ask...

If you happen to have a large customer database, newsletter, emailing list, or something similar, launch a poll or questionnaire and ask your customers directly what they would like to see on your mobile site.

Once you have the answers to the questions above, you will have a better idea of what content you should place on your mobile website, and where.

Business Objectives

Examine your goals, resources, and other factors that may have a bearing on how you develop your mobile website. To that end, answer these questions:

What are your immediate goals?

There may be a number of angles you can take with your mobile site. Use this opportunity to refine your goals. For example, if you have a retail business with local outlets and also sell products online, you should prioritize whether your goals are to drive customers to your retail locations or sell online products. Keep in mind that mobile device users are not necessarily going to navigate around your mobile site—you may only have a few seconds to solicit an action from them.

What are your resources?

Include a detailed estimate of how much time and money you can allocate to your mobile site. Also include ongoing time and money that can be budgeted for upkeep of the site.

Are there any other factors that may restrict how you develop your mobile site?

For instance, is your business restricted from making specific calls to action or from advertising your location?

Features to Consider

Armed with the content you want to prioritize on your mobile site, you can now look at specific features that can help you present your content in a convenient way to your visitors. There are some features only available to mobile browsers like the "click to call" feature, while other features—like how you display multimedia—will need to be altered to work properly on mobile browsers.

The following list is not exhaustive, but outlines some of the most important features you will likely want on your mobile website. Add a list of relevant features to include on your site in your mobile website strategy.

Click-To-Call Buttons

This feature is *only* available to users browsing with a mobile device. It allows a user to click on a phone number to place the call with their mobile phone.

Social Media Buttons

Recall that mobile device users spend a lot of time on social media sites. Be certain to place buttons to your social media profiles where they can be found easily.

Share and Enjoy

Make it easy for visitors to share your site with their own social networks by including sharing badges or "email a friend" options.

Google Maps

Offering visitors an interactive map with directions to your location is a must-have feature for any business with a physical address.

Forms

Since mobile device users are very likely to take action once they land on your mobile site, make it easy for them to do so by offering online forms where applicable.

SMS

Many mobile device users prefer using SMS (text messaging) over email, even for subscription services like RSS feeds and newsletters. If you typically send notifications to a mailing list, consider adding SMS to your campaigns, and offering SMS subscription options on your mobile site.

Event Calendars

If your business or organization hosts events, offer an easy way for them to access event information and add it to their personal calendar.

Location Check-In

Location-based tools like foursquare, Yelp, and Google Places are very popular among mobile device users and can drive a lot of traffic to a local business. Allow visitors a way to "check in" from your location on your mobile site if applicable. See page 195 for more on location-based services.

Multimedia

Keep in mind that one of the goals of a mobile-friendly website is to present the most relevant content to site visitors without a lot of clutter getting in the way of it. To that end, you should consider not placing a lot of images or video on your site. If, however, multimedia is relevant to getting the message across about your business, use the practices discussed in the following section to choose the best method for placing multimedia on your mobile site.

News/Blogs

As we already discovered, mobile device users like to access news and blogs from mobile browsers. If you have a blog, RSS feed, or regular newsletter, make it easy for visitors to find a method for subscribing to it.

E-Commerce

If one of your goals is to sell products on your mobile site, make certain whatever e-commerce method you use works on mobile browsers. PayPal and Google Checkout both have mobile options, as do many popular shopping cart services. Research the service you are presently using to confirm they have a mobile-friendly option, or plan to use a different method.

Industry Specific Features

Check for mobile-friendly versions of features that are necessary to your industry. For instance, if you are a real estate agent and use a database service that provides listings for your website, contact the service to find out if there is a different API you must use to access their database from a mobile browser.

Another scenario may be that you are an author or publisher and want to sell Amazon books on your site. Rather than using the Amazon widgets designed for desktop browsers, use widgets or applications specifically designed for mobile websites.

This step may take a bit of research, but it will be worth the effort to be fully prepared when the time comes to build your site.

Mobile Website Best Practices

> ### ► Bootstrapper's Guide ◄
> ✔ A mobile website should load fast, have no Flash, and very few images.
> ✔ Design for simplicity: Avoid scrolling, horizontal menus, and clutter.
> ✔ Prioritze content, be concise, and make it easy for users to take action.
> ✔ Take advantage of mobile features, and check your site for errors.

Regardless of the specifics of your strategy or the solution you choose to create your site, there are some best practices that should be applied to all mobile websites. Follow these practices when developing and designing your mobile website, or use them as a guide when choosing a service to create and/or host your site.

Keep It Simple: Simple=Good

First and foremost, keep your site simple. If you plan to design your own mobile site or create a mobile version of your existing website, you may be tempted to create something clever or innovative, but that could seriously damage the user experience of your site. This does not mean that you can't create something beautiful and unique, just don't ignore the suggestions in this section as you do so.

In general, keeping your site simple means eliminating most images; simplifying navigation, layout, and design elements; eliminating Flash and other proprietary software; keeping your site free of clutter; and breaking up text and other content. These tactics will keep your site size and load time to a minimum, which is essential to user experience and good search engine placement. This approach will further improve user experience by making the overall functionality of your site more conducive to the mobile experience.

You may be thinking, "So, what is left to make my site stand out from the crowd?" That is a good question. Many of the services we explore later in the chapter offer templates that can be customized to reflect your personal or business branding. If you plan to create your own site, HTML5 and CSS3 can help you create very attractive sites while still keeping your site fast loading and free of proprietary scripting. CSS3 is especially handy for creating gradients, rounded corners, drop-shadows, and many other design elements. We explore this in more detail later in the chapter.

Prioritize Content: 1, 2, 3

Use your mobile website strategy to help you choose the most important content to feature on your site. Space is in high demand on a mobile site and site visitors are on the go, so you need to anticipate what content users will most likely want to access. Choose the three most important content items and make those items easy for users to find and act upon.

Focus on Conversion: Easy Action

Your mobile website should offer a more action oriented experience than its desktop counterpart. Recall that users are not *browsing* your mobile site—make it easy for them to *do* the things they are most likely wanting to do, like find store locations, buy or review products, review menu items, place calls to your business, or request additional information.

Use the click-to-call feature to make it easy for customers to call a store location or customer service representative. Keep forms simple and easy to complete by eliminating unnecessary fields and using radio buttons and check boxes wherever possible. Make your "calls to action" prominent with large buttons and/or bulleted lists.

Take Advantage of Mobile Features: Location, location, location

Like the click-to-call button, there are features specific to mobile devices that can be used to improve your site user experience. The most useful of these features is location, both yours and the customer's. By accessing user location information, you can offer a more personable experience. Other native phone functionalities like GPS, camera, audio/video players, and notepad can also prove useful as each can be utilized to offer quick access without a lot of wasted space.

Think "Tap-able" not "Clickable:" Oops free

Design your site's buttons, navigation items, and links for touch screens, not for a mouse. This will improve the user experience and prevent accidental navigation away from your site.

Make sure your links and buttons have plenty of padding, and are large enough to be pressed by thumbs. Your call-to-action buttons should stand out from the rest of the links on a page. Label buttons descriptively so users know exactly what a button does or where it will take them.

Do not use hover-over features on your mobile site. A thumb cannot "hover" over an item on a mobile site, so avoid integrating that feature altogether. This includes the use of drop-down navigation menus that require the user to hold down the main navigation items in order to access sub-navigation elements.

Navigation: Go Vertical

Figure 1.1:
Vertical navigation example.

Pay special attention to the navigation on your mobile website. Keep in mind the "tap-able" issues discussed above, as well as scrolling and readability issues. Also keep in mind that typing is not always easy for users on mobile devices, so your navigation methods are critical to your visitors finding their way around your mobile site.

Your navigation menu should not scroll left or right. If your menu items are too long to fit horizontally, create a vertical navigation structure (see Figure 1.1). Keep your text readable, so users know what each navigation item does.

Always include a "back" button on the pages of your mobile site. Mobile devices do not make it easy for users to navigate back and forth like desktop browsers do.

Scrolling: Minimize It

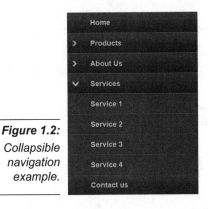

Figure 1.2:

Collapsible navigation example.

Mobile users prefer to scroll from top to bottom, so design your site so that left to right scrolling is eliminated. Smartphones have the option of changing to landscape orientation to accommodate wider sites, but a smart design should not force a user to do so.

You should keep the need for scrolling—even top to bottom scrolling—to a minimum. One tactic you can employ to reduce scrolling is collapsible navigation (see Figure 1.2). If you have a lot of information on your site, you can organize the content into large chunks that can be expanded or contracted by the user by tapping on accordion style modules.

Much scrolling can also be eliminated or reduced by formatting your content wisely. The next section addresses this issue.

Formatting Content: Be Concise

Content is still king, even on the mobile web, and there are plenty of ways to keep your valuable content available to your visitors while still maintaining a simple, readable, and error-free mobile site.

While many of these tactics also apply to the standard version of your website, they are *critical* to a well-designed mobile website:

- Make headers prominent and concise. Remember that you have even less time to grab a reader's attention on a mobile site, so don't try to be clever with your headers or headlines—they should reflect exactly what the reader will garner from further reading.

- Text should be readable at arm's length, and broken up with "read more" links or collapsible navigation (see previous section). Use bulleted lists when formatting your text, and avoid the use of images wherever possible.

- Shorten excerpts for blog posts and news items, providing readers an option to tap a link to read the full post or story.

- Avoid placing too many links within the body of your text, especially if the links are close together.

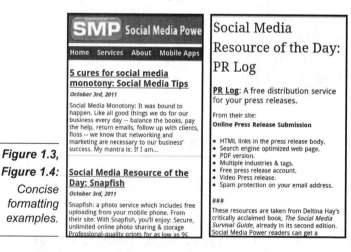

Figure 1.3, Figure 1.4: Concise formatting examples.

Overall Site Design: Simple Usability

Your mobile website design should focus on simplicity and usability. Designing for a smaller screen can be challenging, and requires eliminating many elements we take for granted on desktop sites. The following best practices can help:

- Do not clutter your site with paid ads or unnecessary elements. Include only buttons or links to popular items, services, or products. Eliminate all other links and ads.

- Use CSS to organize content on your mobile site. HTML tables will not render properly on mobile devices. Do not use them.

- Use plenty of white space on your site, and use lighter colored backgrounds. Lighter colors create a roomier feel on any website. Avoid using background images on mobile sites.

- Place a search box prominently on your mobile site. This will make it easier for visitors to navigate your site, and can cut down on the amount of content needed to be visible on any given page.

- Avoid placing images, audio, or video directly on your mobile site, but if it cannot be avoided use the best practices discussed in later sections.

- Single column layouts are the best choice for mobile websites. If you have multiple columns or "sidebars" on your desktop website that you want to use, they will work best below the main content area on your mobile site.

Proprietary Technologies: Beware

Be careful when choosing proprietary software to use on your mobile site. Many smartphones and tablets will not render Flash or Silverlight, which are programs that help create animation and other multimedia for the web. You may run into issues with third-party scripts as well.

Some developers are even concerned that JavaScript will not work on future smartphones, but that is unlikely. The main reason Flash and software like it is not supported is that they tend to take up a lot space and a lot of bandwidth. JavaScript, on the other hand, is more efficient in those areas.

Test any software or scripts you are considering on a mobile device to make sure it renders properly, or research its documentation and check forums to see if others are using it successfully on their mobile sites. We discuss testing on page 24 and in detail on page 90.

Page Size: Smaller Is Better

Page load time (how fast a page renders in a mobile browser) plays a major role in how well a site places in mobile search engines, and can also determine if someone stays on your site or not. Recall that a website designed for desktop browsers can take up to 40 seconds to load on a mobile device, a far cry from an optimized mobile site that should take around four seconds.

The optimum page size for a mobile site is no more than 25 kilobytes (KB); 10 KB or less is a very good number to shoot for.

Images: Crunch 'Em

The two main factors to consider when deciding to include images on your mobile site are space and speed. Recall that fast load times are essential to an optimized mobile site, and images tend to take a long time to load. Also recall that mobile users are content motivated—they are not necessarily "browsing" or "admiring" your mobile site, rather, they are there for a purpose.

This doesn't mean you should avoid images altogether, just rethink whether they are necessary to the goals of the site. A few images are fine, but excessive use will degrade your site's efficiency.

If you are going to include images, here are some guidelines to follow to assure they are as optimized as possible:

- Use only .jpg or .gif formatted images.
- Reduce the size and resolution of images as much as possible.
- Use an image crunching service like Crunch4Free[6] to help reduce image sizes.
- Recall that the optimum page size is around 20KB; images can exceed that size very quickly.
- Always include alternate text for images—many mobile browsers will not display images; including alternate text will keep your site looking complete.

You may also find that your goals require the use of image galleries to display your products, art, events, etc. Some of the services we explore later in the chapter offer built-in image gallery options, and there are some other mobile-friendly image gallery solutions you can explore, such as Galleria[7].

Make certain any gallery solution you choose is specifically designed for use on the mobile web or has a mobile web option. Also make certain it does not use Flash or other proprietary software as discussed earlier.

Video/Audio: Make Them Ask for It

Just as for images, including video and audio on your mobile site can affect load times and usability. And even though smartphones and tablets handle audio and video very efficiently, the mobile browser rendering your mobile website may not do such a good job.

These rich media sources can be valuable for delivering an effective branding message, so it is understandable if you need to include them. Here are a few considerations to keep in mind if you plan to include audio or video on your mobile site:

- Do not use Flash, Silverlight, or other formats that are not compatible with mobile devices.
- Optimize your audio and video files so they are as small as possible.
- Never auto-download or auto-play audio or video files—wait until it is requested.

Use YouTube or HTML5 to Render Video

YouTube does a good job of serving up video on mobile devices. Rather than streaming the video yourself or relying on other proprietary software, consider using YouTube to place video or full video galleries on your mobile site. See page 77.

HTML5 has a video tag that renders video very efficiency. This is a good choice if you are creating your own mobile site. See the example on page 77 for more information.

URL: Dotmobi Versus Sub-domains

You have a few choices for what type of URL to use for your mobile site. You could purchase a domain name using the "dotmobi" or ".mobi" extension so your site would have a URL like "yoursitename.mobi." Or, you could place your mobile site in a directory on your main website and assign it a name like "m.yoursitename.com," "mobile.yoursitename.com," or "yoursitename.com/mobile." See the "Configuring Custom Domains" section on page 79 for more information on how to accomplish this.

If you choose to create your mobile site using one of the services we explore later in the chapter, you may be forced to use a domain name that they assign to you, like "yourname.theirsitename.com." Some services give you an option of pointing your own domain name to your mobile site, in which case you could use one of the options mentioned above.

It is most common to find a website's mobile version at a URL like m.example.com. The advantage to this approach is that site visitors do not get confused when redirected to the mobile version of the site, and if this practice becomes standard, people will be able to find your mobile site more easily if they do not know the direct URL offhand.

Redirecting Visitors to Your Mobile Site: Let Them Choose

When someone accesses your website using a mobile device, there are ways you can make sure the mobile version of your site is what they see. One way is to redirect them to the mobile version of your site, while another way is to use methods that serve up different versions of your site, depending on what device a visitor is using to access the site. We discuss these methods in detail in the "Detection and Redirection" section on page 81.

Regardless of how you redirect visitors to your mobile site, it is always best to allow them the option of viewing the standard version of the site. Since many devices display standard websites with no problems (even if a bit small), some of your visitors may prefer to view that version of your site rather than the mobile version. To accommodate this, you should place links at the bottom of your website that directs visitors to either the standard or mobile versions of the site.

Testing Your Mobile Site: W3C It

Mobile browsers are not as forgiving as desktop browsers when it comes to errors. Your site may not render at all if it does not validate (pass a web standards test).

The best place to test your mobile website for errors is the W3C mobileOK Checker[5]. This tool not only checks your site for errors, but checks page sizes, load times, image sizes, and many other factors that can keep your mobile site from displaying properly in mobile browsers.

Use this tool to test your mobile site, even if you are using a service to create and host your site. If you find problems on a site provided by a service, bring the errors to their attention.

We discuss testing mobile websites, including emulators that allow you to see how your site looks on different devices, in more detail on page 90.

Options for Creating Your Mobile Website

> ### ▶ Bootstrapper's Guide ◀
> √ Create your mobile website yourself as a stand-alone mobile site.
> √ Use responsive web design to create a site that resizes for any device.
> √ Use a service to create/host your site, or to convert your existing site.
> √ For a WordPress or CMS: Use a plugin or service, and be selective.

There are a number of options available to create your mobile website, but not all solutions are going to be a good fit. At this stage of your strategy, take a look at your needs and choose a solution based on those needs. Detailed examples of each solution outlined here are featured later in this chapter.

Creating the Site Yourself

If you already manage your own website, you may want to create the mobile version of the site yourself. You can create either a brand new site from scratch and redirect mobile users to it, or you can incorporate responsive web design to accommodate mobile device and tablet users alike.

Responsive Web Design

The general idea of responsive web design is to do the overall design of your site one time, then incorporate methods of serving up different versions of your site depending on the device that is accessing the site.

The most common method used to achieve responsive design is to create different style sheets for different devices. You might have one style sheet for the desktop version of your site, another for the tablet version, and yet another for the smartphone version.

Using methods such as the media query tag in your CSS style sheets, you can control the look of your site based on the screen size or other characteristics of the device accessing your site. We demonstrate this method in detail on page 62.

Stand-Alone Mobile Site

If you decide that your existing site—even with responsive design—is not a good fit for mobile devices, yet you still want the control of creating the site yourself, there are a couple of decisions to make ahead of time.

First, which URL structure will you use? We discuss those options in the best practices section on page 23. If you do not want your mobile site affiliated with your desktop site, create a unique domain name for the mobile version. Otherwise, it is becoming standard for the mobile version of a website to be found at m.yoursitename.com.

Second, how will mobile device users access your mobile site? If you have decided on a truly stand-alone site that is not affiliated with your existing site, then this is not an issue for you. If you want your desktop site visitors to be automatically directed to the mobile version of your website, then there are scripts you can use to make this happen. If you prefer not to use redirection, you can place a button on your desktop site that takes visitors to your mobile site.

See page 69 for a detailed example of a stand-alone mobile site. You can learn more about redirection of your mobile site in the "Detection and Redirection" section on page 81.

Using a Service

There are quite a few services that can create your mobile website for you (see the resource section of this chapter). There are even some nice do-it-yourself (DIY) platforms that we demonstrate later in the chapter. If you choose to use a service, be sure to use the best practices section (page 16) from this chapter as a guide when deciding.

The DIY services come with different levels of complexities and can be broadly categorized into two types: hosting services and conversion services.

Hosting Services

You can create your mobile website using the host's platform. Some platforms are very basic, offering only a few features, while others are robust enough to host enterprise solutions. Costs can vary widely.

There are other variations in these services, too. Some of them host your site for free in exchange for placing ads on your site, while others offer you the opportunity to become part of a community of mobile sites. Beginning on page 34, we demonstrate a representative sample of these services. Which of these platforms you choose depends on your strategy.

Once you create a mobile site using this type of service, you usually have the option of redirecting your existing site visitors to your hosted mobile site. The service typically provides you with a bit of code to add to your desktop site that detects mobile devices and redirects them to your mobile site accordingly (see page 81 for details). Some services do not offer redirection, so do your homework if you need this feature.

Conversion Services

This type of platform recreates one or more pages of your existing website, optimizes those pages for mobile devices, then provides you with a method for redirecting your existing site users to the mobile version of your site. There are variations of this method among services, but this is the most common procedure.

Conversion can be a good solution if you already have a lot of pages on your site that you want to offer on the mobile web. This solution also offers you a consistent branding experience across all devices and browsers. However, many conversion services use a process called "transcoding." This process can adversely affect search optimization efforts. Read more about this issue on page 89. Go to page 56 for a detailed example of this type of service.

CMS Solutions

If you use a CMS (Content Management System) to power your website, then you have a few options available. There are a number of plugins available to help you accommodate mobile device users, especially if you use WordPress, Joomla!, or Drupal. You can use some of the DIY services demonstrated in this chapter for certain CMSs. There are even some services that specialize in optimizing CMS sites for the mobile web.

When choosing a plugin, don't choose one because it seems the most convenient solution. As our examples on page 57 demonstrate, there are big differences in individual plugin solutions. Since there is usually little effort involved in setting up CMS plugins, it may be worth setting up a few and weighing them against the best practices list in this chapter.

There are demonstrations of WordPress solutions beginning on page 57. Drupal and Joomla! solutions can be found in the resource section of the chapter.

Deciding Which Option Is Best for You

Refer to the previous sections of your strategy and investigate whether a solution fulfills your strategy requirements. Specifically, does a solution:

- Satisfy user expectations?
- Align with business objectives, including cost and time to maintain?
- Have all—or the most important—desired features?

Compare your solution choices against the best practices outlined in this chapter. It is unlikely you will find a solution that passed all of these practices with flying colors, but a good solution will come pretty close.

Design Limitations: Colors And Logos Matter

Consider the design limitations of your solution choices. Though you don't want to overdo design elements on your mobile site, you still want a solution that allows you to have a consistent branding experience—even if it is only custom colors and logos.

URL: It Matters

Pay special attention to the URL structure and redirection options available for each solution in consideration. Does the solution allow you to choose or point your own domain name or sub-domain structure (e.g., m.yoursitename.com or yoursitename.com/mobile)? Does the solution offer a way to redirect your desktop site visitors to your mobile site?

URL: Who Gets the SEO Hit

URL structure is particularly important to good search engine optimization (SEO). If you expect the mobile version of your site to increase the search engine placement of your desktop site, then make certain your solution allows you to create your own URL structure. If your mobile URL structure uses the service's domain name, that is not helping your placement, it is helping theirs.

URL: Redirection (yes) and Duplication (no)

Site redirection and duplicate content are some other factors that can affect good SEO of your desktop and mobile sites. Refer to the "Search Optimization Considerations" section on page 84 for a more detailed discussion and effective workarounds.

Validation: They Should Know Better

If you are paying a service to host or convert your mobile website, the resulting site should validate. Service providers should stand behind their products and offer you a site that is up to industry standards. If possible, check a demo site from a service on the W3C mobileOK Checker to see how the site rates.

Metrics: Make Sure It Counts

Does the solution offer a way to check analytics and metrics for your mobile site? Most of the hosted and conversion services have a way for you to link your own Google Analytics account to your mobile site so you can track the performance of your site. Some services have their own built-in tracking methods.

Marketing: Have QR, Will Widget

Marketing is an important factor to consider once your site is complete. If you are choosing a service, check that it offers features like QR Codes and custom widgets to help market your site. See page 186 for more on QR codes.

Include your option choice(s) in your mobile website strategy. If you have more than one preference, include the pros and cons of each.

Solving Conflicting Issues: Research First, Happy Later

Your site may need a feature that conflicts with mobile website best practices. If that is the case, you should explore as many alternate solutions as possible.

For example, if a site must have an image gallery, how can that be achieved while still keeping page sizes within standards? Possible solutions are to:

- Find a hosted solution that offers an efficient gallery feature.
- Provide a link to an external gallery like Flickr or Picasa.
- Offer a link to a mobile-optimized gallery page on your desktop site.

Or perhaps the site needs a shopping cart, which could slow the load time of the site. In that case, it would be best to do one of the following:

- Sell products directly from an optimized stand-alone site.
- List links to a third-party site like Amazon or Ebay.
- Provide a link to a mobile-optimized page on your desktop site.

Preparing Your Strategy

You are now ready to create a thorough strategy for your mobile website. Below is a worksheet to use as a guide. An online version of this worksheet can be accessed from QR Code 1.1 on page 33 or from the resource section of this chapter. Sample strategies can be found by accessing QR Code 1.3 on page 34, or from the resource section of this chapter.

Mobile Website Strategy Worksheet

This worksheet can help you plan an effective strategy and solution for your mobile website. Refer to the corresponding sections of the book for examples and clarification of specific questions.

I. User Expectations

Answer the following questions about prospective site visitors:

- Why are they most likely coming to your site?
- What information are they most likely seeking?
- What type of actions are they most likely to take?
- If you sent a questionnaire to your mailing list, what did they suggest?

II. Business Objectives

Answer the following questions about business goals, resources, and limitations regarding your mobile website:

- What are your immediate goals?
- How much money can you invest in the set-up of your mobile site?
- How much money can be budgeted for hosting and maintenance of the site (per month)?
- How much time can be allotted to this project, initially?
- How much maintenance time can be allotted (per month)?
- Are there any industry specific limitations that should be placed on this site? See page 14 for examples.

III. Features

Select the features that should be included on your mobile website:

- ☐ Click-to-call
- ☐ Social Media Buttons
- ☐ Sharing Badges
- ☐ Google Maps
- ☐ Forms
- ☐ Event Calendar
- ☐ Location Check-in
- ☐ Multimedia (photos/music/videos)
- ☐ News/Blogs
- ☐ E-commerce
- ☐ SMS
- ☐ Industry Specific (specify below)
- ☐ Other (specify below)

List industry specific or other features to include on your site, if applicable.

IV. Mobile Website Options

Use the respective section in the book to help decide which option to use to create your mobile website.

How will you create your mobile website?

- ☐ Create the site yourself
- ☐ Use a service
- ☐ Use a CMS solution

If you plan to create the site yourself, will you:

☐ Use responsive web design
☐ Create a stand-alone site

If a stand-alone site, what will be the URL structure of the site?

☐ Unique domain name
☐ Sub-domain like m.yoursitename.com
☐ Sub-directory like yousitename.com/mobile

If a stand-alone site, how will visitors to your desktop site access your mobile site?

☐ Automatically be redirected using a script
☐ Access via a button or link

If you plan to use a service, will it be a:

☐ Hosting Service
☐ Conversion Service

If you need a CMS solution, will it be a:

☐ Plugin
☐ CMS conversion service
☐ Theme

V. Solution Criteria

Refer to the previous sections of this strategy and answer these questions for each solution you are considering.

Specifically, does a solution:

☐ Satisfy user expectations
☐ Align with business objectives, including initial cost and maintenance
☐ Have all—or the most important—desired features

Additionally, does a solution:

☐ Offer design choices sufficient for branding needs
☐ Have the desired URL structure options
☐ Provide preferred redirection methods
☐ Offer methods to track analytics and metrics
☐ Provide features like custom QR Codes to help market your site

Are there any conflicting issues to resolve (see page 29 for an example)? If so, list alternatives here.

VI. Best Practices

Rate your solution for each of the relevant mobile website best practices found on page 16. How well does a solution adhere to or help accomplish these practices?

VII. Weighing Options

List your final choice(s) here. If you are considering more than one solution, list the pros and cons of each option.

Solution	Pros	Cons

VIII. Conclusion

What is your final choice?

What compromises were made in favor of this solution?

Discuss conflicting or unresolved issues as they relate to your final choice, and list alternative solutions to resolve them.

Briefly outline the next phase of your strategy, if applicable.

Preparing Your Content

▶ Bootstrapper's Guide ◀

√ Prepare shorter bios, business, product, and services descriptions.
√ Prepare metadata sets including keywords, titles, and descriptions.
√ Use image crunchers to reduce image sizes, prepare alt text for images.
√ Gather URLs to social media, blogs, geo-location sites, and products.

Once your strategy is in place, use it to prepare the content you will need. Try to resist the urge to just "wing it." Proper preparation of your descriptions, biographies, metadata, and other content will help to optimize your mobile site. Follow QR Code 1.2 to an online preparation form.

Text

To cut down on page size, you should conserve the amount of content on your mobile site. Prepare abbreviated and edited versions of:

- Your business description
- Personal biographies
- Product descriptions
- Services

Metadata

Prepare metadata sets for your mobile site. A "set" of metadata consists of a list of keywords, a meta title, and a meta description. If you are creating your own site, prepare a metadata set for each page of your site. If you are using a service, you will likely only need one set. Refer to page 84 for more information on metadata. Prepare each metadata set using the following guidelines.

- Prepare a list of 20 one, two, and three-word keywords, listed in order of relevance. Keywords are the terms that help search engine robots properly categorize your website in the search engines.
- Prepare a meta title that contains one or more of your keywords. Meta titles should be no longer than 60 characters.
- Prepare a meta description that contains as many keywords as possible. Meta descriptions should be no longer than 160 characters.

Images

Gather the images you want to use on your mobile site. For each image:

- Use an image cruncher[6] to reduce the file size as much as possible.
- Rename each using some of your best keywords for optimization purposes.
- Prepare alternate text that includes keywords.

QR Code 1.2:
Complete your prep online[2].

QR Code 1.1:
Complete your strategy online[1].

Links

Gather relevant links to:

- Social media and location-based service accounts
- Multimedia you want to feature
- Products
- Blogs or RSS feeds

Mobile Website Strategy Examples

Follow QR Code 1.3 to view mobile website strategies based on real world examples, including the examples featured throughout the book. Look in the resource section at the end of the chapter for a link to these strategies and for a form you can use to help develop your own strategy. Strategies include a local restaurant, consulting service, online retail sales, affiliate link site, personal branding, news/blog site, landing pages, lead generation, performance, PR, retail, and more.

Mobile Website Service Examples

▶ Bootstrapper's Guide ◀

There are many hosting and conversion services, but set-up is similar:
✔ Set up the account, set up features, customize menus and design;
✔ Set up custom domain, redirect from your main website, optimize;
✔ Test your site, promote your site, track your site using analytics tools.

Featured here are some representative samples of hosting and conversion services you can use to create your own mobile websites. Hosting service examples begin on page 35. A conversion service example can be found on page 56.

We discuss the use of services in detail on page 26. Refer to the "Deciding which option is best for you" on page 27 for recommendations on how to choose the right service for you.

QR Code 1.3:
Example
strategies[3].

These examples are meant to give you an idea of how to set up a mobile website using a hosting or conversion service. They are not intended to show preference to any specific service. Individual platforms will change, and new ones will sprout up, so the intention of this section is to walk you through a number of scenarios so you know what to expect once you choose a service. Though each platform is different, the general process for creating your mobile site remains the same. Here is an outline of the steps you will likely take to create your site using a service:

- Set up your account.
- Choose and set up features (hosting services).
- Configure navigation and content (conversion services).
- Customize your design.
- Choose domain/publishing options: choose your domain name and point it to your mobile site, if applicable.
- Set up redirection of mobile visitors from your desktop site to your mobile site.
- Populate metadata and other settings for search optimization and directory listings.
- Test your mobile site prior to publishing, if applicable, and certainly after publishing.
- Set up synching with Google analytics or investigate other analytics and metrics features.
- Take advantage of all marketing features offered by the service such as widgets and QR codes.

goMobi

GoMobi[8] is a hosted solution with a lot of features, but it does not have a free option. GoMobi uses partners—Internet hosting providers like Network Solutions and Name.com—as a way to offer their platform. You need to get an account with one of their partners to get the service. We chose Network Solutions[9] for our example—they offer the service for $5.99/month with a 30-day trial. See QR Code 1.4 for goMobi examples.

QR Code 1.4:
GoMobi
examples[4].

Setting Up Your Account

Go to the goMobi site and click on "Get goMobi." This takes you to a list of their providers or "partners." Choose the partner you want and get an account. If you choose Network Solutions, your main account screen should look like Figure 1.6. Click on "Launch Setup Assistant" to create your mobile site. The platform for creating your mobile site (whether you choose Network Solutions or not) should look similar to Figure 1.7.

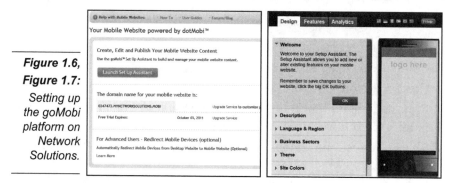

Figure 1.6,

Figure 1.7:

Setting up the goMobi platform on Network Solutions.

Customizing Your Design

The goMobi platform is very straightforward. As shown on Figure 1.8, there are three tabs on the main platform: Design, Features, and Analytics. From the "Design" tab, click "Description" (see Figure 1.7). Enter a site name and description as shown in Figure 1.8.

Figure 1.8,

Figure 1.9:

Choosing a goMobi theme.

Use a short blurb or tag line for your description so it does not interfere with the features you place in the next step. Set your language, region, and business section (category) on this tab before moving on to choosing a theme and site colors.

Click on the "Themes" feature. Figure 1.9 shows the available themes. GoMobi produces icon-driven sites, where each of the navigation items and other features are represented by icons on the main page. Choosing a theme, therefore, means choosing the icon styles that most appeal to you.

Click on "Site Colors." With the "Site Colors" tab open, click on "Options" (see Figure 1.10). This gives you more control over your site colors. Figure 1.11 shows how to upload your logo once you click on the "Logo" option.

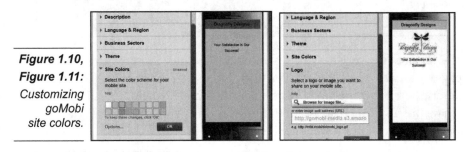

Figure 1.10,

Figure 1.11:

Customizing
goMobi
site colors.

Setting Up Features

Go to the "Features" tab as shown in Figure 1.12. GoMobi has a lot of features to choose from, so refer to your strategy to help decide which ones you need for your site. Many of the features are simply icons that represent actions such as clicking to visit a full website, as seen in Figure 1.12.

Figure 1.12,

Figure 1.13:

Setting up
goMobi
features.

Other features are more robust and require more set up. Figure 1.13 shows part of the process for setting up a gallery in goMobi.

All of the features have an "Options" link that opens to more options for each feature. These options vary depending on the feature, but all of them include options to change the position of the feature on the main page, the icon that represents the feature, and the display name for the feature. See Figure 1.14 and Figure 1.15.

Figure 1.14,

Figure 1.15:

Setting up goMobi features (2).

The features are very easy to set up, and if you need to create customized pages, you can place HTML (for formatting or adding links) within the description boxes in many of the features (see Figure 1.16). Figure 1.17 shows the resulting page when the "invitations" icon is clicked. Figure 1.18 shows the "Leave a Message" feature.

Figure 1.16,

Figure 1.17,

Figure 1.18:

Setting up goMobi features (3).

Custom Domain Options

Return to your main account area (see Figure 1.19), and click on "Customize Domain Name." You are given two options: purchase a new domain name or point a domain name you own to your mobile site (see Figure 1.20). You can use a sub-domain like m.yoursitename.com, if you like.

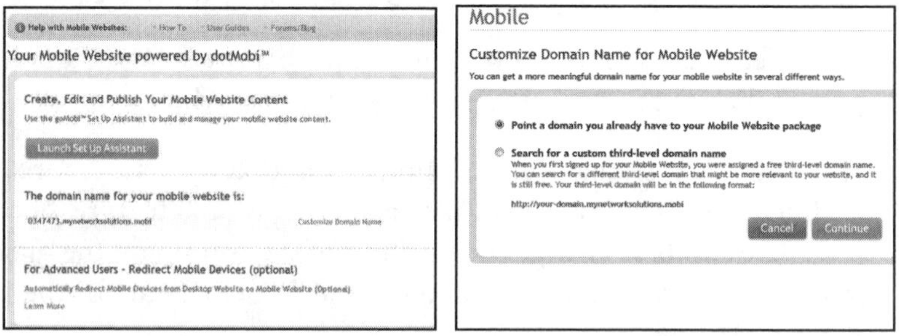

Figure 1.19,

Figure 1.20:

Custom domain options in goMobi.

Click "Continue" to enter the domain name you wish to use, and enter the name on the next screen as shown in Figure 1.21. Click "Continue" again and you are taken to the screen that contains the CNAME record information you need to point your domain name (see Figure 1.22).

Figure 1.21,

Figure 1.22:

Setting up a custom domain in goMobi.

Make a note of the information on this screen and go to the section "Configuring Custom Domains" on page 79 for instructions on how to finish this task.

Setting Up Redirection

GoMobi offers code for redirecting mobile device users to your mobile site from your desktop site. From the main account page (see Figure 1.19), click on "Learn more..." under the section called "For Advanced Users." Figure 1.23 shows the result. Figure 1.24 shows the instructions once you click on "See instructions for enabling redirect...."

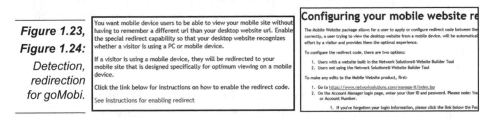

Figure 1.23,

Figure 1.24:

Detection, redirection for goMobi.

On this screen (see Figure 1.24) there is a PDF file (not shown) you can download with instructions and the necessary code needed to redirect your mobile traffic. Download this file, and refer to the "Detection and Redirection" section on page 81 if goMobi's instructions are unclear.

Search Optimization Settings

Figure 1.25 shows the "Traffic Booster" feature (under "Features"). Here is where you add your best keywords and description for your mobile site.

Figure 1.25:

goMobi optimization features.

Analytics Features

Figure 1.26 shows how you can synch your goMobi mobile site with an existing Google Analytics account (under "Features"). To use this feature you need a Google Analytics ID. Go to Google Analytics[10] to set up your account and enter the ID in this feature once you have it. GoMobi also has its own analytics feature. Click on the "Analytics" tab to access the feature.

Figure 1.26, Figure 1.27: goMobi analytics features; Marketing a goMobi site.

Marketing Options

GoMobi has a QR code feature you can use to generate and download a QR code to place on your desktop site or on print materials to help market your site (see Figure 1.27). Go to page 186 for more information on QR codes.

Testing Your Site

Use W3C mobileOK[5] and ready.mobi[11] to test your new mobile site's URL. The sites we tested from goMobi passed both tests. Refer to the "Testing Your Mobile Website" section on page 90 for more information.

mobiSiteGalore

MobiSiteGalore is a hosting service that offers quite a few features and still has a free option. The one thing it does not offer, however, is an automatic redirection solution. See QR Code 1.5 on page 46 for examples.

Setting Up Your Account

Once you have an account, click on "Add New Website." Figure 1.28 shows the resulting screen. From here, enter the name of your new mobile website. The name you enter here is only for your reference; you choose the actual domain name later. Choose the "pack" you want. "Pack" refers to pages. You can have a 3-page site, a 10-page site, etc. The 3-pack option is free, while the 10-pack option runs $156/year.

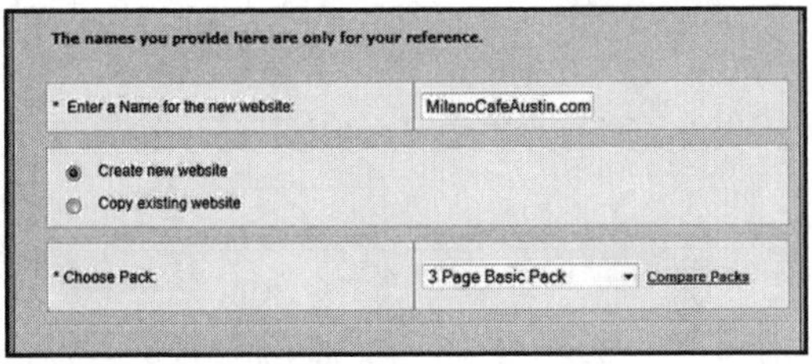

Figure 1.28:

Setting up mobiSite.

Customizing Your Design

Click on the "Manage Website" button from the next screen. From here (see Figure 1.29), you can choose a theme—only certain themes are offered at the free level. Available color schemes are limited to the choices you see once you click on a theme (see Figure 1.30). From this screen you can also view how the theme looks on various phones and tablets.

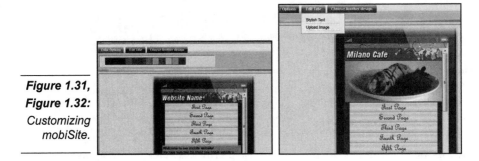

Figure 1.29,
Figure 1.30:

Choosing a mobiSite theme.

Click on "Choose This Design" once you have decided on the theme you want. Figure 1.31 shows the next screen, which allows you to choose a color scheme, customize the title, and add a header image if you like. Click on "Edit Title" and you can change or remove the header text and upload an image. Figure 1.32 shows our finished design.

Figure 1.31,
Figure 1.32:

Customizing mobiSite.

Setting Up Your Features

Clicking "Next" brings you to where you can choose your pages. Figure 1.33 shows how you can label and build your own pages, or choose from a large selection of ready-made pages offered by the mobiSiteGalore platform. At the free level, you only have two additional pages other than the home page, so refer to your strategy as to the best choices. Once you choose your pages, click on "Submit."

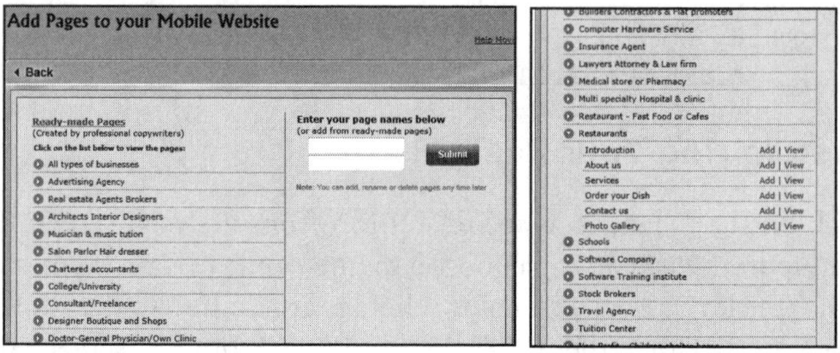

Figure 1.33:

Setting up pages in mobiSite.

Figure 1.34 shows our example site with pages. You can change page names or add more pages (with an upgrade) later. Click "Accept Design" to continue populating your pages.

Figure 1.34:

Setting up pages in mobiSite (2).

Figure 1.35 shows the resulting screen. From here (the "Website Manager") you can add features to your site, edit pages, edit design options, and more. Click on "Goodies" to see the available features.

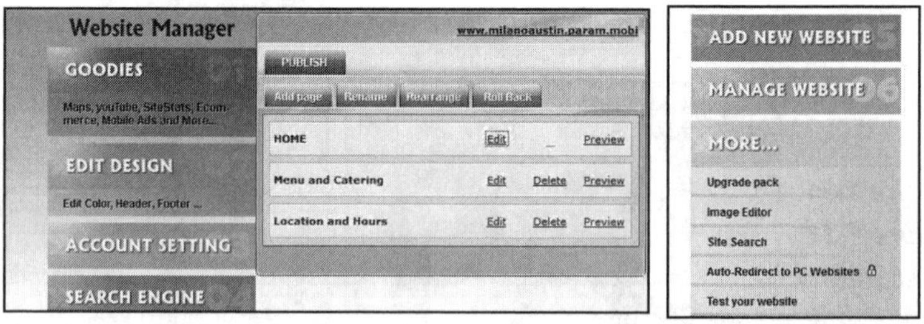

Figure 1.35:

Setting up features in mobiSite.

MobiSiteGalore has a nice selection of features as shown in Figure 1.36, though many of them are not available at the free level. All of the general features are available, save for the RSS feed feature, and the only feature available from the other categories is the YouTube video option. These limitations can work for some strategies, but if you need to import blog posts or sell products, you will need to upgrade.

Figure 1.36:

Setting up features in mobiSite (2).

To place a feature on your site, click on the feature. You can then place it on whichever page you choose, and in the position you wish as shown in Figure 1.37 and Figure 1.38.

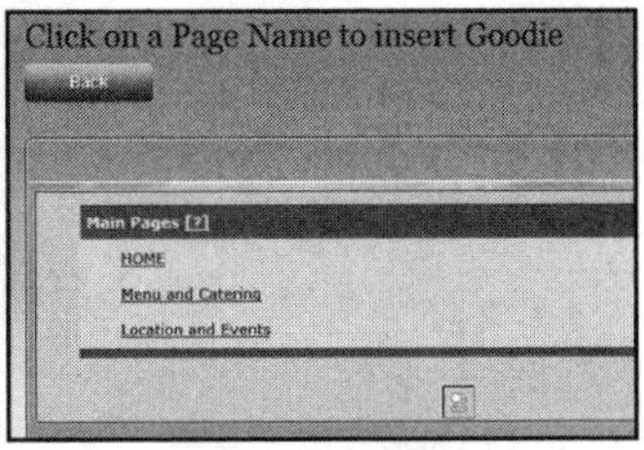

Figure 1.37,

Figure 1.38:

Setting up features in mobiSite (3).

Once you place your first "goodie" you can continue editing content, adding goodies, and customizing your pages from the formatting platform shown in Figure 1.39. When finished, click "Submit Changes."

Figure 1.39:

Setting up features in mobiSite (4).

Figure 1.40, Figure 1.41, and Figure 1.42 show our completed pages for Milano Cafe.

Figure 1.40,

Figure 1.41,

Figure 1.42:

Finished mobiSite pages.

Search Engine Optimization Settings

MobiSiteGalore has a search engine optimization feature, so our next step is to populate our meta title, description, and keywords for each of our pages. See page 84 for information on creating good search engine metadata.

Click on "Search Engine Optimization." Figure 1.43 shows the results. This service also has links to submit your site to the Google and Yahoo! search engines—click on these once your titles, descriptions, and keywords are in place.

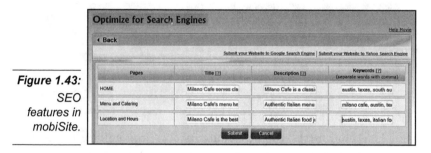

Figure 1.43: SEO features in mobiSite.

Domain/Publishing Options

MobiSiteGalore offers several publishing options. Figure 1.44 shows the resulting screen once "Publish Options" is clicked. Your choices are to:

- Use a domain name that mobiSiteGalore offers. This results in a domain name as shown in Figure 1.45.
- Use your own domain name that points to your mobiSiteGalore mobile website.
- Host the mobile website yourself using your own domain name.

The second and third options require you to upgrade your account, but could be worth the expense if you want your mobile domain name to be affiliated with your desktop site (such as m.yoursitename.com). If you choose one of these options, refer to the "Configuring Custom Domains" section on page 79 for additional help.

Once you have decided on a publishing option, click "Submit." Figure 1.45 shows the URL where your mobile site is live.

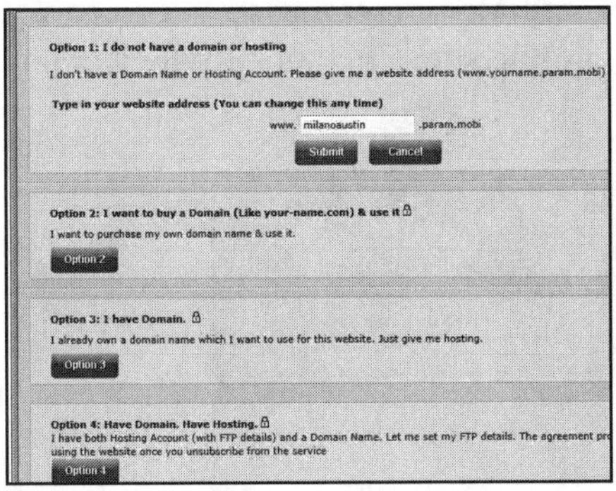

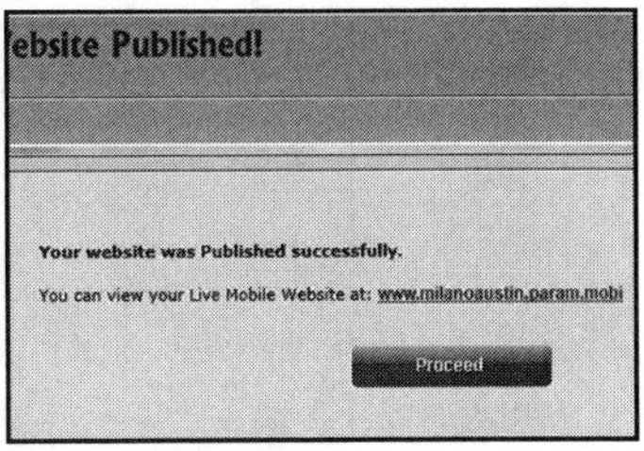

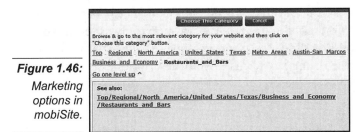

Figure 1.44,
Figure 1.45:
Publishing
options in
mobiSite.

Redirection

Unfortunately, mobiSiteGalore does not offer its own redirection solution, but you can use an alternative method of redirection on your desktop site. See the "Detection and Redirection" section on page 81 for solutions.

Testing Your Site

MobiSiteGalore lets you test your mobile site prior to publication. Click on "Test your website." From here, you can see how your site validates with the service ready.mobi[11]. Once your site is live, it is recommended that you also validate it with W3C mobileOK[5].

Marketing Your Site

This service offers a feature that allows you to place your mobile site in mobile search directories. Click on "Search Engine Submission & Directory Listings" and select the categories that are relevant to your mobile site. See Figure 1.46.

Figure 1.46:
Marketing
options in
mobiSite.

Take your time choosing the correct category, especially if your business is local. As seen in Figure 1.46 above, it can take some trial and error to find the right categories and sub-categories.

MobiSiteGalore also has a template you can use to send to your mailing lists announcing your new mobile site. Click on "Invite Contacts" for this option (see Figure 1.47).

Figure 1.47:
Marketing options in mobiSite (2).

It is important that you offer a link from your desktop site to your mobile site if you are not redirecting mobile visitors. Offer a direct link, or use a QR code, as explained on page 100.

See QR Code 1.5 for mobiSiteGalore examples.

Winksite

Winksite[12] is a mobile website creator that also serves as a community. In addition to hosting your mobile site with Winksite, you become part of a community or social network of mobile site owners. This solution does not include custom URLs or redirection options, but may be a good choice if you want some added exposure, or a mobile landing page. See QR Code 1.6 for Winksite examples.

Setting Up Your Account

Once you create an account with Winksite, click on "Dashboard/Create Site" to create your first mobile site. You can have up to five sites on your account. Figure 1.48 shows the screen for creating a site. Be sure to fill out the options completely using key terms in your description so people can find your site easier in searches.

QR Code 1.5:
MobiGalore examples[5].

QR Code 1.6:
Winksite examples[6].

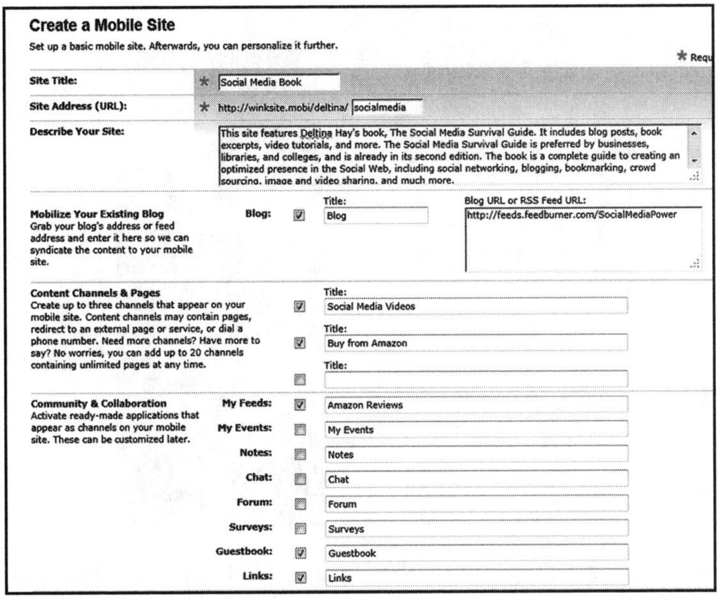

Figure 1.48:
Setting up a Winksite account.

Content channels on Winksite are essentially menu items. They contain items like incoming RSS feeds, click-to-call links, links to external websites, or custom page content. There are also a number of built-in content channels that you can add to your site, as seen in Figure 1.48.

When creating menu items, keep the titles as short as possible, but with as many key terms as you can. In our example, we want our site visitors to access video tutorials and to buy the book on Amazon, so we include them as menu items or content channels. Since Winksite does not have shopping or video features, these options are represented as externals links.

Customizing Your Design

Figure 1.49 shows the next step in creating our Winksite mobile website. Here, we choose the colors and overall design of the site. If you want to use a header image—like a logo or book cover—make it as small as possible. You may need to get creative with your existing images to make them work on a mobile site. In our example, we cropped the book cover to include only the title of the book so it would not overwhelm the site. This interface allows you to upload a background image for your site as well. If you must use a background image, make the image as small as possible and use an image with very little detail. Remember to keep it simple!

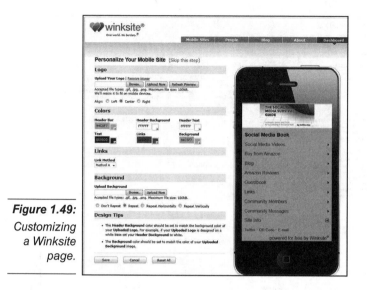

Figure 1.49:
Customizing a Winksite page.

When you are happy with the design, click "Save." The next step is to complete the settings for your content channels. Click on "Edit Channel" for the content channel you want to complete. This takes you to the screen in Figure 1.50.

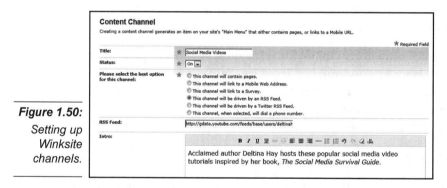

Figure 1.50:
Setting up Winksite channels.

Setting Up Your Features

From this screen you control what happens when a menu item is clicked. In our example, we want to feature video tutorials that are inspired by the social media book, so we enter an introduction and an RSS feed from our YouTube channel that produces a list of videos to feature.

Populate your remaining channels this way until your site is complete. You can turn on or off any of the ready-made applications as shown in Figure 1.51, or add new channels.

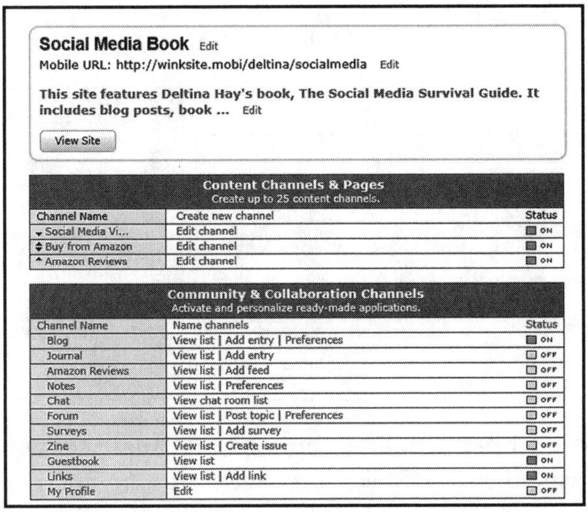

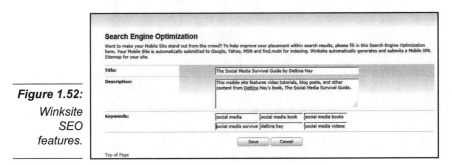

Figure 1.51:

Setting up Winksite channels (2).

Once your content channels are complete, take the time to check out the other features and settings. There are settings specific to the Winksite community, ways for you to monetize your site, settings for geo-location, and search engine optimization (SEO) settings.

Search Optimization Settings

Figure 1.52 shows the search optimization settings for our social media book site. We use our best meta keywords, titles, and descriptions, keeping in mind that our titles should be no longer than 75 characters, and descriptions no longer than 160 characters. Read more about search engine best practices on page 84.

Figure 1.52:

Winksite SEO features.

Custom Domain and Redirection

Other settings you should complete on the Winksite platform are the copyright options and the desktop site option. The desktop site option allows you to set a URL that visitors are redirected to if they access your

Winksite mobile site from a desktop browser. This will likely be your main website. Figure 1.53 and Figure 1.54 demonstrate these features.

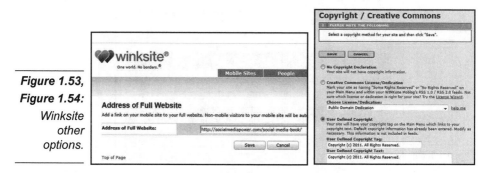

Figure 1.53,
Figure 1.54:
Winksite
other
options.

Winksite does not offer a redirect option (that redirects your desktop visitors to your mobile site). Make sure you place a link or a QR code on your main website so people can find your mobile site. Read more about QR codes on page 186.

Marketing Your Site

When you access the direct URL of your Winksite, you get a page as seen in Figure 1.55. On this page is a QR code. We can copy this code and use it as a way to market our site. Read more about QR codes on page 186.

Figure 1.55:
A Winksite
page in
action.

Winksite offers a way for you to place a Winksite widget (a graphical link) on your website by copying the embedded code and placing it on your site. Learn more about how to do this and other marketing techniques in the "Promoting Your Mobile Website" section on page 100. Take advantage of Winksite's community features by inviting others in your network to become a part of the community as well.

Testing Your Site

Use W3C mobileOK[5] and ready.mobi[11] to test your new mobile site's URL. Refer to the "Testing Your Mobile Website" section on page 90 for more information.

Mofuse

Mofuse[13] is a robust service that offers a lot of features. They do not offer a free version, and their starter plan runs $7.95/month. This plan gets you one site with ten elements (similar to a module, discussed below) and 1,500 hits a month. The next plan offers 50,000 hits and 100 elements for $39/month. See QR Code 1.7 on page 56 for Mofuse examples.

Setting Up Your Account

Once you have an account, click on "Launch a New Mobile Site." The platform is fairly user-friendly, and walks you through the process of creating your mobile site. Figure 1.56 shows the opening screen. Choose a site name and URL for your mobile site, and upload your logo. You can change the URL later to one that is more conducive to your strategy.

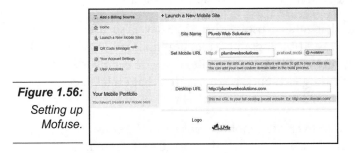

Figure 1.56:
Setting up
Mofuse.

Setting Up Your Features

The next screen, shown in Figure 1.57, shows some of the features available to create, modify, promote, and analyze your site. The next step, though, is to set up the elements for your site. Click on "Add Elements" to proceed.

Figure 1.57:
Setting up
Mofuse
features.

Figure 1.58 shows some of the elements you can add to your site. Some of them are only available at upgraded levels, such as Google Checkout, Form Builder, and Store Locator. The Mofuse platform uses a modular concept to help you build your site. Each of the elements you create can be placed—like a module—on a page of your mobile site in the "Layout Site" mode.

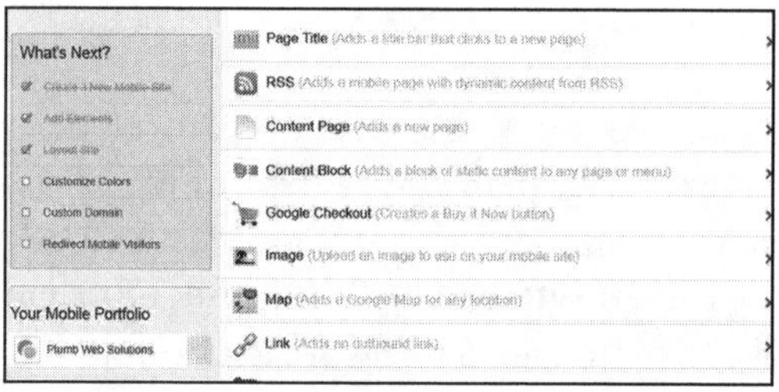

Figure 1.58:
Setting up
Mofuse
features (2).

Most of the elements are self-explanatory, but there are a couple that may be a bit confusing. You have the option of placing your elements on the home page of your site, or creating pages that contain elements or custom content. To create a page that contains elements, use the "Page Title" element. To create a page that has custom content (not elements), use the "Content Page" element. Both options create a link to a sub-page from the home page. We demonstrate both of these options below.

You only have ten elements to use at the $7.95 level, so use elements sparingly if you don't need to upgrade. You should already have a good idea which elements you need from your strategy, so you can plan your site before you begin activating elements. Keep in mind that each "Page Title" and "Content Page" is counted as an element as well.

In our example, we want to create a mobile website for the consulting firm, Plumb Web Solutions. Based on the required features from our strategy, here are the Mofuse elements we plan to use:

- Content block with short company blurb (one element)
- Click-to-call (one element)
- Click-to-text (one element)
- Contact via email (one element)
- RSS feed from two blogs (two elements)

Because we don't have too much text cluttering any one page of the site, we will use three of the remaining elements to create a contact page for the call, text, and email elements, and two separate pages for the blogs.

Figure 1.59 shows the content block element. Place content in this element that does not need to be on a page by itself. You can embed images and links in these blocks as well as format text and background colors. There is also an option of having a "Live Image" in a content block. That means you can place a link to an image that you can change on your own server whenever you like without having to update the mobile site.

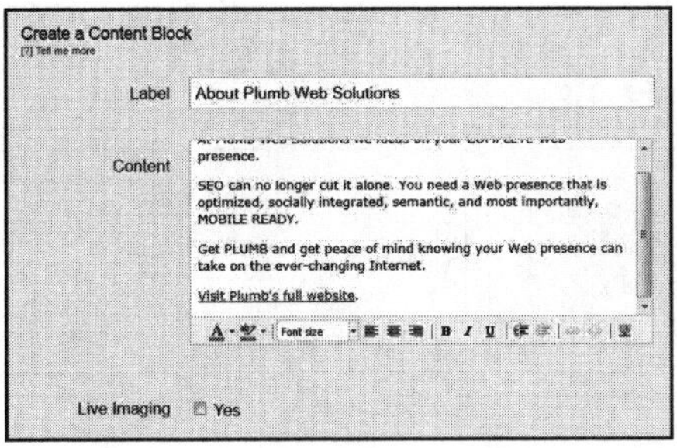

Figure 1.59:

Setting up Mofuse elements.

Figure 1.60 demonstrates the click-to-call element we need for our contact page. The click-to-text element is set up similarly. Figure 1.61 shows how to utilize the link element to create an email option.

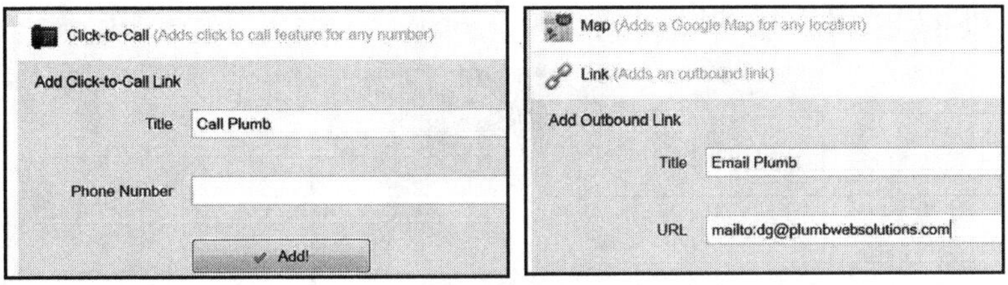

Figure 1.60,
Figure 1.61:

Setting up Mofuse elements (2).

In Figure 1.62 we demonstrate how to create an RSS feed element. Click on "Advanced Options" to reveal all of the options available for this element. You can control how many items appear, as well as how images are displayed. Unless images are a vital part of your blog posts, it is recommended that you do not display them at all.

We also create three "Page Title" elements. The element entitled "Contact Plumb" will contain the click-to-call, click-to-text, and email elements. The two additional page title elements will contain the blog elements.

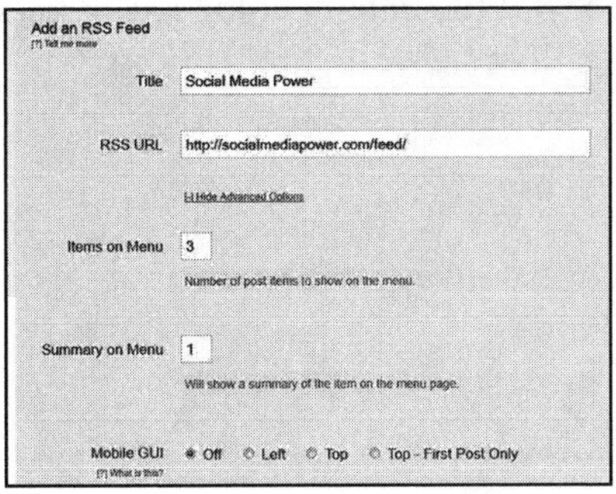

Figure 1.62:

Setting up Mofuse elements (3).

Customizing Your Design (Laying Out Your Site)

Once your elements are created, click on "Layout Site." Figure 1.63 shows the elements we created for our example site. All we do now is move each element either onto the home page of the site, or into the page where they belong.

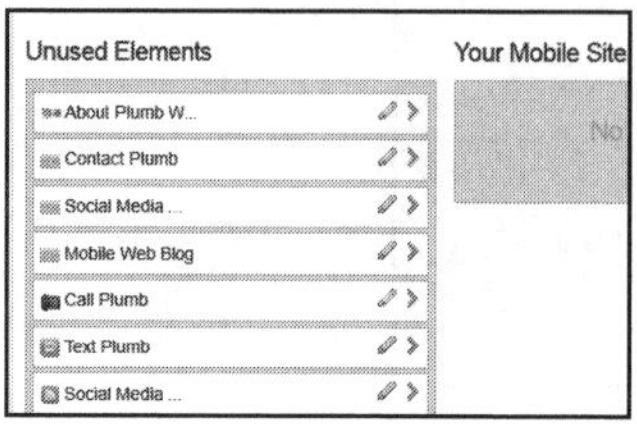

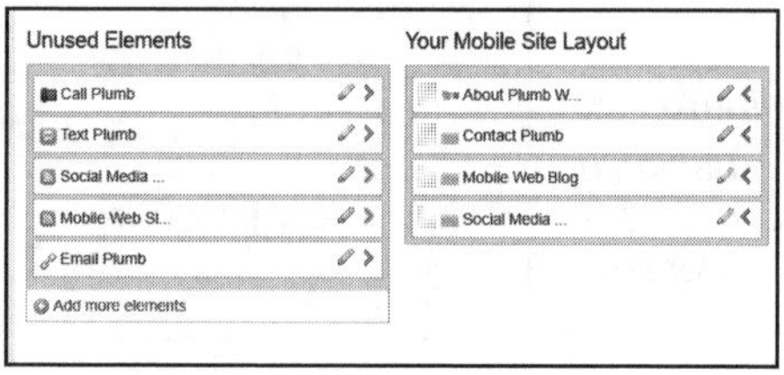

Figure 1.63,
Figure 1.64:
Setting up
Mofuse
pages.

As Figure 1.64 shows, we first move over the elements that go onto the home page. Figure 1.65 shows some of the sub-page elements placed under their respective pages. To move a sub-page element onto a page, drag it slightly to the right.

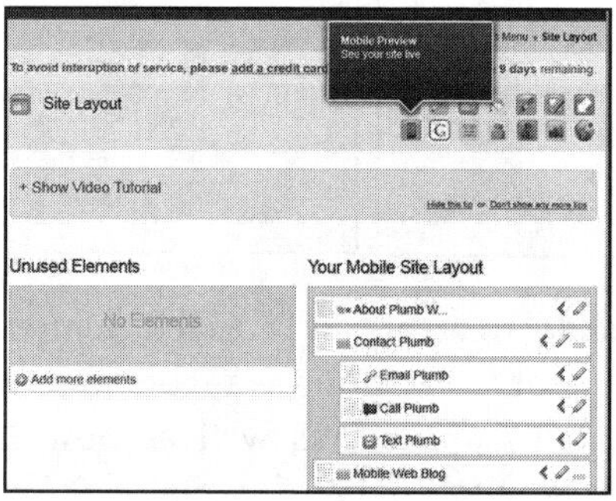

Figure 1.65:
Setting up
Mofuse
pages (2).

Get a preview of your page by clicking on the "Mobile Preview" button, as shown in Figure 1.65. Use the preview as a guide when customizing your colors.

Click on "Customize Colors." Figure 1.66 shows part of the resulting screen. Comparing the preview images with the default color settings should serve as a guide for customizing the colors for your site.

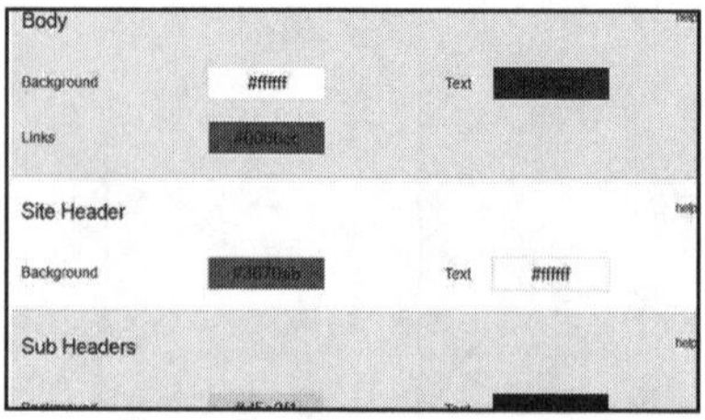

Figure 1.66:
Setting up
Mofuse
colors.

Figure 1.67, Figure 1.68, and Figure 1.69 show the preview images for our example Mofuse site.

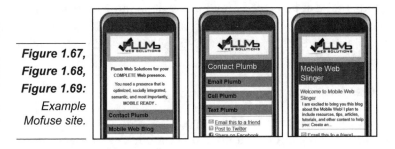

Figure 1.67,
Figure 1.68,
Figure 1.69:
Example
Mofuse site.

Custom Domain

Click on "Custom Domain" and follow the instructions for setting up a sub-domain on your main domain that will point to your mobile site. If you do not have a main website then this step does not apply.

Figure 1.70 shows the custom domain name we want to assign to our mobile site, and the CNAME entry information provided by Mofuse. Make a note of the CNAME entry and refer to the "Configuring Custom Domains" section on page 79 for instructions on how to create the CNAME record on your server or hosting account.

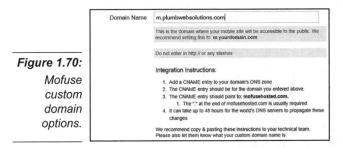

Figure 1.70:
Mofuse
custom
domain
options.

Redirection

Click on "Redirect Mobile Visitors." Figure 1.71 shows the resulting screen.

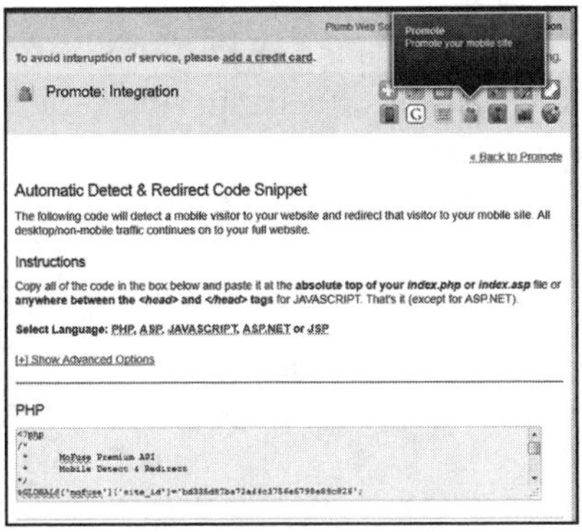

Figure 1.71:
Mofuse
redirect
options.

Mofuse offers code that can be placed on your site depending on whether your site is powered by PHP, ASP, JavaScript, ASP.NET, or JSP. Refer to the "Detection and Redirection" section on page 81 for help if their instructions are not adequate.

Marketing Your Site

Mofuse has a QR code manager that can help you create QR codes to place on your desktop site or on print promotions that mobile device users can use to find your mobile site. Read more about QR codes on page 186.

Analytics

Mofuse offers a way for you to check site analytics from their site, but to synch your site with Google Analytics and access other analytics features you need an upgraded account.

Testing Your Account

Use W3C mobileOK[5] and ready.mobi[11] to test your new mobile site's URL. The Mofuse sites we tested did very well on both tests. Go to the "Testing Your Mobile Website" on page 90 for more details

See QR Code 1.7 below for Mofuse examples.

bMobilized (A Conversion Service)

Figure 1.72: *bMobilized conversion service.*

BMobilized[14] is a conversion service that runs $19.95/month. The platform is pretty straightforward and offers a lot of ways to fine tune the mobile version of your site once it is converted.

QR Code 1.7: *Mofuse examples[7].*

QR Code 1.8: *bMobilized demo[8].*

Since this type of service literally converts an existing website to a mobile website, the process is different than setting up a hosting service. Steps are added that include configuring content and navigation pulled from the existing desktop site that needs to be customized for the mobile counterpart. Search optimization and marketing aren't emphasized as much for conversion services since those efforts are typically reserved for the mother site. See page 84 for more on search optimization issues.

To initiate the conversion process, enter the URL of the desktop site you want converted to mobile on the bMobilized home page (see Figure 1.72).

We continue this example online (see QR Code 1.8), since the bMobilized platform relies heavily on color coding, and we cannot do it justice in black and white.

CMS Solution Examples

> ### ▶ Bootstrapper's Guide ◀
> ✔ A plugin, responsive theme, or service can prepare a CMS for mobile.
> ✔ Choose a plugin or theme that adheres to mobile website best practices.
> ✔ Choose a plugin that addresses the features found on your CMS site.
> ✔ Test potential plugins, themes, and services on devices and the W3C.

If you power your website using a content management system (CMS) like WordPress, Joomla!, or Drupal, then you have a few options available for getting your site ready for the mobile web. You can use a plugin, choose a responsive theme for your site, or use a hosting service that integrates with your CMS.

The discussion in this section assumes you are using WordPress to power your website, but the concepts can be applied to any CMS. The section also assumes that you have a working knowledge of using WordPress as a CMS.

Using Plugins

There are a number of good plugins that can get your website quickly and easily ready for the mobile web—see the resource section at the end of this chapter. When choosing a plugin, however, resist the urge to choose one based only on aesthetics.

Since most WordPress powered sites are composed of blogs, static pages, sidebars, plugins, and widgets, there are some specific issues that should be addressed when mobilizing a WordPress site. Below are some guidelines to help you choose a plugin that will help your WordPress site adhere to mobile website best practices, while addressing issues specific to the WordPress platform.

Your final choice will likely depend on which features are most important to you, but make certain you test the finalists before making your decision.

Theme Customization

Some plugins allow you to customize your mobile theme, while others offer a variety of generic themes to choose from. Still other plugins give you a choice of themes that can be further customized using style sheets.

Blog Post Configuration

A good plugin should offer many ways for you to control how your blog posts are organized and formatted, including excerpt length, how to display titles, how to handle images, and whether or not the mobile site lists categories and tags. You should also be able to choose which categories to include or exclude on your mobile site.

Static Pages

A plugin should give you the option of choosing which of your static pages you want to show on your mobile site. Some of your pages may not be suitable for viewing on a mobile device. You may even want to create pages that only appear on the mobile version of your site.

Of particular concern is your home page. A plugin should give you control over what you want featured on the home page of your site—be it blog posts, a specific page, a list of categories, etc.

Navigation

You should have the option of selecting which of your static pages appear in the navigation of your site's mobile version. Some plugins also allow you to use categories and tags as menu choices. Also consider how much control you have over the styling of your navigation: whether you can use icons for navigation or have to settle for the style a plugin chooses for you.

Sidebars and Widgets

Most mobile plugins will eliminate sidebars and widgets since displaying them may not adhere to mobile website best practices. There are some plugins, however, that allow you to display sidebars below the main content area. Some plugins also let you choose which of your widgets you wish to display.

Be warned that many widgets and plugins you activate on a WordPress site may not validate on a mobile version of the site. Be very selective if you plan to use widgets on a mobile site, and test after activating each plugin or widget.

Image Handling

Some plugins eliminate images altogether, while others allow you to control how the plugin handles images—by selecting only one image per post or reducing all images by a selected percentage. Since you want to keep your pages as small as possible, it is recommended that you use as few images as necessary.

Search Optimization Settings

You want a plugin that gives your site the best possible placement in the mobile search engines. It is best to choose a plugin that offers ways you can set metadata specific to the mobile version of your site. An added bonus would be a plugin that integrates with your existing SEO plugin.

Analytics

Most mobile plugins offer some way for you to check the analytics of the mobile version of your site. Some even integrate with Google Analytics[10] and other analytics plugins.

Mobile Feature Integration

Some mobile plugins offer ways to integrate mobile features like Google Maps[15] or push notifications using services like Prowl[16]. Refer to page 113 to read more about push notifications.

Detection and Redirection

Most mobile plugins detect when a mobile device accesses your site and serve up the mobile version of the site automatically. This is usually the most convenient way to go, but you may want more control over that. Some plugins allow you to turn this function off.

Monetizing

If you are monetizing your site using Google AdSense[17], you should make sure that AdSense for mobile is set up on the mobile version of your site. A good mobile plugin will have that feature built in.

Testing Plugins

Since you are already weighing the options of one or more plugins, you should make the effort to test them using the W3C mobileOK Checker[5].

You can activate a plugin on your site and test it before making any major customizations to get a feel for how "healthy" a plugin is before proceeding.

Comparing Two WordPress Plugins

To give you an idea of the different types of plugins available, we prepared a comparison of two popular WordPress plugins: Wapple Architect and WPTouch. Both of these platforms have pro versions that can increase the functionality of the free versions shown here.

Wapple Architect[18] is an extension of the sophisticated mobile website and app builder, Wapple[19]. The Wapple plugin has just about all of the features you would want to see in a mobile plugin, including customizable style sheets and Google Analytics integration.

Figure 1.73 and Figure 1.74 show two pages from the mobile version of the WordPress powered site SocialMediaPower.com using the Wapple plugin with a customized theme. You are given a lot of control over navigation, pages, blog formatting, redirection, and more using this plugin.

Figure 1.73,
Figure 1.74:

Wapple
Plugin.

One drawback is that you are required to register with Wapple and acquire a key in order to activate the plugin. This is not much of a drawback, however, once you realize that linking to the Wapple infrastructure means your site will be driven by the most updated algorithms. This is apparent when we check the W3C mobileOK score of 99% for this plugin.

WPTouch[20] is a plugin designed to work well with smartphones and other touch screen devices. It, too, has just about any of the features you would want to see in a good mobile plugin, including custom menu icons, stylish themes, and push notification integration.

Figure 1.75 and Figure 1.76 show the same pages from SocialMediaPower. com with the WPTouch plugin activated. As you can see, it has a very different look and feel to it, and is ideal for touch screen browsing.

Figure 1.75, Figure 1.76: WPTouch Plugin.

The biggest drawback of this plugin is that it does not rank well on the W3C mobileOK Checker. In defense of this plugin, however, it is important to recall that the plugin is designed specifically for touch screen devices. The W3C mobileOK Checker is meant to check the mobile readiness of a website for all mobile devices, not only touch screen devices.

Using a Responsive Theme

Some WordPress themes are mobile-friendly in the sense that they are responsive, meaning that they respond appropriately to the screen size of the device accessing the site.

Figure 1.77 and Figure 1.78 show the top and bottom of the WordPress powered site MobileWebSlinger using a responsive theme called Yoko[21] on a mobile device. Figure 1.79 shows the site on a desktop browser.

Figure 1.77, Figure 1.78: Yoko theme on mobile device.

Figure 1.79:
Yoko theme on desktop.

Responsive themes typically flow the main content area first and the sidebar elements underneath in the mobile version of the theme (see Figure 1.77 and Figure 1.78). Some even have theme options that allow you to control which sidebars to include in the smaller screen versions.

While these themes scale well for different devices, they do not necessarily take care of the other mobile website best practices. You need to make certain you are tending to those other tasks yourself, like keeping your page sizes small, and making certain your plugins validate.

Using a Hosting Service for a CMS

There are many mobile website hosting services that integrate with CMS sites quite effectively. The Mofuse[13] tool we examined on page 51 has procedures for integrating with the most popular CMSs. Wirenode[22] is another hosting service that lets you use your blog as the basis of your entire mobile site.

These hosting services can be especially good solutions for WordPress sites that are not blog-centered (use a static page as a home page instead of blog posts). The Mofuse example on page 51 is a good example. The site in the example is a WordPress powered site.

Responsive Web Design

> ### ▶ Bootstrapper's Guide ◀
> ✔ Use media queries in HTML to assign style sheets for different devices.
> ✔ Use separate style sheets for desktop, tablet, and smartphone.
> ✔ Use JavaScript libraries in case browsers do not support queries.
> ✔ Test your responsive theme thoroughly on all targeted devices.

A major challenge for web designers today is trying to accommodate all the different devices accessing the Internet, especially devices with very small screens. Responsive web design is one solution to that challenge.

Designing responsively means attempting to design a website that not only scales to the screen size of a device, but takes best practices into account as well, especially as they apply to page size and load time.

In the CMS section on page 61, we demonstrated a responsive theme that adjusts the width of the theme depending on the screen size of the device accessing it. True responsive design does more than simply adjust the width of a site, it also adjusts typography, optimizes images, and more.

This section assumes that you have a working knowledge of HTML and CSS. The author makes no attempt to explain the basic HTML or CSS concepts demonstrated in the following example. See QR Code 1.9 on page 64 for the sample code used in this example.

The Figures below are screen shots of a site designed using responsive web design concepts. Figure 1.80 is the desktop version; Figure 1.81 is the tablet version; Figure 1.82 is the smartphone version; and Figure 1.83 is the handheld (or feature phone) version. Each version uses the same HTML file, but accesses a different style sheet and different images.

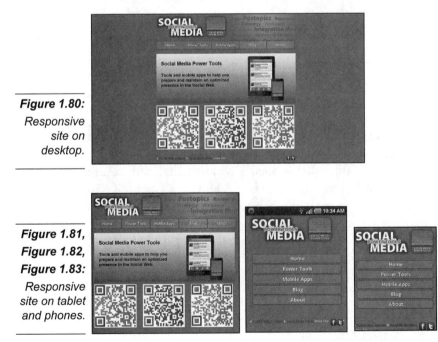

Figure 1.80:
Responsive site on desktop.

Figure 1.81,
Figure 1.82,
Figure 1.83:
Responsive site on tablet and phones.

The general process of our responsive web design example is as follows:

- Create one HTML file for each page of the site
- Create four style sheets: one style sheet for desktop, one for tablet, one for phone, one for handheld

- Create three sets of images: one set for desktop, one set used for both tablet and phone, and one for handheld
- Use media queries to determine the screen size of the device accessing the site
- Serve up the appropriate style sheet according to the screen size
- The style sheets adjust the element styles according to the respective screen size
- The style sheets access appropriate images depending on screen size

Using the Media Query

The media query is used within a style sheet link declaration and should be in the <head> section of your HTML pages. Here is an excerpt from our example index.html file:

```
<!DOCTYPE HTML>
<html>
<head>
...
<link rel="stylesheet" type="text/css" href="css/desktop.css" >
<link rel="stylesheet" type="text/css" media="screen and (min-width: 0px) and
(max-width: 320px)" href="css/handheld.css" >
<link rel="stylesheet" type="text/css" media="screen and (min-width: 321px)
and (max-width: 480px)" href="css/phone.css" >
<link rel="stylesheet" type="text/css" media="screen and (min-width: 481px)
and (max-width: 768px)" href="css/tablet.css" >
...
</head>
```

The media query consists of a media type and optional expressions that check for conditions of particular media features. Media types are "screen" and "print," and some of the media features that can be used include "width," "height," "resolution," "color," and "orientation." Using media queries allows you to control how a web page displays by determining the features of the device accessing the page.

In our example, the appropriate style sheet is used depending on the screen width of the device accessing the page:

QR Code 1.9:
Responsive
example
sample code[9].

- If the screen width is between 0 and 320 pixels, the handheld.css style sheet is used (for feature phones).

- If the screen width is between 321 and 480 pixels, the phone.css style sheet is used (for smartphones).

- If the screen width is between 481 and 768 pixels, the tablet.css style sheet is used (for tablet computers).

- If none of the conditions are met, the default style sheet, desktop.css, is used.

You can use the same process to test for screen resolution, screen orientation, aspect ratio, etc. Read more about media queries on the W3C website[23].

Most modern browsers support the media query, but not all in the same way. For instance, there is a media feature called "device-width" that is more appropriate for mobile devices, and most mobile browsers prefer to test this media feature rather than the plain "width" feature we demonstrated above. The problem is that iPhone browsers act more like desktop browsers, and will often ignore the "device-width" test. Our solution was to add the following media queries to our index.html file to cover all bases:

```
<link rel="stylesheet" type="text/css" media="screen and (min-device-width:
0px) and (max-device-width: 320px)" href="css/handheld.css" >
<link rel="stylesheet" type="text/css" media="screen and (min-device-width:
321px) and (max-device-width: 480px)" href="css/phone.css" >
<link rel="stylesheet" type="text/css" media="screen and (min-device-width:
481px) and (max-device-width: 768px)" href="css/tablet.css" >
```

These lines are identical to the previous queries, save for using "device-width" rather than "width."

The lesson here is to make certain you test your responsive website on as many different devices as you can before you launch your site. See page 96 for more details on testing a responsive website.

The HTML File and Style Sheets

To get a feel for how media queries are applied, let's take a look at our example site step-by-step. An excerpt of our example index.html file is shown below. Since most of the page functionality is controlled within the style sheets, this file is pretty sparse.

```
<body>
<div id="container">
  <header id="logo">
    ...
    <nav>
    ...
```

```
    </nav>
  </header>
  <div id="maincontent">
    <div id="vision"></div>
    <div class="pod1"></div>
    <div class="pod2"></div>
    <div class="pod3"></div>
  </div>
  <footer>
    ...
  </footer>
</div>
</body>
```

The #container and #logo elements are formatted within each style sheet by accessing their respective images and adjusting the size, margins, and padding of the elements accordingly. There are two background and three logo images that are accessed by their respective style sheets.

Since the desktop style sheet is the default, we only need to change the image URLs and adjust other element style changes for our tablet, phone, and handheld style sheets. Most images are eliminated in the phone and handheld versions to keep the page sizes as small as possible. Here is the relevant CSS code from each style sheet:

desktop.css

```
#container {
    background-image: url(/images/bg_smpt.jpg);
    background-repeat: no-repeat;
    background-position: right top;
    width: 840px;
    margin-top: 0px;
    margin-right: auto;
    margin-bottom: 0px;
    margin-left: auto;
}
#logo {
    background-image: url(/images/logo.png);
    background-repeat: no-repeat;
    height: 138px;
    width: 100%;

}
```

tablet.css

```
#container {
    width: 700px;
    background-image: url(/images/med/med_bg_smpt.jpg);
}
#logo {
    height:100px;
    background-image: url(/images/med/med_logo.png);
}
```

```
phone.css

#container {
    width: 400px;
    background-image: none;
}
#logo {
    width: 100%;
    background-image: url(/images/med/med_logo.png);
    margin-left:auto;
    margin-right:auto;

}
```

handheld.css
```
#container {
    width: 100%;
    background-image: none;
}
#logo {
    height:100px;
    width:320px;
    background-image: url(/images/sml/sml_logo.png);
    margin-left:auto;
    margin-right:auto;
}
```

The navigation elements are designed using CSS, so there are no images to worry about resizing. All we do to the tablet, phone, and handheld stylesheets is adjust the top position of the main navigation area, adjust the width of the navigation items, and adjust the size of the fonts. Additionally, in the phone and handheld style sheets, we eliminate the "float left" attribute so it runs vertically down the page (refer to Figure 1.82 on page 63).

Within the #maincontent element is the #vision element which contains the large image with the title and tag line, and three smaller class elements below it: .pod1, .pod2, and .pod3 that contain the QR codes in the desktop and tablet versions. See Figure 1.80 and Figure 1.81 on page 63 for reference.

There are two relevant images for the #vision element: a large one for the desktop style sheet and a medium-sized image for the tablet style sheet. As seen in Figure 1.81 on page 63, the image is not present on the phone or handheld versions of the site.

Below are relevant excerpts from the style sheets:

desktop.css
```
#vision {
    background-image:url(/images/big_phones.jpg);
    background-repeat:no-repeat;
```

```
    width: 450px;
    height:280px;
    padding: 5px 450px 0 40px;
    margin-bottom:10px;
}
```

tablet.css

```
#vision {
    background-image:url(/images/med/med_phones.jpg);
    width: 350px;
    height:222px;
    padding-right:350px;
}
```

phone.css

```
#vision {
    clear:both;
    background-image:none;
    height:auto;
}
```

handheld.css

```
#vision {
    clear:both;
    background-image:none;
    height:auto;
}
```

The tablet style sheet grabs the medium-sized image and adjusts the width, height, and padding of the #vision element. The phone and handheld style sheets declare no image, and adjust the height of the element so padding does not result in white space.

A similar process is used for the three QR code images contained within the pod class elements. Large images are used in the desktop style sheet, medium-sized versions are used in the tablet style sheet, and no images are used in the phone and handheld style sheets.

Finally, the only styles adjusted within the footer element are font size and position for all style sheets.

JavaScript Backup

Unfortunately, not all browsers support the media query. Most modern browsers do support this feature, but if you want to support legacy browsers, you should add backup. There are some good JavaScript libraries you can use to solve the issue, like css3-mediaqueries.js[24].

Testing Your Responsive Website

You may be disappointed if you use the W3C mobileOK Checker[5] or ready. mobi[11] to test your responsive website. The problem is that those tools do not look for the media query statements. The tools typically grab the main style sheet and base their scores on it—which in our case is a style sheet for a desktop computer, not a mobile device. You should still test your site using the traditional W3C validators, however—see page 96 for details.

Alternatively, you can use an app called ProtoFluid[25] that emulates responsive websites. Figure 1.84 shows our example site once we enter the URL into ProtoFluid—this is how our example site looks on the iPhone.

You can see how your site looks on many phones, tablets, monitors, and televisions. Figure 1.85 and Figure 1.86 show our example site on a Blackberry and a Motorola Droid, respectively.

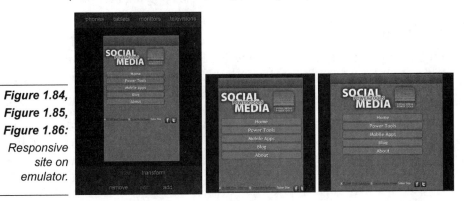

Figure 1.84,
Figure 1.85,
Figure 1.86:
Responsive
site on
emulator.

Exploring Further

Responsive design concepts are constantly evolving, and this section is only meant to give you a general understanding of some of the concepts used to achieve it. There are a number of good articles, books, and sites listed in the resource section of this chapter if you would like a more advanced introduction to this topic.

Creating a Stand Alone Mobile Website

► **Bootstrapper's Guide** ◄

√ Good at HTML and CSS? Create your site using best practices.
√ If you dabble in HTML and CSS, there are mobile templates to use.
√ Take advantage of mobile features like click-to-call and Google Maps.
√ APIs can help add functionality that perform well on mobile devices.

The best way to create a stand-alone mobile website is with HTML5 and CSS3. If you are proficient at HTML and CSS, then refer to the best practices section of the chapter and apply them to your new mobile site. You may even find some useful tips in this section. For those of you who dabble, there are some nice templates—many of them free—that can help you create your mobile site.

Since a full tutorial on HTML and CSS is beyond the scope of this book, we demonstrate how to create a stand-alone mobile site by customizing a template. If you proceed with this section, be warned that it is assumed that you have at least a general understanding of HTML and CSS, and that you have FTP access to where your website is hosted.

The template you choose may be quite different from this example, but the process outlined here can help you choose, customize, test, troubleshoot, and implement just about any template while applying best practices.

Choosing Our Template

Our example stand-alone mobile website is for Quill Driver Books. They are a publisher of nonfiction books and have quite a few titles under their belt. Refer to the example strategies in the resource section of this chapter.

It is important to resist the urge to choose a template based only on aesthetics. Check prospective templates against the best practices listed in this chapter, and pretest them prior to investing the time to customize.

We decided upon a template by QRdvark called Fone[26]. They have a number of stylish and clean templates and frameworks to choose from. We opted for the free version, but there is also a pro version you can purchase for $29. If you do use the free version, do not ignore the creative commons license agreement that requires a link to the author's website if you use the template. Refer to the resource section of this chapter for additional template sources.

Pretesting the Template

If a prospective template has a demo, use the demo URL to test the site against mobile web standards using the W3C mobileOK Checker[5]. Our example template does not have a demo so we need to download the files, upload them to a folder, and run the test using a temporary URL.

Figure 1.87 shows the contents of the template folder once it has been downloaded and unzipped. The template comes as a fully functional site, including an index HTML file, a CSS style sheet, several buttons you can customize for your site, and sample images.

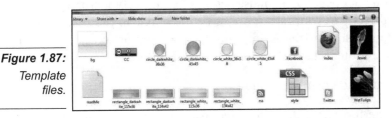

Figure 1.87:
Template files.

To test the template, upload the contents of the folder to a temporary directory on your server—just as you would for any website. If you place the template files in a directory called "fone," then the URL of the test site is "yoursitename.com/fone." Enter that URL in the W3C mobileOK Checker.

Testing the Fone template using W3C mobileOK Checker reveals a score of 76%, including a few errors that we address later in this section. We want to get it to at least 90%, but wait until your site is complete before attempting to correct any of the errors.

Customizing the Template

Figure 1.88, Figure 1.89, and Figure 1.90 show part of the template before our customization. Open the index.html file with a browser to see the template. The template demonstrates all of the CSS styles available, as well as a demonstration of the buttons and the navigation link styling.

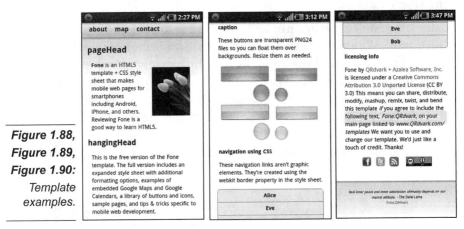

Figure 1.88,

Figure 1.89,

Figure 1.90:

Template examples.

One of the reasons we chose this theme is that it is very well documented. If you know enough about HTML and CSS, you should have no problem altering a template like this to fit your needs. Follow QR Code 1.10 on page 72 to see the template code before and after customization.

Edit the index.html and style.css files using your favorite HTML editor or any text editor. Be sure and only use styles from the style sheet to format elements on your pages. Do not use tags like "bold type" to format elements directly in your pages; use or define a style in the style sheet for bolding text instead. This is important for validation purposes and to ensure your content displays properly on mobile devices.

Our customization plan is as follows:

- Use the top menu items to direct users to contact information, the company blog, and home.
- Style the home page using a logo image and a description of the company.
- Use the navigation link styling to direct users to learn more about the books by category.
- Use the social media buttons to point to the company's Facebook page and blog.
- Add a "newsletter" button to encourage subscriptions.
- Use the footer area for copyright information and a link to the full website.
- Create a "contact" page that includes a submission form and click-to-call link.
- Create book category pages that feature several books and links to the full website.

The Home Page

Using the template's index.html file, we add a logo image and the company description. We alter the main menu area to include the home, contact, and blog menu choices, and use the navigation link styling to include a way for users to explore the books. We point the Facebook icon to the company's Facebook page, the RSS icon to their blog, and add a "Newsletter" button—using one of the button images supplied by the template—that links to the contact page. We add a copyright statement in the footer area as well as a link to the full website. Figure 1.91 and Figure 1.92 show the customized index.html (home) page.

QR Code 1.10:
Sample HTML5
template
code[10].

Figure 1.91,

Figure 1.92:

Customized

home page.

The Contact Page

Figure 1.93 and Figure 1.94 show our contact.html page. We duplicate the index.html page and add contact information. Below the contact information, we offer a click-to-call option for discounted sales.

The following syntax will trigger a mobile device's capability to call a phone number when clicked:

```
<a href="tel:+phonenumberhere">
```

Here is the HTML we used on our contact page for the "click-to-call" functionality:

```
For retail, wholesale, or educational discounts<a href="tel:+18003454447">
call us directly</a>.
```

We also add a form that allows users to inquire about different aspects of the publishing company or subscribe to the company newsletter. We demonstrate an easy way to add forms to your mobile site later in this section on page 77.

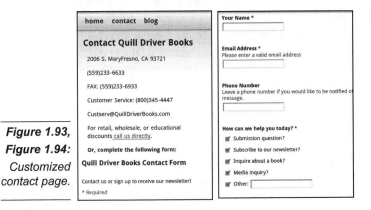

Figure 1.93,

Figure 1.94:

Customized

contact page.

The Book Category Pages

The book category page requires the most customization. Figure 1.95 and Figure 1.96 show how the page is formatted. We want to create a page that highlights a couple of books within a category, provide links to a selection of additional books from that category, and add a link to the full website in case the user wishes to explore all of the books in the category.

Figure 1.95, Figure 1.96: *Customized books page.*

In keeping with best practices, we only offer two book cover images on each category page so our page sizes remain small. We also format the book images and titles in a one-column design for easier browsing on small mobile devices.

Instead of adding shopping features, we link each book to its Amazon.com page. This cuts down significantly on the size and complexity of the site, and could yield more sales since the mobile demographic is more likely to buy from Amazon.

Figure 1.96 shows how we also add a link back to the home page underneath each of the featured books. These category pages require more scrolling than we would like, so we compensate by adding a way for the user to return to the main page without needing to scroll to the top of the page.

Testing Our Mobile Site

Place all of your files in a directory on your site—something like yoursitename.com/mobile—and test your customized site using the W3C mobileOK Checker[5]. Figure 1.97 shows the results of our customized site for Quill Driver Books. Luckily, we only added one additional error during our customization so our site is still ranked at 76%. We still want to get it to at least 90%.

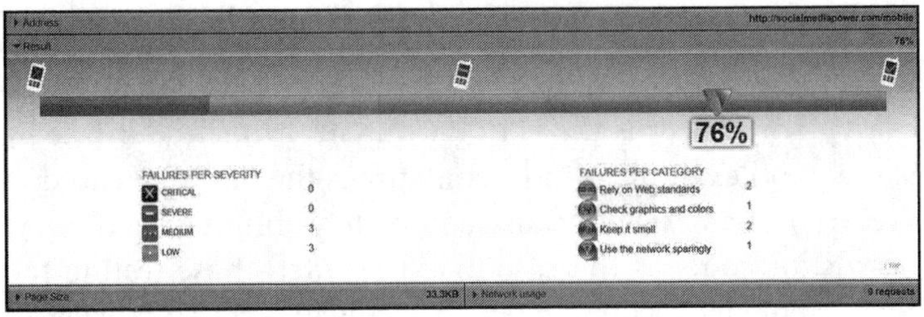

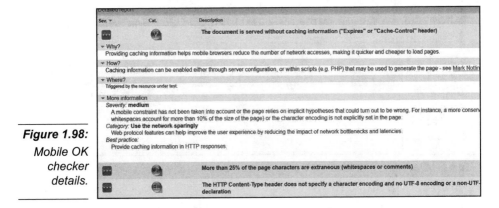

Figure 1.97:

Mobile OK checker results.

There are many types of errors you can encounter when attempting to validate your mobile site, and we can't address them all in this section. Instead, we want to demonstrate some troubleshooting techniques you can apply to help keep your site mostly error free.

Figure 1.98 shows the list of errors encountered by our example site. We don't have any critical or serious errors, but there are a few medium and low level errors that can be addressed. We will tackle them one at a time.

Figure 1.98:

Mobile OK checker details.

The first error warns that our site does not use caching. As Figure 1.98 demonstrates, clicking on an error within this tool reveals a lot of information on the error as well as recommendations for fixing it. After some research using the tool, we discover that there is no need to implement a caching script on a site as small as ours, so we add a basic line of code into the <head> section of our HTML files, like this: <meta http-equiv="Cache-Control" content="public"/>. This will allow browsers to cache our page information however it sees fit. If we wanted more control as to how and what we wanted a browser to cache, we would need to use a script.

The next error points out that "More than 25% of the page characters are extraneous (whitespaces or comments)" (see Figure 1.98). The cause of this error is the documentation that the template author placed in the index. html file. Though this was helpful while we were customizing our site, it is no longer necessary, so we remove the comments from all of our HTML files.

The last error concerns the HTTP Content-Type header (see Figure 1.98). This is a good example of how sometimes the best one can do is to lessen the severity of an error because completely eliminating the error is not in the cards, or code, as the case may be. Often these testing tools will not validate elements within newer protocols like HTML5, even if the syntax is correct.

We can improve upon this particular error, however, by moving the HTTP Content-Type header statement just under our <head> tag. This is a tactic we discovered while investigating this error within the validation tool.

The last issue we address is one of the low level errors that warns that our page size is too large. We lessen the severity of the error by running our images through an image cruncher[6] to reduce the page sizes.

All of these changes improves our ranking to 90%—as seen in Figure 1.99—which is a very respectable score.

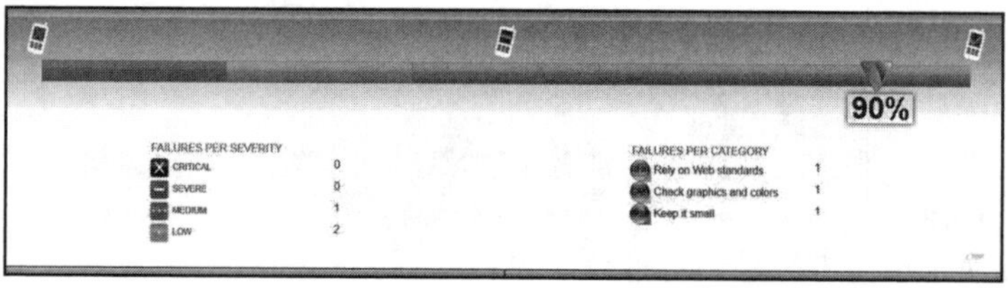

Figure 1.99:
Mobile OK
checker
results final.

Search Optimization

Figure 1.100 shows part of the metadata already in place in the index.html file of our example site. We need to change the values for each of our site files to reflect our own best search engine optimized titles, descriptions, and key terms. Figure 1.101 shows how we change it for Quill Driver Books' index.html file. Change or add the title, description, and keyword metadata in every one of your files using SEO best practices. See page 84 for more details.

Figure 1.100,
Figure 1.101:

Template
metadata;
Quill Driver
metadata.

```
<title>Fone HTML5 mobile template</title>
<meta name="keywords" content="Fone HTML5 mobile template, QRd
<meta name="description" content="Fone is an HTML5 mobile web tem
free Creative Commons web page template, at www.QRdvark.com/temp

<title>Quill Driver Books Publisher of Books on Business, Writing, and
<meta name="keywords" content="Quill driver books, independent publ
publishing, writing books, publishing books, books on business, californi
<meta name="description" content="Quill Driver Books is an award win
life after fifty, and California history.">
```

Custom Domain Name

Since this is a stand-alone site on your own server or hosting account, just point a CNAME record to the directory your site resides in—yoursitename. com/mobile in our example. It is recommended that you use a sub-domain name like m.yoursitename.com. See page 79 for more information. This step is not applicable if your mobile site is the primary domain on your server or hosting account.

Redirection

The method you use for redirection depends on the type of server or hosting account you have. Refer to the "Detection and Redirection" section on page 81 for details.

Adding Special Functionality to Your HTML Site

You may want to add special functionality to your mobile site, either right away or in a later phase of your site strategy. Though we can't show you how to implement all possible features, we can give you a glimpse at where you might find solutions to some of them. Below is a sampling of features you can add to your site with little effort or specialized knowledge.

Look in the resource section of this book for other books that can help you create advanced functionality for your mobile sites.

Forms

In the Quill Driver Books example, we used Google Docs[27] to create our form. This is an easy and convenient way to place forms onto any website. You can embed the form on your site, receive notifications of completed forms, and access the form data from a Google Docs spreadsheet.

Click-to-call

Most mobile browsers support the following syntax that should trigger a mobile device's capability to call a phone number when clicked:

```
<a href="tel:+phonenumberhere">
```

Embedding Videos

Videos can be embedded into a mobile site with the HTML5 video tag or by using a service like YouTube.

When embedding YouTube videos, grab the embed code by clicking on "embed" under any video on YouTube as shown in Figure 1.102. The only customization you need to make is to change the size as shown. Once you have the code, place it in your website where you want the video to appear. See QR Code 1.11 for a video on how to place YouTube video embed code.

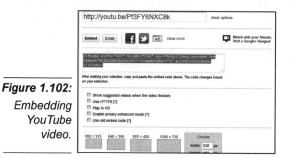

Figure 1.102:

Embedding YouTube video.

The problem with the YouTube embed method is that it uses frames, which don't work on some mobile devices, and a site will not validate very well as a result.

Embedding video using HTML5 can solve the validation issues, but there is another issue. Not all mobile devices and browsers render the HTML video tag properly. It is best to find a solution that has fall back methods. There are a number of open source solutions that can help, like Video For Everybody[28]. Refer to the resource section for additional solutions.

Google Maps

To embed maps in your mobile site, use the Google Maps API[15]. They have a good tutorial that can run you through how to set up and configure your embedded maps, as well as provide you with sample code. Don't be intimidated by using APIs—especially Google APIs—as the process is not that difficult if you follow the tutorials closely.

Additional APIs

There are a lot of APIs you can utilize to add nice features to your mobile site. Look through the Google Code directory[29] for ideas. You can find solutions for embedded calendars, payment solutions, analytics, monetizing your site with ads, and more. When you add functionality of any kind to your site, be sure to retest for errors.

QR Code 1.11:

Embedding YouTube video[11].

Configuring Custom Domains

▶ **Bootstrapper's Guide** ◀

√ Choose the type of domain name you want for your mobile website.
√ If you want a subdomain like m.yoursite.com, create a CName record.
√ Have your host service create your CName record for you, if needed.
√ Most services provide the CName info you need to direct your site.

As we discuss throughout this chapter, you have several choices for the URL (or domain name) of your mobile site. Ideally, you want to create a custom domain name (also called a sub-domain or alias) like "m.yoursitename. com" for the mobile version of your website.

If you use a hosting or conversion service to create your mobile site, they will assign their own URL for your site and (in most cases) offer you information that allows you to create your own custom domain name that replaces the one they assigned. You then need to "point" this custom domain name to your mobile site. This section is dedicated to showing you how to create and point such a custom domain name using CNAME records.

It is important to understand that only you can create a custom domain name associated with any domain name you own. A hosting or conversion service will simply provide you with what is called the "CNAME record destination" that you can use when creating the CNAME record for your custom domain name.

Domain Name System (DNS) is the naming system used to translate and manage domain names used by the Internet. A CNAME record (Canonical Name record) is used to establish an alias of an existing domain name. It is this alias we use as our custom domain name.

In our example, the main domain name is http://plumbwebsolutions. com. The alias (custom domain name) we want to create is http://m. plumbwebsolutions.com. If we entered the custom domain name (http://m. plumbwebsolutions.com) in a browser without establishing it as an alias, we would be taken to the main site (http://plumbwebsolutions.com). But if we tell the DNS to assign the alias to another destination, then entering the custom domain name in a browser will take us to that established destination.

The goal of our example is to create a custom domain name for Plumb Web Solutions that will take visitors to the mobile site we created using the hosting service Mofuse. See the original example beginning on page 51.

In that example (see Figure 1.103), we made a note of the CNAME information provided by Mofuse. Now we can use that information to create our custom domain name that will ultimately point to our Mofuse mobile site.

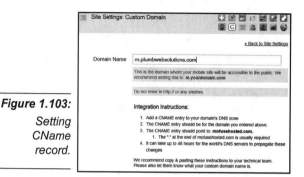

Figure 1.103:

Setting CName record.

The next step is to go to the control panel (or site manager) of your hosting service (the service where your domain is registered) and create the alias using a CNAME record. Once in the control panel of your hosting service, look for an option called "DNS Records" or "Manage Domains" or something similar.

Figure 1.104 shows how we create the CNAME entry in the control panel of our hosting service after selecting the option "DNS Records" under the "Domain Settings" options. Our "subdomain name" or "alias" is "m" and our destination is the address that Mofuse provided us: "mofusehosting. com." (Note that the trailing "." at the end of "mofusehosting.com" is necessary.)

Your hosting provider's control panel will probably look very different from ours, but the concept is the same—just look for similar menu choices. If you do not know how to access this area of your hosting account or are unsure about any part of the process, contact your hosting provider support services.

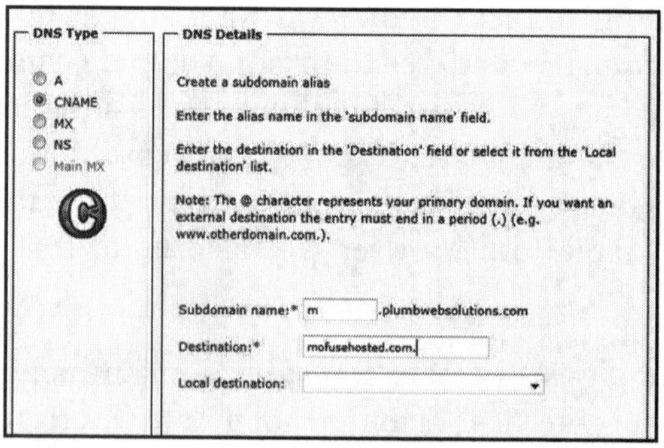

Figure 1.104:

Setting CName record (2).

If you need to contact your hosting provider for tech support to complete this task, the following statements should keep the conversation short and to the point:

"I need to create a CNAME record that points to my new mobile site. The main domain name is _____ (your main domain name) and the sub-domain I want to create is _____ (the custom domain name like "m.mysitename.com"). Here is the CNAME record information provided to me by the mobile hosting service: _____ (in our example, this would be "mofusehosting.com.").

If you created a stand-alone mobile site in a directory on your main site, like on http://yoursitename.com/mobile, and want to point a sub-domain or custom domain name to the directory, use the same process as above, but replace the destination with the full URL of the directory (http://yoursitename.com/mobile or wherever the mobile site it located).

See QR Code 1.12 for a video on how to create custom domains.

Detection and Redirection

▶ Bootstrapper's Guide ◀

√ Try to use a server-side script to redirect traffic to your mobile site.
√ An alternative is to use a JavaScript script placed in your HTML.
√ Direct users with a link on your desktop site, or with a QR code.
√ Always give visitors a choice between your mobile or standard site.

The purpose of this step in the mobile website preparation process is to "detect" what type of device is accessing our website, and "direct" the device to either the desktop or the mobile version of the website.

What we need is a script (a small program) on our main website that determines the type of device accessing the website and seamlessly redirects the user to the appropriate version of the site. This section is meant to give you a general idea of how to accomplish this task; no attempt is made to show you how these scripts work.

QR Code 1.12:
Creating custom domains video[12].

QR Code 1.13:
Using redirection scripts video[13].

The general process to get your mobile site traffic redirected to your mobile website is as follows:

- Determine which server-side scripting language is available to you (by asking the tech support department of your hosting service).

- Acquire the script necessary for redirecting your site visitors (either from your mobile website hosting/conversion service, or from another source).

- Place the script on your main website's server (ask your hosting service for instructions on how to do this).

- If you do not have server access to your site, place a JavaScript script after the <head> tag of your index.html file.

See QR Code 1.13 on page 81 for a video on redirection scripts.

Server-Side Scripts

Website hosting services offer "server-side scripting languages" to assist users in developing websites. The most common server-side scripting languages are PHP, JSP, ASP, ASP.NET, Python, and Ruby. Most likely, your hosting service makes at least one of these languages available for you to use. The first step in the detection and redirection process is to find out which of these languages are available to you.

The next step is to find a script to do the "detect and redirect" task. If you are using a hosting or conversion service for your mobile website, the service will most likely generate a script for you to use on your server. We have already demonstrated this process in many of the hosting examples in this chapter.

On page 55, we demonstrate how to acquire the necessary detection and redirection code using Mofuse. Figure 1.105 shows the redirection instructions from Mofuse. They offer "server-side" redirection scripts for PHP, ASP, ASP.NET, and JSP.

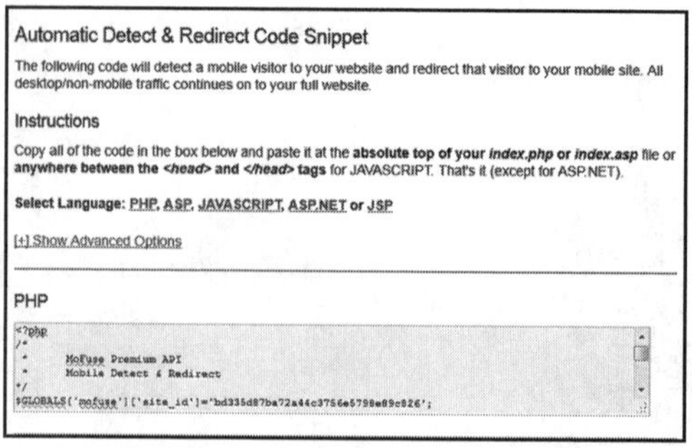

Figure 1.105:

Redirect code

from Mofuse.

Finding Scripts and Services

If you are creating a stand-alone site, or your hosting/conversion service does not provide you with redirection scripts, there are other options available. There are quite a few open source mobile detection scripts you can use and alter to fit your needs.

A couple of good sources for finding scripts are Sourceforge[30] and Hotscripts[31]. If your site uses ASP.NET, you should also check out 51degrees[32]. When choosing a script, look for one that a lot of other folks are using and is rated well among its users.

If you get a lot of traffic to your site, or are running an enterprise level site, you might consider investing in a cloud detection service like DeviceAtlas[33], or purchasing a premium detection script like Detect Mobiles[34]. Look in the resource section of this chapter for additional sources of mobile detection scripts and services.

Placing Your Script

With script in hand, the final step is to place the script on your hosting server. If you have a PHP or ASP script (classic ASP, not ASP.NET), find the index.php or index.asp file in the root of your server, and paste the code at the very top of the file. If you are unsure how to do this, or for other server-side scripting languages, contact your hosting service tech support for instructions, or follow the instructions provided by your mobile hosting service.

Using JavaScript

If you do not have server access to your site, but do have access to the index. html file of your website, you can still detect and redirect using a JavaScript script. Most hosting/conversion services offer JavaScript alternatives (see Figure 1.105 above) in addition to their server-side solutions, and you can find JavaScript solutions at the open source resources mentioned above.

Once you have a JavaScript mobile detection script, place it at the very top of the "head" section of your index.html file (just under the <head> tag). Though using a script like this seems easier than using a server-side script, there are some disadvantages:

- Users can disable JavaScript in their browsers, in which case your script will not work.
- Some mobile browsers (especially older browsers) do not support JavaScript at all.

- Mobile device users can set their phones to modes (WAP and WML modes) that do not support JavaScript (many feature phones and BlackBerries have this option).

As a result, you should only use a JavaScript mobile detection script as a last resort.

No Redirection

There is no hard and fast rule that says you must redirect mobile device users to your mobile site. You could just as easily offer them a nice big button to click that takes them to your mobile site. The problem with this option is that your desktop site may not display properly on mobile devices, so visitors may not get a chance to see the button.

Give Your Visitors a Choice!

Regardless of how you direct (or redirect) your visitors to your mobile site, you should still give them an option of viewing the desktop or the mobile version of your site. Many smartphone users prefer to view the desktop version of a website rather than the mobile version, while some tablet computer users prefer mobile versions over desktop versions. Always offer buttons or links at the bottom or top of your site so users can choose which version of your site they wish to view. (See the discussion on page 24.)

Search Optimization Considerations

▶ Bootstrapper's Guide ◀

√ Use best practices like small images, good metadata, error-free code.
√ Optimize keywords for suggested search features like Google Instant.
√ Create a mobile sitemap so Google's mobile robots can list your site.
√ Research any service you plan to use for the "transcoding" issue.

Search engines like Google, Yahoo, and Bing use different bots (search engine robots) and algorithms for their mobile search engines than they do for their traditional search engines. Mobile search bots place emphasis on how well a website renders on mobile devices.

In the chapter examples, we address best practices that can help a mobile website render well on mobile devices and place well in mobile search engines. Some of these tactics include:

- Keeping images and page sizes as small as possible

- Using keywords in page titles, descriptions, file names, and image names
- Using titles and alt names for images
- Making sure the HTML and CSS is error free
- Avoiding proprietary scripts and Flash
- Using detection and redirection

In this section, we discuss some additional search optimization issues that are specific to mobile websites. We also look at some search optimization considerations that may affect your mobile website solution choices.

Existing Search Optimization Efforts

One of the best search strategies you can use for your mobile site is to keep applying traditional search engine optimization techniques to your existing website. Regardless of the solution you ultimately choose for your mobile site, driving traffic to your existing website will also drive traffic to the mobile version of your site, that is, as long as you are properly redirecting and/or promoting your mobile website as discussed on pages 81 and 100 respectively.

For an introduction to effective search optimization techniques, read Google's "Search Engine Optimization Starter Guide"[35]. And watch for the next book in this series, *The Bootstrapper's Guide to the New Search Optimization*, for a practical down-to-earth framework for achieving great results across a spectrum of search engines.

Relevancy

One major element of a good search optimization framework is relevancy. This area includes the relevancy of your web content to your meta keywords, titles, and descriptions, as well as the relevancy of your outgoing links, the "friends" you keep in social media realms, the topics you blog about, etc.

Your mobile website content should also conform to this type of relevancy, and this starts with your metadata. Focus on "organic" search optimization when developing your metadata—this means you find keywords based on your content, rather than forcing keywords into your content. Use the following strategy to accomplish this:

- Research the best keyword and keyword phrases to use for your overall website (look in the resource section for tools to help you achieve this).

- When choosing keywords for each page of your website, make certain the keywords (or synonyms of them) are contained within the content of the page itself.

- Write each page title and description using as many keywords as possible without sacrificing clarity.

- Your titles and descriptions should tell potential visitors exactly what they will find on a page.

- Remember to limit your titles to 60 characters, and your descriptions to 160 characters.

If you are creating your own mobile website based on an existing desktop site, you should keep the metadata as similar as possible for each site. Though, as demonstrated in the next section, you might want to revisit some of your keyword choices specifically for your mobile web pages.

Google Instant and Related Searches

Google Instant is the feature where a person starts to type into a search box in Google search and Google offers them "instant" choices based on what they are typing (see Figure 1.106 and Figure 1.107). Other search engines provide similar "suggested search" features. This feature is of particular interest when optimizing for mobile search, since people tend to type as few characters as possible on a mobile device. As a result, they are far more likely to use Google Instant than desktop computer users.

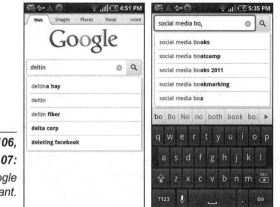

Figure 1.106,
Figure 1.107:
Google
Instant.

Optimizing for Google Instant can be tricky and time consuming. Use the following strategy to help improve your mobile website's placement in Google Instant search results:

- Go to Google.com on a mobile device

- Type in the first few letters of your best "short" keywords (see Figure 1.106)
- Type in the first couple of words of longer keyword phrases (see Figure 1.107)
- Note the relevant recommendations offered by Google Instant for both scenarios
- Use the resulting (and relevant) keyword phrases as your own meta keywords and within your meta titles and descriptions

Even if a site is ranking well in initial search results, it is the title and description that will ultimately grab the user's attention. Figure 1.108 shows our search results when we choose Google Instant's first suggestion in our first example. In the first result of our example, "Deltina Hay social media and Web 2.0 author, speaker, educator, ..." is the meta title, and the meta description is "Deltina Hay helps to empower you with the tools of social media with her books, presentations, and videos."

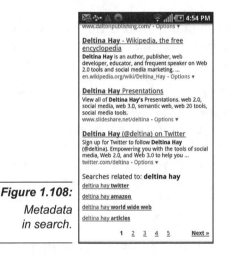

Figure 1.108:

Metadata in search.

Not only should your titles and descriptions contain relevant keywords, they should accurately represent the content on the web page they represent.

Figure 1.109 and Figure 1.110 show the same search results in our examples, but further down the page. Here we see Google's suggested "Related Searches." Again, mobile device users are more likely to click on one of these links rather than type in longer search terms themselves. This is another tactic you can use to gather relevant and effective keywords for your websites.

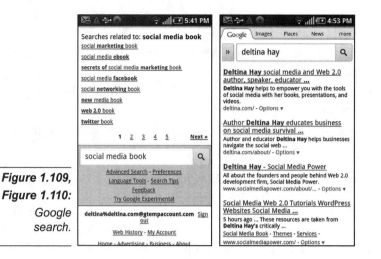

Figure 1.109,

Figure 1.110:

Google

search.

Consistency

Another tactic that is important to good search optimization is to keep your desktop and mobile sites as consistent as possible. This means you should mimic the pages of your desktop site on your mobile site as much as possible—especially if you are detecting and redirecting (see page 81).

If you are creating your own mobile site, keep each page content as similar as possible to the respective pages of the desktop site. You still want to adhere to mobile website best practices, but the crux of the information should remain the same. If your site is large, you probably shouldn't recreate every page of your desktop site on your mobile site, but the ones you do create should serve up similar information to their desktop counterparts. You should also link individual mobile pages directly to their desktop counterparts and vice versa, when applicable.

Many hosting services let you create individual pages that can help you maintain more consistency, and CMS plugins should handle this issue with ease. Consistency is not an issue if you are using responsive design techniques, as long as you are only altering styles (and not content) using responsive techniques.

Mobile Sitemaps

Google Sitemaps are an important part of any good search optimization strategy. In its simplest form, a Sitemap is an XML file you create and place on your server that tells Google about the pages on your website. This helps the Google search bots find and crawl all of your web pages more efficiently. Once your Sitemap file is in place, you need to submit it to Google. You can learn more about how to create and submit Sitemaps at Google Support[36].

In addition to a standard Sitemap, you should submit a mobile Sitemap to Google. Mobile Sitemap requirements can also be found on Google Support[37]. This is a great way to let Google's mobile search bots know about the mobile version of your website.

If you are creating your own mobile website or are using a conversion service, you need to create and submit a Sitemap yourself to let Google know about your mobile site. If you are using a hosting service, check with the service to find out if they submit Sitemaps to Google for you (most of the services do).

Your mobile Sitemap should only include the pages of your site that are mobile friendly. Google's mobile bot will ignore all other pages. So if you are using responsive design techniques, you should still create a mobile Sitemap but only include pages that are mobile ready.

There are third-party services that can create Sitemaps for you[38], but you should check that they are using the most up-to-date mobile Sitemap standards set by Google[37]. CMSs like WordPress have plugins that create and maintain Sitemaps for you, but again, check that they include mobile Sitemaps in addition to standard Sitemaps.

Transcoding

Search engines prefer to offer all the content in their indexes to mobile browsers, even if that content is not optimized for mobile devices. But to ensure all content displays properly on mobile devices, Google and other search engines display web search results through a "transcoder." Transcoding means that a search engine may resize, adjust, or convert images; reformat text; suppress Flash and other incompatible scripts; and alter other functionality of a website that does not conform to mobile standards.

Transcoding should not be a problem if you are following mobile website best practices, but it can be an issue if you use a conversion service or responsive web design. As previously discussed, a conversion service may be a good choice for your website if you have a large site and have good search engine placement that you want to maintain. But many conversion services actually use transcoding when converting your site.

Search optimization issues arise when conversion services convert images and files, as they may be renaming them and stripping them of their titles and alt text, which are key elements to good search optimization. Before deciding on a conversion service, you should ask them how they handle transcoding, and be assured that your search optimization efforts will be preserved.

If you are using responsive web design, mobile search bots may not recognize your media queries, and attempt to transcode your site based on the standard (or desktop) style sheet instead of your mobile style sheets. In this case, you should use a "no_transform" directive in the cache-control header of your web pages. This indicates to transcoders not to modify your pages since they are already mobile-ready.

You should place the directive like this (and in this position) in the header section of your web pages:

```
<head>
    <meta http-equiv="Content-Type" content="text/html; charset=utf-8" />
    <meta http-equiv="Cache-Control" content="no-transform" />
    ...
</head>
```

Getting good search placement requires commitment. If you painstakingly optimize each of your web pages, every blog post you create, all of your social media profiles and updates, and every other element of your web presence, you are well on your way. But frequency and diversity are also key. Posting to a blog and social networking sites regularly and establishing a presence in as many applicable places online as you can are equally as important in today's real-time Internet environment. This method of complete search optimization is the topic of the next book in the Bootstrapper's Guide series.

Testing Your Mobile Website

> ### ► Bootstrapper's Guide ◄
> √ Determine the devices you want to target and focus testing accordingly.
> √ Device emulators can depict how your site renders on mobile devices.
> √ Use W3C validation tools to test and troubleshoot HTML and CSS.
> √ Use testing tools like the W3C mobile site checker and mobiReady.

We have demonstrated many testing and troubleshooting methods throughout the examples in this chapter. In this section, we explore some additional troubleshooting techniques and tools you can use to test your mobile website.

Determining Your Target Devices

Before testing your mobile website, determine the types of phones and other mobile devices you want to target. Do you want to target all tablet, smartphone, and feature phone users? Or, are you only interested in the most popular models?

Figure 1.111 and Figure 1.112 show the mobile browser and mobile OS (operating system) stats for the United States from August 2010 to July 2011 from StatCounter[39]. Use stats like these to determine what part of the market you want to target.

Another tactic you can use to determine your target device market is to look at the analytics for your current website. You can get a lot of insight into which devices your site visitors are using to access your site. See the "Mobile Site Analytics" section on page 97 for more information.

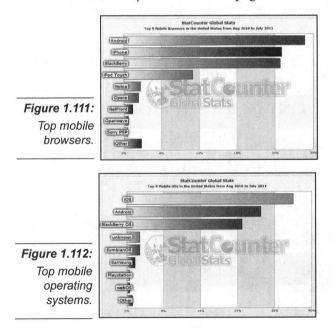

Figure 1.111:

Top mobile browsers.

Figure 1.112:

Top mobile operating systems.

Mobile Device Emulators

Chances are, you don't have access to every type of mobile device you are targeting. This is where mobile device emulators can help. Emulators help you get a feel for how your site will actually look and behave on various mobile devices.

It is particularly important to use emulators to test sites that don't do well on the testing tools—like HTML5 and/or responsive websites, as we demonstrate later in this section.

There are a lot of emulators out there, and one could go nuts trying to test a mobile site on every mobile device in existence. You want to focus on emulators for your target devices, but choose more than one emulator. Testing your site on a variety of emulators and getting consistent results is the goal.

If you are targeting the majority of operating systems and browsers (see Figure 1.111 and Figure 1.112 on page 91), then the following emulators are good places to start. If you want a larger selection, there are more emulators listed in the resource section.

The emulators featured here are free and come with easy-to-follow instructions. For most, just enter the URL of the site you want to test, press Enter, and get the results.

Figure 1.113 shows our responsive site example on the IphoneTester emulator[40]. This emulator is only good for testing iPhone devices. Figure 1.114 shows our example site on MobileWebsites.com's mobile preview[41]. This tool emulates iPhone, Droid, and Blackberry devices.

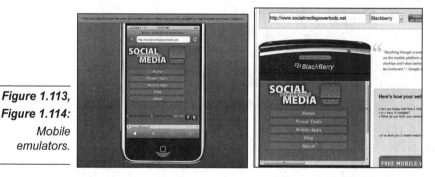

**Figure 1.113,
Figure 1.114:**

*Mobile
emulators.*

Figure 1.115 and Figure 1.116 show the example site on the Mobile Phone Emulator[42] for a Samsung phone and a smaller LG feature phone, respectively. This emulator offers many more options. You can set your current monitor size to help keep things in perspective and choose from many smartphone and feature phone models.

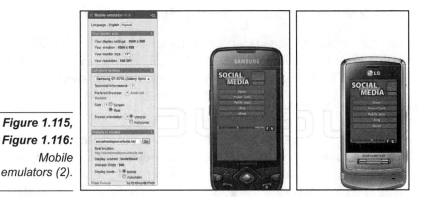

Figure 1.115,
Figure 1.116:
Mobile
emulators (2).

W3C Validation Services

A host of validation tools is offered by the World Wide Web Consortium (W3C)[43]. These validation tools are most relied upon by web developers since they are managed by the organization that sets the standards for HTML and CSS. The tools we are most interested in for this book are the mobileOK Checker[5], the markup validator[44], and the CSS validator[45].

W3C mobileOK Checker

We have seen this tool demonstrated a lot in this chapter, and for good reason. It is one of the best ways to test your mobile site for many issues that can affect how well your site performs on mobile devices. The mobileOK Checker uses a number of basic tests that the W3C defines on their site[46]. Some of these tests include:

- Redirection; caching; character encoding
- Valid markup and style sheets; use of external resources
- Graphics; use of tables
- Image and file sizes; use of pop ups

The entire list pretty much sums up the best practices you want to apply to any mobile website (see the "Mobile Website Best Practices" section on page 16).

W3C Markup Validator

The Markup Validator is a free tool and service that validates markup. In other words, it checks the syntax of web documents, written in formats such as HTML, (X)HTML, etc.

W3C CSS Validator

The W3C CSS Validation Service is a free software created by the W3C to help web designers and web developers check for errors on Cascading Style Sheets (CSS) and (X)HTML documents with embedded style sheets.

Using the W3C Validation Tools

In this section, we explore some issues you may encounter when using the W3C validation tools to test stand-alone mobile websites and responsive websites. It is assumed in this section that the reader has a general knowledge of HTML and CSS. To test your site as demonstrated here, simply go to the validation tool and enter the URL of the site you wish to test.

Stand-Alone Sites

In our stand-alone mobile website example beginning on page 69, we demonstrate some troubleshooting techniques you can use to help your site score better on the W3C mobileOK Checker. Note that regardless of how your mobile site scores on the mobileOK Checker, when creating your own mobile website, you should validate the HTML and the CSS.

Our stand-alone site eventually scored 90% on the mobileOK Checker, but we want to make certain that the HTML and the CSS are valid for the site. Figure 1.117 shows the results of the W3C markup validator for our stand-alone mobile site. The validator recognizes the code as HTML5 and uses the experimental HTML5 conformance tester to validate the site.

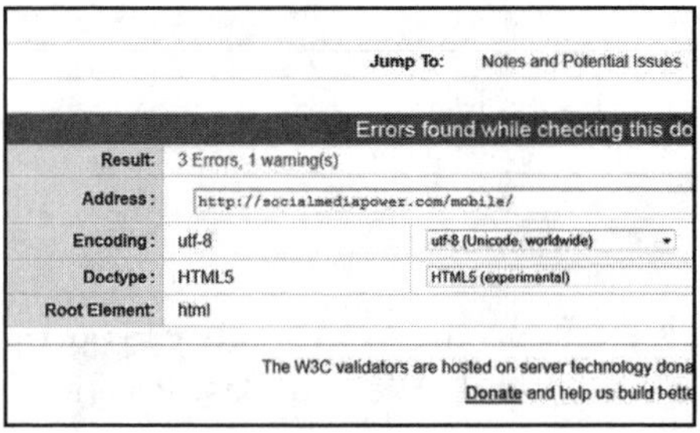

Figure 1.117: W3C Validation.

Even though we are confident there are no errors, the site does not validate. The problem is not necessarily with the markup code, but more likely with the experimental nature of the HTML5 validator. We intentionally used an HTML5 template to design this site, mainly because most mobile browsers support HTML5. Using the latest (but not necessarily the standard) version of HTML can often result in these types of issues.

The solution is to go back to the most recent "strict" (no longer experimental) version of the HTML validator to see if your site passes. Figure 1.118 shows how to do this. Clicking on "More Options" on the validator tool reveals some ways you can control how the tool validates your site. We choose to attempt a validation using the last strict version of HTML (4.01), just so we know there are no errors. Figure 1.119 shows that the site does validate, if tentative, using this option.

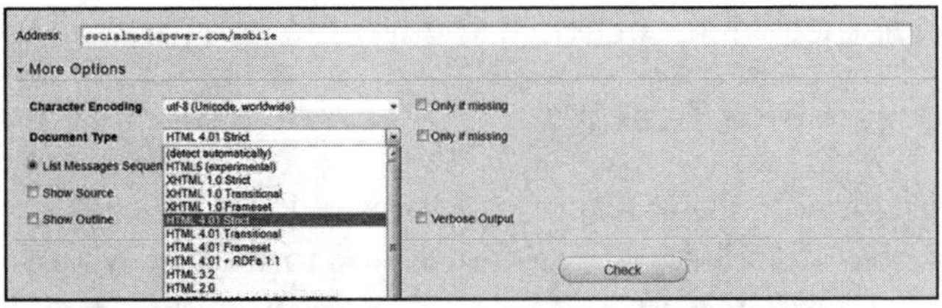

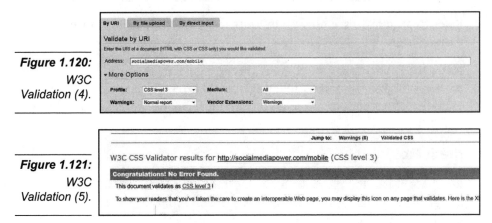

Figure 1.118: W3C Validation (2).

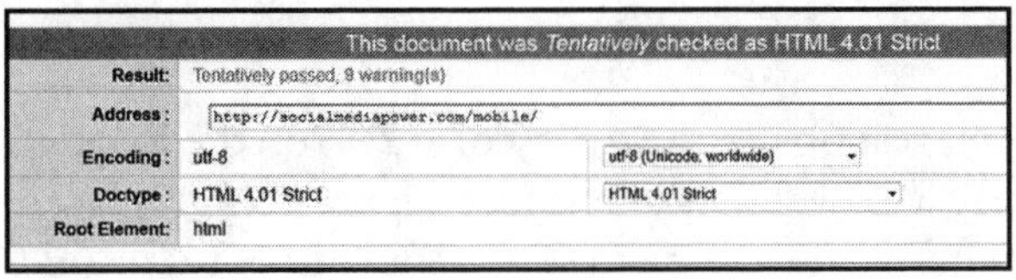

Figure 1.119: W3C Validation (3).

Our next step is to try to validate the CSS for our stand-alone mobile site. Figure 1.120 shows the W3C CSS validator. We click on "More Options" so we can let the validator know to test this as CSS level 3. If you are using a template or your own CSS that uses external styles from libraries like Webkit, as we do in this example, it is best to change the "Vendor Extensions" option to "warnings." Figure 1.121 shows that our CSS validates.

Figure 1.120: W3C Validation (4).

Figure 1.121: W3C Validation (5).

There is always a risk of your site not validating or rendering properly when implementing the latest features of HTML and CSS, as we have seen here, especially as it applies to legacy browsers. But the advantage to coding for mobile browsers is that they are all fairly new, so legacy isn't that much of an issue.

If you want to use the most recent features of HTML5 and CSS3—even if legacy browsers don't support them yet—there are things you can do to find out whether a feature is in use on the browser accessing your site, and there are alternatives you can offer if not. It is beyond the scope of this book to go into more detail on this topic, but there is a tool you can use called Modernizr[47] that can help if you want to know more.

Responsive Site Testing

As we discovered in our responsive website example beginning on page 62, the mobileOK Checker does not know to look only for the relevant (phone or handheld) style sheets when testing the site. As a result, responsive sites do not score well.

Even though our responsive site only scores 21% on the mobileOK Checker, it passed the HTML5 validation test (see Figure 1.122). Just as with stand-alone mobile sites, you should make certain your HTML and CSS validate for your responsive mobile sites.

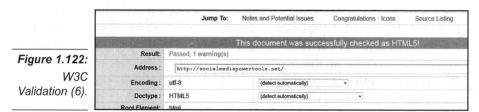

Figure 1.122:
W3C
Validation (6).

Refer to page 69 to see how we test our responsive site using a responsive design tester.

Note: The target devices for the previous examples are mainly smartphones. As a result, we focus on validating for HTML5. If your target devices include feature phones as well, you should focus on validating for strict XHTML.

readyMobi

ReadyMobi is a mobile website testing tool offered by MobiForge[48], and is a great resource for all things mobile. ReadyMobi tests your site for all mobile phones—feature phones and smartphones alike. This means that even if you plan only to target the larger screen smartphones, your score with readyMobi will reflect how your site will likely perform on all phones.

Figure 1.123 shows the basic readyMobi page tester with the highest score of 5 for our Wirenode example site. You can test individual pages (by entering the direct URL to the page), or get a free account with MobiForge to get access to the more sophisticated site tester.

On the site tester, enter the home page URL of your mobile site and it will return results for the entire site. Figure 1.124 shows the results of our stand-alone site for Quill Driver Books (see page 69). At this level, the tool can give you valuable insight into problems your site may encounter when displaying on mobile devices.

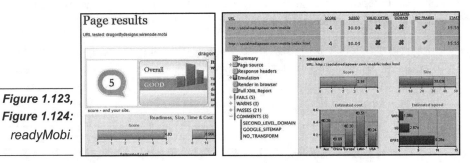

Figure 1.123,
Figure 1.124:
readyMobi.

In our example, our main target devices are smartphones, so we are not too concerned with some of the stricter criteria of this testing tool. There are some comments we take notice of, though, including the "Google sitemap" and "no transform" comments. These are issues we discuss in the "Search Optimization Considerations" section beginning on page 84. If you plan to target all types of mobile phones, you should investigate all of the errors recorded by readyMobi.

A responsive website will encounter the same problems with this tool as it does with the W3C mobileOK Checker, where the tool accesses the wrong style sheet to base its score upon. For the sites that do not score well on these types of tools, be certain to test them on a few good emulators.

Mobile Site Analytics

▶ **Bootstrapper's Guide** ◀

√ Use the new version of Google Analytics to see your mobile traffic.
√ Use analytics reports to see which mobile devices visitors use most.
√ Many services allow you to add Google Analytics code for tracking.
√ Use mobile analytics tools like PercentMobile in addition to Google.

Mobile site analytics can give you insight into what types of mobile devices your site visitors use to access your site. You can use these metrics to see how well your SEO and promotional tactics are working, improve the performance of your site, or get an idea of which devices you need to target for optimization.

Google Analytics

Google Analytics[10] has long been the most popular way to track and analyze website traffic. If you do not use Google Analytics yet, set up an account with them. The Google Analytics tool provides you with "tracking code" that you place on your website. The code tracks your site traffic, and the results are reports that give you details on how many people are visiting your site, how they are getting there, and much more.

Google just recently added mobile analytics to their tracking algorithms. In order to see mobile analytics for your site, you need to use the "New Version" of Google Analytics (see Figure 1.125). Once on the new platform, you can access mobile analytics from the main menu (see Figure 1.126).

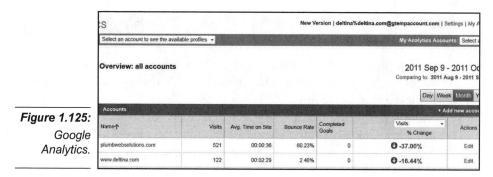

Figure 1.125:
Google Analytics.

Figure 1.126 shows the mobile analytics overview for one of our example sites. Toward the bottom of the screen it shows how many of our visits were from mobile devices. Clicking on "Devices" reveals the actual mobile devices that accessed our site (see Figure 1.127).

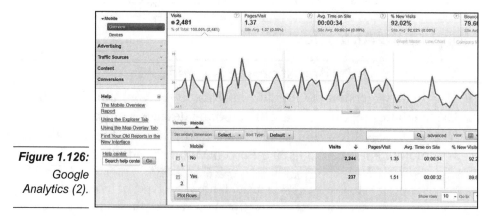

Figure 1.126:
Google Analytics (2).

Figure 1.127:
Google
Analytics (3).

This is how you can gain insight into how visitors are accessing your standard website when deciding on a device target for your mobile site (see page 91 for more information).

If you are using a hosting or conversion service for your mobile website, you can still take advantage of Google Analytics. Many of the hosting services we feature beginning on page 34 allow you to input your own Google Analytics code so you can conveniently gather insight into how your mobile site is performing.

Mobile Analytics Services

There are other tools that specialize in helping you gather mobile analytics. PercentMobile[49] is a mobile analytics tool that still has a free level. Figure 1.128 shows the same example and date range as the Google Analytics example above.

Figure 1.128:
Percent
Mobile.

The results are a bit different. The PercentMobile results show nearly 100 more mobile visits than Google Analytics. If you need to get very specific or accurate analytics for your site, you may consider using more than one tool. Refer to the resource section of this chapter for a list of free and paid mobile analytics tools.

Promoting Your Mobile Site

▶ **Bootstrapper's Guide** ◀

√ Promote on your desktop site and blogs using links and QR codes.
√ Use built-in promotion features of hosting and conversion services.
√ Promote your mobile site on your online and social media presence.
√ Add your mobile site to mobile website directories and "top lists."

Don't let all your efforts go to waste! Once your mobile site is launched, optimized, and tested, be sure to promote it as much as possible.

Promote on Your Desktop Site and Blog

Many of the hosting services we demonstrate in this chapter offer QR codes or widgets that can be used to promote your mobile site on your desktop site, blog, or any other place you can post images or widgets.

On page 46 we create a mobile site on the Winksite platform for the author's social media book. The Winksite service offers both a QR code and a widget we can use to promote this site on other websites and blogs.

Figure 1.129 shows the home page of the social media book Winksite mobile site. To use the QR code associated with this site, we right click with our mouse placed over the QR code image and "save image as" a file on our computer as shown, on Figure 1.129. We can now place this QR code (which is an image file) on any website or social media site where we want to promote our mobile site.

Figure 1.130 shows how we "place" the QR code image on the author's WordPress blog site by using HTML in a WordPress text widget. When placing a QR code on a desktop website or blog, make certain it also links to the source site. In our example, the image links to "http://winksite. mobi/deltina/socialmedia/" which is the home page of the Winksite. Even though the code is meant to be scanned by a mobile device, placing the code image this way allows visitors without a mobile device or QR code scanner to use it as a graphical link to your mobile site.

QR Code 1.14:
Placing code
on a website
video[14].

Figure 1.129,
Figure 1.130:

Placing a
QR code.

Figure 1.131 shows some "embed code" offered by Winksite that we can also copy and place on a website or blog to help promote our Winksite mobile site. We copy the embed code and place it in a text widget on the author's WordPress blog site (see Figure 1.130). See QR Code 1.14 for a video on how to place embed code on a website.

Figure 1.132 shows the Winksite logo on the author's site that links to the social media book Winksite, along with the QR code that can serve as a link or be scanned by a mobile device and take users to our mobile site. Read more about QR codes on page 186.

Figure 1.131,
Figure 1.132:

Placing
embed code.

You can use the method outlined above for any hosting or conversion service that offers QR codes and embeddable widgets. If a service does not offer such features or you have a stand-alone or CMS mobile site, you should still create a conspicuous button or link to your mobile site on all of your other relevant websites and blogs. You can also create your own QR code to direct mobile visitors to your site (see page 186).

Take Advantage of Built-In Features

If you are using a hosting or conversion service, use whatever promotion options they offer to get extra exposure for your mobile site. In the examples we feature in this chapter, we saw many built-in promotion options to take advantage of—here are a few:

- Mofuse offers a QR code manager (see page 56).

- Winksite has a community feature to tap into (see page 50).
- MobiSiteGalore offers an option to add your mobile site to directories as well as an email template you can use to promote your mobile site in campaigns (see page 40).

Promote to Your Existing Network

Reach out to your social media audience, professional networks, email lists, and other sources to let them know about your mobile web presence. Include a QR code in all your campaigns to make it easier for folks to bookmark your mobile site on their mobile device.

Read more about using QR codes to market your mobile site on page 186.

Mobile Directories and "Top Lists"

You can get extra exposure for your mobile website by submitting it to mobile website directories like idibidi[50] and seego[51]. Many of these directories are difficult to get listed in—they tend to be particular about the sites they include. That can be a real advantage if your site is chosen.

Top lists like Mobile Awesomeness[52] and surfwap[53] are crowd-sourced directories (individual sites are rated by site visitors and move toward the top of the directory based on the votes they receive). Your site will do better on these sites if they become popular with the site visitors, so encourage your supporters to vote for your site.

Look in the resource section of this chapter for a list of additional directories and top lists.

Mobile Shortcuts

You can instruct your site visitors on how to add your mobile site as a shortcut on their mobile device home screen. See page 147 for instructions on how to do this.

Other Tactics

Refer to the "Mobile Marketing Tactics" chapter on page 186. Many of these tactics can be applied to promoting and marketing your mobile website.

Endnotes

1. Mashable Tech. "Google:Desktops Will Be Irrelevant in Three Years' Time." http://mashable.com/2010/03/04/google-desktops-irrelevant

2. comScore, Inc. "2 out of 5 Smartphone Subscribers now Use Android Platform." http://www.comscore.com/Press_Events/Press_Releases/2011/8/comScore_Reports_June_2011_U.S._Mobile_Subscriber_Market_Share

3. Gartner Newsroom. "Gartner Highlights Key Predictions for IT Organizations and Users in 2010 and Beyond." http://www.gartner.com/it/page.jsp?id=1278413

4. Google Mobile Ads Blog. "Smartphone user study shows mobile movement under way." http://googlemobileads.blogspot.com/2011/04/smartphone-user-study-shows-mobile.html

5. W3C. "mobileOK Checker." http://validator.w3.org/mobile

6. Crunch4Free. http://crunch4free.net

7. Galleria. http://galleria.aino.se

8. goMobi. http://gomobi.info/home.html

9. Network Solutions. http://www.networksolutions.com

10. Google Analytics. http://www.google.com/analytics

11. mobiReady. http://ready.mobi/launch.jsp?locale=en_EN

12. Winksite. http://winksite.com/site/index.cfm

13. Mofuse. http://www.mofuse.com

14. bMobimized. http://bmobilized.com

15. Google Maps JavaScript API V3. http://code.google.com/apis/maps/documentation/javascript/

16. Prowl. http://www.prowlapp.com

17. Google Adsense. http://adsense.google.com

18. Wapple Architect Mobile Plugin for WordPress. http://wordpress.org/extend/plugins/wapple-architect/

19. Wapple. http://wapple.net

20. WPTouch Mobile Plugin for WordPress. http://wordpress.org/extend/plugins/wptouch

21. Elmastudio. http://www.elmastudio.de/wordpress-themes/yoko

22. Wirenode. http://www.wirenode.com

23. W3C Media Queries. http://www.w3.org/TR/css3-mediaqueries

24. css3-mediaqueries-js. http://code.google.com/p/css3-mediaqueries-js

25. ProtoFluid. http://app.protofluid.com

26. QRdvark Templates. http://www.qrdvark.com/templates/fone

27. Google Docs. http://docs.google.com

28. Video for Everybody!. http://camendesign.com/code/video_for_everybody

29. Google Code Site Directory. http://code.google.com/more

30. SourceForge. http://sourceforge.net

31. HotScripts. http://www.hotscripts.com

32. 51Degrees.mobi. http://51degrees.codeplex.com

33. DeviceAtlas. http://deviceatlas.com

34. Detect Mobile Browsers. http://detectmobilebrowsers.mobi

35. Google's Search Engine Optimization Starter Guide. http://www.google.com/en//
webmasters/docs/search-engine-optimization-starter-guide.pdf

36. Google Webmaster Tools Help. "Creating Sitmaps." http://www.google.com/
support/webmasters/bin/answer.py?answer=183668#2

37. Google Webmaster Tools Help. "Creating Mobile Sitemaps." http://www.google.
com/support/webmasters/bin/answer.py?answer=34648

38. Sitemap-generators. http://code.google.com/p/sitemap-generators/wiki/
SitemapGenerators

39. StatCounter Global Stats. http://gs.statcounter.com

40. iPhone Tester. http://iphonetester.com/

41. MobileWebsites. http://mobilewebsites.com/mobile-preview

42. Pixmobi. http://www.mobilephoneemulator.com

43. W3C. http://www.w3.org

44. W3C Markup Validation Service. http://validator.w3.org

45. W3C CSS Validation Service. http://jigsaw.w3.org/css-validator

46. W3C mobileOK Basic Tests 1.0. http://www.w3.org/TR/mobileOK-basic10-tests

47. Modernizr. http://www.modernizr.com

48. mobiForge. http://mobiforge.com

49. PercentMobile. http://percentmobile.com

50. idibidi. http://idibidi.com/directory.aspx

51. Seego. http://www.seego.com/home

52. Mobile Awesomeness. http://www.mobileawesomeness.com

53. SurfWAP. http://surfwap.com

QR Code Notes

1. Mobile Website Strategy Worksheet. http://goo.by/wZO6Mc/bgmw1-1

2. Mobile Website Preparation Form. http://goo.by/wkiCMF/bgmw1-2

3. Mobile Website Strategy Examples. http://goo.by/wJeM0B/bgmw1-3

4. GoMobi Mobile Website Examples. http://goo.by/wWcx1t/bgmw1-4

5. mobiSiteGalore Mobile Website Examples. http://goo.by/wEmqD8/bgmw1-5

6. Winksite Mobile Website Examples. http://goo.by/wQFZya/bgmw1-6

7. Mofuse Mobile Website Examples. http://goo.by/wwXmb6/bgmw1-7

8. bMobilized Demonstration. http://goo.by/wZmS3p/bgmw1-8

9. Responsive Website Sample Code. http://goo.by/w5zj9g/bgmw1-9

10. Sample HTML5 Template Code. http://goo.by/wM7QGk/bgmw1-10

11. Embedding YouTube Code Video. http://goo.by/w4yC9f/bgmw1-11

12. Custom Domain Video. http://goo.by/w5ImJE/bgmw1-12

13. Redirection Scripts Video. http://goo.by/w5jAYP/bgmw1-13

14. Placing Code Video. http://goo.by/w8w7Wf/bgmw1-14

15. Chapter One Resources. http://goo.by/wdAwxM/bgmw1-15

Additional Resources

Resources for the topics covered in this chapter can be found at TheBootstrappersGuide.com under the categories listed below. Additional resources and examples are added to the website on a regular basis.

Mobile Website Resources

- Mobile Website Creation Services
- Mobile Website Conversion Services
- Mobile Website Hosting Services
- WordPress Mobile Solutions
- Joomla! Mobile Solutions
- Drupal Mobile Solutions
- Responsive Web Design
- Mobile Website Templates
- HTML5 and CSS3 Tutorials
- Mobile Detect and Redirect Scripts
- SEO Tutorials
- Mobile Device Emulators
- Mobile Analytics Tools
- Mobile Website Directories

Mobile Website Worksheets

- Mobile Website Strategy Worksheet
- Mobile Website Preparation Worksheet

Mobile Website Examples

Mobile Website Strategy Examples
- Local restaurant, online sales, affiliate sales
- News/blog, personal branding
- Landing pages, lead generation
- Retail, PR, performance, local, and more

Mobile Website Service Examples
- bMobilized
- Google Sites
- Wirenode

QR Code 1.15:
Chapter one resources[15].

2 Mobile Applications

"THERE'S AN APP FOR THAT"® —trademark by APPLE, Inc. 2009[1]

In This Chapter

What Is a Mobile Application?

Classifications of Mobile Apps: Native, Web, or Shortcuts

But Do You NEED a Mobile Application?

Planning Your Mobile App

Mobile App Strategy Worksheet

Native App Solutions with Examples

Web App Solutions with Examples

Creating Mobile Shortcuts

Preparing App Assets

Redirecting, Promoting, Monetizing, Testing, Supporting, and Analyzing

Bootstrapper's Guide

I know what an app is, help me decide if I need one: Skip to page 118

What are my options for creating an app? See pages 114 and 116

I have a plan for my app, help me outline a strategy: Skip to page 125

Show me how to create apps to distribute in app stores: Skip to page 129

How can I use my HTML skills to create a web app easily? See page 133

I want to create a mobile shortcut for my website: Skip to page 147

How can I take advantage of the mobile app marketplace? See page 172

Mobile Applications

In the introduction to this book, we saw some staggering figures for existing mobile app usage and the expected growth in mobile app downloads. Specifically, ABI Research reports that "Global app downloads for year-end 2011 are expected to balloon to 29 billion, compared to only nine billion in 2010."[2]

In the previous chapter, we cited a study showing that mobile device users use mobile apps about as much as they use mobile search (see page 10). However, another study by Flurry shows that time spent on mobile apps continues to exceed time spent browsing (both PC and mobile browsing)[3]. See Figure 2.1.

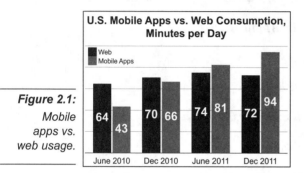

Figure 2.1: Mobile apps vs. web usage.

Before you get too excited and start building an app today, let's look at how that time was spent. Figure 2.2 shows a breakdown of Flurry's results by mobile app category.

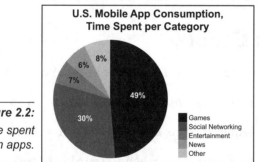

Figure 2.2: Time spent on apps.

Figure 2.2 reveals that consumers spent nearly 80% of their mobile-app time using games and social networking apps combined. The Flurry study further reveals that "consumers use these two categories more frequently, and for longer average session lengths, compared to other categories."[3]

These numbers are very encouraging if you plan to create a game or a mobile app related to social networking. But as we discuss in this chapter, creating, launching, and maintaining a mobile app that can be placed in the leading app stores requires investment, and should not be undertaken lightly.

Still we don't want to discourage you from creating your own mobile apps! Mobile apps offer businesses an opportunity to engage a target market whether online or not, and in ways a mobile website cannot. Plus, you can easily create mobile apps for less time and money—if they don't need to appear in the leading mobile app stores—and without a lick of programming.

In this chapter, we show you ways to create, deploy, and launch mobile apps all the way to those leading app stores and markets, if you are so inclined. We also show you how to create apps that your customers can download from your website or from app directories, galleries, and independent stores. We even show you how to serve up your mobile-optimized website as a mobile shortcut.

Though this chapter is a good introduction to mobile app development, its main focus is on how you can create and utilize mobile apps for your marketing efforts. If you are looking to develop more sophisticated apps for profit, refer to the resource section at the end of the chapter for further reading suggestions.

What Is a Mobile Application?

> ### ▶ Bootstrapper's Guide ◀
>
> ✓ A mobile application is a small program residing on a mobile device.
> ✓ Users download apps from app stores like iTunes and Android Market.
> ✓ Apps are developed on platforms for devices like iPhone and Android.
> ✓ Apps can work on specific platforms (native) or on all platforms (web).

A mobile application (mobile app) is a small program that resides on a mobile device, similar to how a software program resides on a desktop computer. You download and install mobile apps for a smartphone, tablet, or other mobile device, just as you would software for your desktop computer.

However, you do not install the *entire* software program when you install a mobile app. A mobile application is a "rich client front-end." That means that most of the program's front-end functionality (what the user sees and interacts with) is installed onto the mobile device, but the more complex, back-end functionality and most of the data are hosted online by the application developer. Most mobile apps store enough information on the mobile device to allow it to work whether the device is online or not.

The Mobile App Marketplace

Mobile device users download applications from a mobile application market or app store, from application directories and galleries, or directly from your website. Many mobile apps are free, and others range in price from $.99 to over $25, averaging around $3.

Each mobile device has its own platform. A platform is like an operating system. Apps developed for a specific mobile device need to adhere to the device's platform. Developers create apps for specific platforms and distribute their apps through the app stores (see page 130 for more details on this process).

App stores typically pay developers 70% of the sales price of an app, and require apps to go through a vetting process before they can be offered for sale (or for free) in a store. There are also independent stores that pay developers more and do not require vetting; however, many cell phone providers restrict download access to the leading stores only. See the resource section of this chapter for a list of mobile app stores.

Though Apple's App Store has dominated the mobile app market since the beginning, other stores are beginning to see a much larger market share. The table below shows the mobile app stores with the largest market share as of January 2012[4].

Store Name	App Store[5]	Android Market[6]	Ovi/ Nokia Store[7]	Black-berry App World[8]	Windows Phone Market-place[9]	Amazon Appstore[10]	GetJar, Pocket-Gear, Han-dango, others
Company	Apple	Google	Nokia	RIM	Microsoft	Amazon	Getjar/ Appia
Platform	iOS	Android	Series 40, Symbian, Maemo, MeeGo, Windows Phone	Black-berry OS	Windows Phone 7	Android	All
Number of Apps	550K+	450K+	117K+	60K+	61K+	22K+	Varies

Mobile App Trends

As shown in Figure 2.2 on page 108, the most popular apps are games and social networking apps, followed by apps that provide news and entertainment. Mobile apps come in a variety of forms. They can be simple feeds that pull information from a website all the way to full-featured financial applications that synch with a user's bank account.

Using data from the leading app stores over a 30-day period in Q2 2011, Nielsen[11] reports the percentage of downloads in each of the major mobile app store categories shown in Figure 2.3 below.

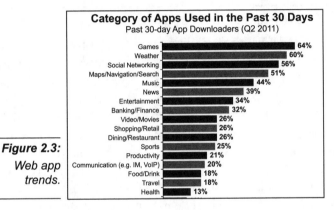

Figure 2.3:

Web app trends.

Current mobile app trends can give you insight into your target market, as well as ideas for your own mobile apps. They can also tip you off to the types of apps your competitors are creating, as well as which categories are already saturated.

Classification of Mobile Apps

There are two distinct types of mobile applications: *native* apps and web apps. And, though technically not a mobile app, a third option is the utilization of mobile shortcuts.

A native app is called such because it is programmed specifically for a native device. This means that it can be installed on a mobile device and can access the device's hardware features. A web app is a "web-based" app that can work on all devices from within a mobile browser. It cannot be distributed by leading app stores, and does not have access to certain features.

Here are the main elements that distinguish a native app from a web app:

- Only native apps can be distributed by the leading app stores.

- A native app has access to certain hardware features built in to mobile devices that a web app does not.
- At this time, you can only send push notifications from a native app.
- A web app cannot be *officially* installed on a mobile device.

As we hint in item number four above, there is a way for users to *unofficially* install a web app on their mobile device using mobile shortcuts. In the following sections we discuss native apps, web apps, and mobile shortcuts.

Native Applications

> ### ▶ Bootstrapper's Guide ◀
>
> √ Native apps are created for "native" devices like iPhone or Android.
> √ Each device has its own platform, and apps are developed for each.
> √ Create apps using SDKs, HTML5, or by using a mobile app service.
> √ Take time choosing a service with features you need now and later.

Native apps are programmed using the platform that is native to a specific mobile device. The table in the previous section shows the platforms used by most mobile devices in the market today. For instance, referring to the table, we see that a mobile app "native" to the iPhone is programmed specifically for the iOS platform, where a native app for Blackberry is programmed for the Blackberry OS platform.

Unfortunately, each of these popular devices use different operating systems (or platforms). This means that developers must write apps in a variety of programming languages in order for their apps to work on all devices.

Each platform, in turn, has its own development environment called a Software Development Kit (SDK). Developers use the SDK to "build" a special binary file that is recognized and implemented by a mobile device with the relevant platform. This file is also referred to as a "build." SDKs are discussed in more detail on page 130.

Only apps created this way (with a binary file) can be added to the leading app stores. Developers need to have a developer account with a store (this runs from $25 to $99 a year) before they can offer their apps in a particular app store. Apps are added to a store by providing descriptive text for the app, uploading application assets (like icons and screen shots of the app), and uploading the binary file (see the AppMakr example on page 151).

Features Only Available to Native Apps

Since a native app is programmed using a mobile device's native platform, it has access to hardware capabilities built in to the device that a web app does not. The following table outlines some of these features.

Feature	Description
Gyroscope	Gyroscope sensors in a mobile device detect the yaw, pitch, and roll of the device. This allows a native app to react to, or interact with, the movement of the device—like when the user twists their smartphone.
Accelerometer	The accelerometer sensor detects the device's acceleration, shake, vibration shock, or fall. This allows a native app to offer features like "shake functions" that let a user control the functions of an app by shaking their smartphone.
Camera	A native app can access a device's built-in camera. This is particularly useful for rich media, augmented reality, and photo sharing apps.
Compass	A mobile app can access the current settings of the built-in compass of a mobile device.
Contacts	Some mobile apps may require access to a user's contact database stored on the user's mobile device.

Push Notifications and Native Apps

Push notifications are another feature that can only be implemented using native apps at this time, though they may be available to web apps in the near future[12].

A push notification is a message sent to a mobile device user through a native app. The message can be in the form of a pop-up window, a sound, a vibration, or all three (see Figure 2.4). The user does not need to have the app open to receive a push notification. A push notification is sent from the app developer's server to the mobile app, and ultimately to the end user who has the app installed on their device.

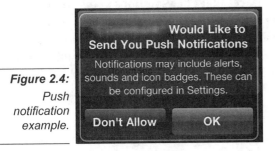

Figure 2.4:
Push notification example.

If you have a smartphone, you are already familiar with push notifications—they are the beeps and vibrations you receive when notified of an event like a new email message or a Facebook update. Push notifications also take the form of messages that pop up on mobile device screens notifying the user of an event relevant to the app—like a to-do reminder, a product price the user has been tracking, or a weather update.

Push notifications usually require a developer account and a special certificate to implement. See an example of adding push notifications to a native app on page 165. Refer to the resource section of this chapter for further reading on push notifications.

Options for Creating a Native App

There are any number of ways you can create a native application. The one you choose will depend on the resources and level of expertise available to you, as well as the features and amount of control you require.

Using the SDK

If you have programming experience, and/or the resources at your disposal to develop native apps using each specific SDK, this may be the solution for you. This option provides the highest level of customization, availability of features, and control of all the options. See page 130 for more details on using SDKs to create your native app.

Using HTML5

There is a way to turn an HTML5 web app into a native app. This process requires the use of a tool like PhoneGap to create the native "build" or binary file from the web app. You would then use that file and your own developer account to create your native app. This process usually eliminates the need for an SDK. See the "Turning Your Web App into a Native App" section on page 140 for more details.

Using a Service

There are a host of tools and services that offer solutions at different stages of the native app process (programming, building, hosting, etc.). Some services require you to upload your own code and only offer build and hosting services, while others offer platforms that let you use your existing RSS feeds to build an app with no programming skills at all, though you still need to have your own developer accounts in the leading stores in order to upload the app builds.

Specific examples of these services begin on page 150. Refer to the resource section of this chapter for a list of tools to assist you in creating native mobile apps.

Choosing Your Native App Solution

Which overall option you choose depends on your resources and level of expertise. There are specific factors to consider when choosing the right native app service. Here are some things to assess about a tool before deciding:

- Programming languages: Some services allow you to code your app in a number of languages, while others restrict you to only one language. Still other tools do not allow custom programming at all.

- Features: Confirm that a tool offers all of the features you will eventually need to support and grow your app. These features might include push notifications, e-commerce solutions, camera access, or GPS.

- Hosting: Some services offer hosting while others require that you download what you have built and host it yourself.

- Platforms: Research which tools create which "builds." If you ultimately want to create apps for all platforms, choose a solution accordingly. This may mean that you choose to use the SDKs or the HTLM5 solution.

- Complexity: You can get a feel for how user-friendly a service is by accessing its demo or getting a trial account.

- Updates: Some services allow you to update minor changes to an app without the need to rebuild and resubmit the build to the app stores.

- Reputation/Support: You can learn a lot about a service by visiting their support forums or wikis.

Web Applications

> ► **Bootstrapper's Guide** ◄
>
> √ Web apps work on all platforms, but cannot be added to leading stores.
> √ Use HTML5, CSS3, and JavaScript for web apps, like for a website.
> √ Web apps become more popular as more browsers adhere to HTML5.
> √ Create web apps using HTML5, with a framework, or with a service.

Web apps are mobile applications that work across all platforms, which is why they are also called cross-platform apps. These apps are created using HTML5, CSS3, and JavaScript—similar to how you would create a website. As a result, web apps work inside of mobile browsers, unlike native apps that need to be programmed in specific languages for each platform, or *native* device. Therefore, web apps work on any mobile device that has access to the Internet.

The catch is that web apps—unlike native apps—cannot be placed in the leading app stores. In addition, web apps do not have access to certain hardware features or push notifications as discussed in the previous section.

Web apps are easier to implement and typically cost less to develop than native apps. And using the right tools, you can even turn a web app into a native app.

The Rise of Web Apps

At this stage in the app development game, there is a lot of debate around native versus web apps: which one is best, which will eventually take over, etc. Unfortunately, there is no definitive answer this early in the game.

Though native apps are more prevalent, current trends indicate that web apps are becoming more accessible and more popular. Mobile browsers are getting faster and including more HTML5 features, and there are mobile web app directories and independent stores popping up almost daily.

Some of the leading app stores, like Apple, even have their own web app directories[13]. And there are new mobile browsers, like MobiUS[14], dedicated to providing an HTML5-friendly environment that allows web apps to access mobile-specific features they can't access while running in traditional mobile browsers.

One thing that contributes to the closing gap between native and web app capabilities are emerging JavaScript libraries and frameworks that help integrate just about any mobile feature or functionality.

Options for Creating a Web App

Using HTLM5, CSS3, and JavaScript

Even novice HTML users can create mobile web apps with little effort thanks to the host of tools and resources available. There are countless HTML5 tutorials, resources, and templates available, as well as JavaScript libraries, dedicated to helping you create mobile web apps. See page 133 for more details.

Using a Framework

HTML5 and JavaScript frameworks offer user-friendly interfaces that allow you to create web apps quickly using built-in libraries and drag-

and-drop features. Some of these frameworks allow you to export native app builds or HTML, CSS, and JavaScript files so you can create your own builds using a tool like PhoneGap. See page 136 for more details and an example framework.

Using a Service

There are services that can help you create your own web apps without any programming or HTML skills. Many of the services also host your app for a monthly fee. Some services allow you to create web apps by simply importing RSS feeds from blogs, YouTube videos, Flickr photos, etc. Other services provide more robust platforms that let you add native features and even convert your web app to a native app. Specific examples begin on page 157.

Choosing Your Web App Solution

The main factor in deciding on a solution for your web app is whether or not you eventually want to convert it to a native app. If you use a framework or a service, you need to make certain you have the option of exporting the web app as HTML, CSS, and JavaScript. You will need those raw files if you are to turn your web app into a native app.

Other considerations include:

- Features: Some web app services are very basic. Research the types of features offered by each service before deciding.
- Hosting: Most web app services also offer hosting, but frameworks usually do not.
- Cost: There is a wide variance in price for hosting web apps. Be careful when choosing a free service, making certain you know what the catch is—for instance, do they place ads in your app?
- Monetizing: If you want to place ads in your apps or sell products, check that a web app solution allows it.
- Promotion: Some services also host directories that can get your app extra exposure.

Mobile Shortcuts

▶ Bootstrapper's Guide ◀

✓ A mobile shortcut is an icon the user places on the home screen of their mobile device that links to a mobile website or a web app.
✓ The process is not intuitive for users, you should provide instructions.
✓ Control the icon used for your site, and use a script to automate.

Even though users cannot install a web app on their device the way they can a native app, they can still save a web app to their home screen using a mobile shortcut. By providing instructions within your web app, you can show users how to save your app and keep it top-of-mind on their home screen.

Similarly, if you have a mobile-optimized website (see the "Mobile Websites" chapter), your site visitors can add your website as a shortcut on the home screen of their device. Though not technically a mobile app, this option gives a mobile device user one-click access to your website, just as they have to the mobile apps residing on their device. This tactic is only recommended for mobile-optimized websites, since you never want to direct a mobile device user to a site that may not render properly on their device.

You can create a special icon to represent your app or website that looks just like a mobile app icon. You can also use a script that prompts users to save your app or website as a shortcut when they visit your web app or site. See page 147 for instructions on how to create mobile shortcut icons, instructions, and scripts.

But Do You NEED A Mobile App?

> ▶ **Bootstrapper's Guide** ◀
>
> √ Mobile apps can be costly to develop; best to be certain you need one.
> √ In many cases a mobile-optimized website can be just as effective.
> √ Pros: native features, closed environment, accessibility, context.
> √ Mobile app cons: cost, resources, limited reach, maintenance.

A mobile-optimized website may be all you need to engage your target market on the mobile web[15]. If your audience can find your mobile-optimized website on a mobile browser, and subsequently save it as a shortcut on their home screen, that is close to having your own web app.

Your time and money may be best put toward search optimization and marketing techniques to get your mobile site more exposure. Many mobile website services help you create mobile websites that even look and feel like mobile apps (see the "Mobile Websites" chapter).

You can also add mobile app advertising campaigns to your overall mobile web strategy. This can give you the opportunity to reach the mobile app target market for specific campaigns or to drive traffic to your mobile-optimized website.

Following are some pros and cons to consider when deciding whether to create a mobile app. Having a mobile-optimized website should be a given if you already have a standard website. Therefore, this argument does not debate whether to develop a mobile-optimized website OR a mobile app, rather whether or not to add a mobile app to your overall mobile web strategy.

Pros	Cons
Device Functionality Since apps are specifically written for mobile devices, native device capabilities can be programmed into them. Functionality like GPS, push notification, shake functions, and camera accessibility are only available using mobile apps.	**Cost and Resources** Developing a mobile app can require a substantial investment. Maintaining an app in the long term can cost even more.
User Experience Mobile apps provide an unencumbered platform from which to engage your audience. Users are not tempted away from your site by ads or outgoing links.	**Distribution/Reach** Mobile apps are limited to the devices they are developed for. This limits the reach of an app to individual mobile app stores.
Top of Mind When users install your app on their mobile device, they will be more likely to access it for its specific purpose, rather than search the web for an alternative.	**Maintenance** Mobile apps require quite a bit of maintenance. Native apps need to be updated for newer versions of each platform.
Accessibility A mobile app can be accessed even if a Wi-Fi, 3G, or 4G connection is not available, since they do not require Internet access to function.	**Accessibility** In order to access your app, a user must download and install it. This can limit your reach to customers.
Control A mobile app is a controlled development environment. A developer controls the look and feel of an app, the way it responds to user input, sounds, video, and more.	**Reputation** If you launch an app and find you do not have the resources to maintain it, it can negatively affect your brand reputation.
Compatibility As we discovered in the "Mobile Websites" chapter, mobile websites have compatibility issues. Mobile apps do not encounter the same issues since they are programmed specifically for mobile devices.	
Context Awareness On page 214, we discuss the trend toward a more context-aware approach to mobile search and development. A mobile app can meet this goal effectively since an app can be programmed to access a user's content and return a more personalized and context-aware experience.	

Planning Your Mobile App

> ### ► Bootstrapper's Guide ◄
>
> √ Decide on a native app or a web app; each has pros and cons.
> √ Plan your app for your target market using trends and market research.
> √ Plan your app for success by designing it to fit users' needs and desires.
> √ Costs depend on your needs and whether you need to hire help.

When planning your mobile app, you should first decide whether it will be a native app or a web app. Your target market, current mobile app trends, type of app to develop, and mobile app costs are also factors to consider when planning your app.

First Things First: Native or Web

On page 113 we looked at some of the features that can only be utilized if you create a native app. If you know you need one or more of these features, you should create a native app or plan to create a web app that can be turned into a native app.

Also recall that only native apps can be distributed by the leading app stores like Apple App Store or Android Market.

Beyond feature and app store limitations, some other factors to consider in your native-versus-web-app decision include:

- Cost: Web apps cost substantially less to develop (see page 123).
- Maintenance: Native apps require more maintenance.
- User Experience: Native apps offer a richer user experience.
- Compatibility: Web apps may have compatibility issues with certain devices.
- Control: Native apps offer the developer more control over the app environment.

Plan for Your Target Market

Once your target market is defined, use current research to determine which platforms your target market is most likely to use. This is particularly important if you plan to create a native app.

Figure 2.5 shows the top smartphone platforms used by the nearly 77 million smartphone users in the United States as of May 2011[16]. Figure 2.6, Figure 2.7, and Figure 2.8 show the demographic breakdown by gender, age, income, and average number of apps installed for the top three platforms (Apple iOS, Android, and Blackberry).

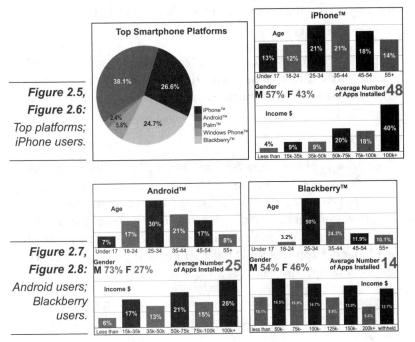

Figure 2.5,
Figure 2.6:
Top platforms;
iPhone users.

Figure 2.7,
Figure 2.8:
Android users;
Blackberry
users.

Some of these demographics are notably different. As we discuss in the "Native Applications" section on page 112, native apps need to be developed separately for each platform. As a result, you can save time and money developing only for the platforms relevant to your target market.

Researching mobile app trends—such as in the "Mobile App Trends" section on page 111—can also give you insight into the types of apps your target market may be using.

Planning for a Successful Mobile App

Finding the right formula for a *successful* app can be challenging. A study by Localytics showed that over a quarter of all downloaded apps were used only once[17]. Part of that formula for success then, should include giving users incentive to return to an app by offering an interactive and engaging brand experience or real-time content they won't want to miss.

When brainstorming your app, start with the following questions:

- Will the app be useful to the user?
- Does the app fill a specific niche relevant to your business?
- Will the app extend user engagement with your business?

- Does the app offer functionality that is not available on your website?
- Will the app provide users with exclusive content or offers?
- Does the app engage the user to encourage brand loyalty?
- How will the app encourage users to return?

A mobile app should be an extension of your current offerings and objectives. Consider creating mobile applications that actually make sense for your brand or business. Following are some general types of apps you might consider.

Content-Driven Apps

Content-driven apps offer real-time content streamed (usually as an RSS feed) to the user's mobile device. For publishers, news sites, and blogs, content-driven apps are a natural fit. These apps can also be useful for businesses that have content that is in high demand. Some examples might include a retail store that offers current sales and availability of in-demand products, or a blogging app that pulls together popular posts by category (see the AppMakr example on page 151).

These apps are perfect candidates for web apps since they don't necessarily require the native functionality of mobile devices.

Rich Media Apps

Mobile devices are the perfect platform for rich media applications that encourage user engagement. These apps combine rich media like video, audio, and images with gaming concepts to create highly interactive applications. Some examples might include a clothing brand app that lets users design their own fashions, or a video blog or podcast that offers exclusive content to mobile users (see the iBuildApp example on page 162).

These apps are especially useful for in-app offers and purchases. An app of this type can encourage users to purchase products, tickets, services, etc. Examples include:

Branded Utility Apps

A branded utility is a tool that extends the services of a brand. This type of app is a natural extension of the existing services of a brand or business, and can improve brand loyalty. Some examples might include a banking app that allows users to check account balances and perform other transactions, or a book publisher's catalog app with built-in video and downloadable excerpts (see the HTML5 example on page 143).

Though a branded utility can be one of the most successful mobile applications for a well-known brand, they are not a good fit for just any business. You should weigh the usefulness of an app to your existing client or customer base before proceeding.

Generic Tools

Unlike branded utilities, generic tools are created as a convenience to users in the hope that the brand sponsoring the tool will gain exposure. Some examples might include a car dealership offering a "best gas prices" app, or a restaurant offering a tip calculator.

While generic tools may be indirectly associated with a brand or business, they don't necessarily encourage brand engagement or loyalty. These types of apps can also get swallowed up by an already saturated app marketplace.

Just for Fun

These are fun, entertaining apps that can get a lot of exposure very quickly for a product or ad campaign, but can lose their appeal just as quickly. Examples might include a virtual Zippo lighter app or a sock monkey cootie catcher (see the Tiggzi example on page 136).

These apps can be useful for short-term or one-off ad campaigns, though there are instances of apps created for short-term campaigns that remain popular a year or more later.

Additional tips for planning a successful app:

- Get feedback from your existing customer base.
- Get ideas from current app trends.
- Personalize the experience for the user.
- Utilize native mobile device features.
- Keep content dynamic and engaging.

Planning for the Cost of Mobile Apps

There are many factors to take into account when estimating the cost of a mobile app. These factors include:

- The type of app
- Whether it is a native app or a web app
- The level of complexity of the app
- Which platforms the app needs to be developed for

- Whether you need to hire someone to help develop the app
- How much maintenance the app will require

The Cost of Native Apps

Native apps can be expensive to develop. The development cost of a native app, like a sophisticated branded utility for the iPhone, can run anywhere from $30,000 to $150,000[18]. Add to that the additional cost of developing the app for Android, Windows, and Blackberry, and you are looking at a major investment.

Later in the chapter we look at some tools that can greatly reduce the cost of developing native apps, especially if you plan to do the work yourself. You could feasibly create a content-driven app for the iPhone and Android platforms for $500 to $3,000, depending on how you value your own time and whether you need to hire additional help.

Maintaining a native app can also get expensive. A full-featured app like a branded utility should be considered a piece of professional software and be managed accordingly. Even a content-driven native app that only imports RSS feeds requires maintenance. These apps should be updated periodically to keep up with the latest versions of the platforms they run on. Some level of support should be offered for any app you create—even if it is a simple comment form. See page 178 for information on offering support.

Many native apps need to be hosted on robust servers that can accommodate the advanced functionality, database management, and potentially high bandwidth of the app. This type of infrastructure can be expensive to maintain, though cloud services like Amazon Web Services[19] can help reduce this cost substantially.

The Cost of Web Apps

Web apps cost substantially less to develop than native apps, especially if you have HTML, CSS, and JavaScript experience. Since web apps are web-based, they do not need to be built for each individual native platform. They are developed and maintained much like a website.

Web app developers tend to charge less than native app developers. Since JavaScript is a more prevalent programming language than some of the languages used to develop native apps (like Objective C for the iPhone), the field is more competitive.

Web apps can be hosted on the same type of hosting service as a website, so hosting costs are also much less than for native apps.

The development cost of a web app will depend on the app's required functionality, but will likely be about a quarter of the cost of a native app with similar features. We demonstrate some tools beginning on page 133 that can help you create and host web apps anywhere from $0 to $25 a month.

Hiring Developers

App developers range in experience as much as they range in price. You can choose to hire a high-end development firm for your project, but expect to pay accordingly. On the other end of the spectrum are developers that mass produce apps using templates. Just keep in mind that you get what you pay for.

For a mid-range solution, look into hiring developers, programmers, or designers from a vetting service like Elance[20]. Using this type of service, you can see how other clients have rated a developer's work, negotiate a fixed price for the job, and manage the entire project inside of the site.

You should be able to judge whether a developer is the best fit for your job by viewing the apps they have worked on or created on their own. You want to see finished work developed specifically for the platforms you want to use.

Look in the resource section of this chapter for places to find developers.

Preparing Your Strategy

You are now ready to create a general strategy for your mobile app. Below is a worksheet to use as a guide. An online version of this worksheet and example strategies can be accessed from QR Code 2.1 and QR Code 2.2, respectively. Online and example strategies can also be found in the resource section of this chapter.

QR Code 2.1:
Complete your strategy online[1].

QR Code 2.2:
Go to sample strategies[2].

Mobile App Strategy Worksheet

This worksheet can help you plan an effective strategy and solution for your mobile apps. Refer to the corresponding sections of the book for clarification of specific questions.

I. Target Market, App Category, Platforms

Defining your target market can help you decide whether to create a native versus a web app and, if you decide on a native app, on which platforms to develop.

Describe your target market:

Will you create a web app or a native app?

If a native app, which platforms will you develop your app for?
- ☐ iOS
- ☐ Android
- ☐ Blackberry
- ☐ Windows Phone
- ☐ Symbian
- ☐ WebOS
- ☐ Other

II. Type of App, App Functionality

After researching mobile app trends, investigating competitors' apps, and reaching out to your existing customers for feedback, discuss the type of app you plan to create and what specific functions it will perform.

What type of app will you create?
- ☐ Content driven
- ☐ Rich media
- ☐ Branded utility
- ☐ Generic tool
- ☐ Just for fun
- ☐ Other

Describe the functionality and purpose of the app you plan to create:

Specifically, answer any of the following questions that are relevant to your app idea:

- How will the app benefit the user?
- Does the app fill a specific niche relevant to your business? How?

- How will the app extend user engagement with your business?
- What does the app offer that is not available on your website?
- Will the app provide users with exclusive content or offers? What?
- Does the app engage the user and encourage brand loyalty? How?
- How will you personalize the app experience for the user?
- How will you keep the app content dynamic and engaging?

III. Native Features

Select the native device features that should be accessible by your mobile app.

☐ Push notifications
☐ Gyroscope
☐ Accelerometer
☐ Camera
☐ Compass
☐ Other

Other features, if applicable:

IV. Budget

Answer the following questions about your overall budget for your mobile app.

- What is your budget for app development and maintenance?
- Will you create the app in-house or hire a developer?
- If a developer, how will you recruit?

V. Native App Options

Use the corresponding sections in the book to help decide which option to use to create your native app.

How will you create your native app?

☐ Use the SDK
☐ Code in HTML5 and convert using PhoneGap or appMobi XDK
☐ Use a service

VI. Web App Options

Use the corresponding sections in the book to help decide which option to use to create your web app.

How will you create your web app?

☐ Use HTML5, CSS3, and JavaScript
☐ Use a framework
☐ Use a service

If a framework, which will you use?

Will you convert your web app to a native app? How?

VII. Mobile App Stores

Depending on the platforms you plan to develop for, in which stores will you distribute your app?

☐ Apple App Store
☐ Google Android Market
☐ Blackberry Market
☐ Ovi/Nokia Store
☐ Windows Phone Marketplace
☐ Amazon Appstore
☐ GetJar
☐ Handango
☐ Other

VIII. Solution Criteria

Refer to the previous sections of this strategy, and answer these questions for each solution you are considering.

Specifically, does a solution:

☐ Align with your target market, app category, and desired platforms?
☐ Fit within your budget constraints?
☐ Align to your vision of the app's main purpose and functionality?
☐ Offer accessibility to the desired native device features?

Additionally, does a solution:

☐ Offer custom programming in appropriate languages?
☐ Offer ways to upgrade or grow your app in the future?
☐ Offer hosting, if a service?
☐ Allow minor updates without the need to rebuild your app, if a service?
☐ Have good support forums, if a service?
☐ Have a gallery to offer your app more exposure?
☐ Adhere to web app best practices?
☐ Provide the opportunity to convert to a native app in the future?
☐ Offer ways for you to monetize your app?

IX. Weighing Options

List your final choice(s) here. If you are considering more than one solution, list the pros and cons of each option.

Solution	Pros	Cons

X. Conclusion

What is your final choice?

What compromises were made in favor of this solution?

Discuss conflicting or unresolved issues as they relate to your final choice, and list alternative solutions to resolve them:

What are your plans for subsequent phases of the app development?

Mobile Application Solutions

▶ Bootstrapper's Guide ◀

✓ Native app solutions include SDKs, HTML5, or using a service.
✓ Web app solutions include HTML5, frameworks, or using a service.
✓ Several solutions are available for turning web apps into native apps.
✓ Mobile shortcuts can help make a mobile website seem like an app.

Beginning on page 112, we discuss options for creating native apps and web apps. We also mention methods for turning web apps into native apps and creating mobile shortcuts. In the following sections, we take a closer look at how to:

- Create native apps using SDKs
- Create web apps using HTML5, CSS3, and JavaScript
- Use HTML5 frameworks for web and native apps
- Use tools to turn web apps into native apps

- Create a web app and a native app from an HTML5 website
- Create mobile shortcuts

Step-by-step examples of native and web app services begin on page 150.

Using SDKs for Native Apps

In this section, we describe the process required to create and distribute native applications using SDKs.

Mobile Device Platforms

Recall that native apps are mobile applications created specifically for "native" devices like iPhone, Android, Blackberry, and Windows, and that each of these devices uses a different platform.

Platforms used on mobile devices can be "open" or "closed." A closed platform is a proprietary platform that can only be used on a specific company's device. This is the case with Apple's iOS, which can only be used for Apple devices like the iPhone and iPad.

An open platform like Android can be used on any device whose company chooses to adopt it. Android was developed by Google and is used on Google products and by many other smartphone and tablet manufacturers, including Motorola, Samsung, and Barnes & Noble (for the Nook).

Software Development Kits

Each platform has its own development tool called a Software Development Kit (SDK). An SDK is software that provides the developer with a set of libraries, programming tools, debugging tools, and sample code specific to the device they are creating an app for.

Installation and set up of SDKs vary by platform. Some SDKs require additional development software to be in place before they can work. For instance, the Android SDK requires the Eclipse IDE[21] (integrated development environment) be in place and an additional plugin to be added to Eclipse that integrates the IDE with the SDK to make the development process run smoother.

It is important to understand that an SDK is not a framework or a programming language; you still need to write the programming code for the app in the language that is required by the app (see the table below). The SDK simply provides an environment to make the programming process easier, and assists the developer with sample code specific to developing mobile apps.

Even if you program your app using a different development environment, you still need the SDK to create the binary file (or build) that is required to distribute your app.

Developers can use the same SDK "build" for each store that distributes a specific "open" platform. This means that once a binary file is created for an Android app, it can be used in the Google Android Market, the Amazon Appstore, or any other store that distributes Android apps.

Distributing to App Stores

Once an app is added to an app store by uploading assets and the build file, the app typically goes through an approval process. There is no approval process for the Google Android Market. Approval in some of the other markets—like Amazon—typically takes several days. Apps for the Apple store, however, can take up to a month to get approval.

The following table demonstrates some of the major companies, platforms, development environments, programming languages, distribution markets, and sample devices.

Company	Google	Apple	RIM/ Blackberry	Microsoft
Platform	Android (open)	iOS (closed)	Blackberry OS (closed)	Windows Phone (open)
Development Environment	Android SDK[22]	iOS SDK[23]	Blackberry Java Development Environment[24]	Windows Phone SDK[25]
Programming Language	Java	Objective C	Blackberry Java	.NET
Distribution	Google Android Market, Amazon App-store, Others	Apple App Store (iTunes)	Blackberry App World	Windows Phone Marketplace
Sample Devices	HTC Legend, Droid Incredible, Google Nexus One, Samsung Galaxy, Barnes & Noble Nook, Motorola Droid	iPhone, iPad, iPod Touch	Blackberry Torch, Blackberry Storm, Blackberry Playbook	HTC Arrive, Samsung Focus, LG Quantum, Dell Venue Pro

The Process: Step-By-Step

Let's assume we want to create a mobile app for the iPhone and iPad, and offer it in the Apple App Store. Here are the necessary steps:

1. Get an app developer account with Apple and iTunes Connect[26].
2. Download and install the latest iOS SDK[23].
3. Write the app program in the Objective C programming language[27] (usually done within the SDK).
4. Upload the program files and supporting assets to your server.
5. Test the application using the SDK.
6. Configure your app for submission to iTunes Connect[28].
7. Create a new app in iTunes Connect, completing all details[28].
8. Build the binary file using the iOS SDK[29].
9. Create the assets for the Apple Store, including icons, splash page, and screen shots (see page 168 for more on this process).
10. Have a Mac computer with a minimum OS version of Mac OS X 10.5.3 (Snow Leopard) on hand.
11. Install the Application Loader on the Mac computer (if you have the iOS SDK installed on this computer, the Application Loader is installed as well).
12. Add your mobile app to the Apple Store by completing descriptive text, adding assets, and uploading the binary file using the Application Loader on the Mac computer[28].
13. Wait for the Apple Store to approve the app[28].

For a complete guide to building and publishing iOS apps, refer to the iOS Developer's Library[29] and the iTunes Connect Developer Guide[28], respectively. See QR Code 2.3 for a presentation.

Now, let's assume we want to prepare and submit the same application to the Android Market and to the Amazon Android Appstore. We would follow these similar steps:

QR Code 2.3:
Publishing
an Apple app
presentation[3].

QR Code 2.4:
Publishing an
Android app
presentation[4].

1. Get a developer account with the Android Market[30] and the Amazon Appstore[31].
2. Download and install the latest Android SDK[22].
3. Write the app program in Java or another allowable language.
4. Upload the program files and supporting assets to your server.
5. Test the application using the SDK.
6. Create a signed certificate for the app[32].
7. Prepare any release keys or materials necessary to run your app[33].
8. Build the binary file (.apk file) using the Android SDK[32].
9. Create the assets for the Android Market and Amazon Appstore, including icons, splash pages, and screen shots (there are size differences between markets—see page 168 for details).
10. Add your mobile app to both the Android Market and the Amazon Appstore by adding descriptive text and assets, and uploading the .apk file using any computer.
11. Wait for the Amazon Appstore to approve the app (the app does not need approval for the Android Market).

For a complete guide to building[33] and publishing[32] Android apps, refer to the Android Developer's Guide. See QR Code 2.4 for a presentation.

Once we have our "build," we can use it to add our app to other stores that distribute Android apps using this same process. Look in the resource section of this chapter for a list of additional app stores.

The same process is required for additional app platforms you want to use (Blackberry, Windows Phone, etc.). To update an app, a new binary file must be created and uploaded to replace the existing binary file in each store that distributes the app.

Using HTML5, CSS3, and JavaScript for Web Apps

HTML5 and CSS3 have features that lend naturally to creating web apps. Add mobile JavaScript libraries to the mix, and you have an environment that is quickly closing the gap between native app and web app functionality. Following are a few of the features that make this possible.

Working Offline

The ability to "work offline" is a feature that HTML5 handles very well. Through caching, local storage, and database support, you can create a web app using HTML5 that can be accessed by your users whether they have an Internet connection or not.

Simplified Styling

Access to web browser engines like WebKit[34] can help you style and animate sophisticated navigation buttons and other design elements using CSS3 without the need to use external graphics. This makes your web app faster and more flexible.

Multimedia Made Easy

Combine CSS3 features with the HTML5 canvas element, and you can even create animations without the need for proprietary software like Flash. The HTML5 video and audio tags allow you to stream video and audio files within your web app without the need to access proprietary software.

Mobile-Specific Functionality

Combining HTML5 and CSS3 features with JavaScript gives you the ability to add mobile-device-specific functions like GPS, camera accessibility, and touch events (tapping, sliding, squeezing, etc.) to your web app. JavaScript is a scripting language that allows you to program more robust functionality into your websites and apps that cannot be accomplished using HTML alone.

Mobile-Specific Meta Tags

Smartphone-specific HTML5 meta tags are already in common use. These tags control things like defining icon images and splash screens, smartphone status bar styles, and controlling the display style[35].

Plenty of Tools and Support

One nice thing about using JavaScript is that there is no need to reinvent the wheel when trying to integrate special functionality into your web apps. There are some very good JavaScript libraries—like jQuery[36] and jQTouch[37]—that can help you integrate just about any mobile feature or functionality. A JavaScript library is a collection of JavaScript plugins (or code snippets) that you reference from within your HTML documents to perform specific functions.

See the resource section of this chapter for many tutorials, books, tools, and frameworks you can use to help create your web app in HTML5, CSS3, and JavaScript.

The Web App Process

The process for creating a web app is substantially less complex than for native apps. The general steps are as follows:

1. Write the program for the application in HTML5, CSS3, and JavaScript.
2. Upload the program files to a server.
3. Create icons and images to use in stores and directories.
4. Add the app to web directories, galleries, independent app stores, and as a link on your website.
5. Convert your app to a native app if needed.

Updating a web app is a simple matter of updating and re-uploading the files to your server—the same way you would a website.

Web App Best Practices

Since web apps run on mobile browsers, you should follow any relevant best practices listed in the "Mobile Website Best Practices" section on page 16. The W3C also has additional best practices for web apps[38].

Because HTML5 is not necessarily standard to all mobile browsers, some features of your web app may not be available to all users. There are ways you can test if a browser supports certain features and adjust your app to accommodate different capabilities using specialized JavaScript libraries like Modernizr[39]. Additional techniques can be found on HTML5 tutorial sites[40].

Performance can be an issue for web apps since they rely on mobile browsers. You can find methods for improving performance of your web app on HTML5 tutorials[41] or on the W3C[42].

If you plan to create a web app in place of a mobile-optimized version of your standard website, you should consider redirecting mobile traffic from your standard website to your mobile web app. See page 172 for more details.

Users cannot upload and install a web app onto their mobile device like they can from the app stores, so you should encourage them to add your web app to the home screen of their smartphone or tablet as a shortcut. See page 147 for more details.

Web Apps Are Not Websites

While web apps are created using HTML, CSS, and JavaScript, just as websites are, they are distinct from mobile websites in that they are programmed specifically to act like mobile applications on smartphones and tablets.

As we discuss in the "Mobile Websites" chapter, a mobile-optimized website should be designed for *all* mobile devices and should be consistent with your desktop website experience. Mobile web apps, on the other hand, target features specific to smartphones and tablets and often store information on a mobile device necessary for the app to work while the device is offline—something you would not do when developing a website.

Using an HTML5 Framework to Create Mobile Apps

HTML5 and JavaScript frameworks like Sencha Touch[43] and jQuery Mobile[44] offer free interfaces that allow you to create web apps quickly using built-in JavaScript libraries. Some services have taken these frameworks a step further by expanding them into full-featured services.

Tiggzi[45] is one such service. Using jQuery Mobile as its base, Tiggzi provides a drag-and-drop platform for creating native apps or web apps that can be turned into native apps. Tiggzi charges $45/month with a 30-day trial. Tiggzi is web-based, so there is no software to install.

The following example is meant to give you a *general* idea of how you can use the Tiggzi platform to create a web app. You should have an understanding of HTML, JavaScript, and XML when using a framework like this.

Figure 2.9 shows the Tiggzi platform. You can watch your app take shape in the center area of the platform as you develop it.

Figure 2.9:
Tiggzi
platform.

From the "Palette" tab on the left, you can add buttons, drop-down menus, navigation menus, links, images, video, maps, and many other elements to your app. Some elements like video, images, or maps require additional steps—like entering additional information or uploading assets.

Once an element has been added (by dragging the element onto the app area), you can change its properties using the "Properties" tab on the right (see Figure 2.10). Each element has its own set of properties. For our button, we can change things like text, position, margins, icon style, etc.

Figure 2.10:
*Button
properties.*

Once an element like a button is styled, you want to assign it a function. To accomplish this, you need to create an "event" and an "action." An *event* is something that happens to the element, usually something the user does, like click on a button, enter a keystroke, re-size a page, or scroll. The choice of events depends on the element. For our button we can choose events like click, focus, key up, and so forth (see Figure 2.11).

Figure 2.11:
Button actions.

An *action* is what happens when an event is encountered. This can be something like navigating to another page, changing the properties of an element, implementing some HTML, running a JavaScript script, etc. (see Figure 2.12). In our case, we associate the "click" event to the "Navigate to Page" action, since we want the user to be taken to another page in the app if they click the button. See Figure 2.13.

Figure 2.12,
Figure 2.13:
*Buttons
events.*

More advanced features of Tiggzi include adding custom HTML5 code, adding and implementing custom JavaScript, and using REST (REpresentational State Transfer) services. A REST service consists of a client and a server. A client initiates a request to a server, and the server processes the request and returns an appropriate response.

In this situation, the client is your app and the server is wherever you are requesting data or some other process from. One example might be that you want to show your latest Twitter updates in your app. In this case, your app is the client requesting a process from Twitter (the server).

In our example, we are creating an app from a widget we created as an example in the author's last book. The app needs to pull data from an XML file in order to provide dynamic responses.

The "Bootee Catcher" app we are creating serves up "fortunes" for the user based on their choice of colors and numbers. The data (bootee images and "fortune" data) is stored in an XML file on the author's server. Figure 2.14 and Figure 2.15 show (generally) how Tiggzi recognizes the XML file and the individual fields from the URL we provide to the XML file. This is the first step in setting up a REST service within Tiggzi.

Figure 2.14,
Figure 2.15:
REST
services.

The REST service allows us to pull data into our app and place it wherever we want within our app. There are more steps involved in this process, but this hopefully gives you an idea of what you can do with the framework beyond just adding buttons and images. See QR Code 2.5 for tutorials.

Using Tiggzi, we can test our app right from our browser. Figure 2.16 and Figure 2.17 show the Bootee Catcher app in action. The user selects a color and a number and is given a fortune by Bootee the sock monkey.

QR Code 2.5:
Tiggzi
tutorials[5].

QR Code 2.6:
Bootee
Catcher
example[6].

The image of Bootee and the fortune text are pulled from the XML file according to the user's choices. This is accomplished by using the REST service described above, and some custom JavaScript code.

You can see the entire process of creating the Bootee Catcher app based on the widget along with the code by following QR Code 2.6. You can also see excerpts from the author's last book as to how the widget was created.

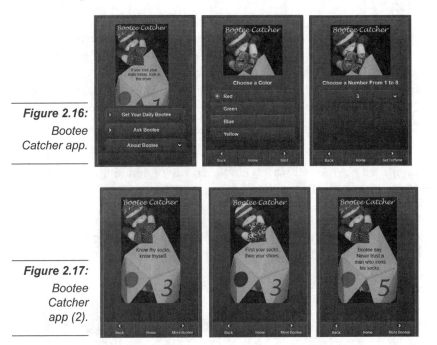

Figure 2.16:
Bootee Catcher app.

Figure 2.17:
Bootee Catcher app (2).

Once your app is complete, click "Export" to download the HTML, CSS, and JavaScript for your app. Figure 2.18 shows the export options.

Tiggzi offers an option to download the Android build file (release binary), Android or iOS development files (source code) that can be used with the platform's SDK, or the web resource files (HTML/CSS/JavaScript files).

Figure 2.18:
Publishing with Tiggzi.

If you choose the web resources option for "other platforms," you can then use the downloaded HTML, CSS, and JavaScript files to turn the web app into a native app using the tactics discussed in the next section.

Turning Your Web App into a Native App

There are services and frameworks available to turn your web app into a native app. These services are sometimes called "cross-platform" services. We discuss a couple of these services in this section. See the resource section of this chapter for additional services and tutorials.

PhoneGap

PhoneGap[46] is open source software that serves as a bridge between web apps and individual SDKs. This means you aren't tied into programming your app using the required programming language of an SDK. You can create an app using HTML5, CSS3, and JavaScript, then use PhoneGap to convert it into a form that allows you to create your build using a specific SDK (see Figure 2.19).

PhoneGap is compatible with almost all of the SDKs, including iOS, Android, Blackberry, Windows, WebOS, and Symbian. PhoneGap also integrates directly with Dreamweaver 5.5.

PhoneGap does not create your builds for you—you still need to use the SDK to do that. The advantage is that you have access to all of the native functionality that the SDK provides while still programming with the web standards you are familiar with. Figure 2.20 shows some of the native features PhoneGap gives you access to while developing your app.

Figure 2.19, Figure 2.20: PhoneGap features.

The general process for utilizing PhoneGap with a specific SDK is as follows:

1. Upload and install the SDK.
2. Upload and install PhoneGap.
3. Configure your SDK to integrate with PhoneGap.

4. Use PhoneGap features within the SDK to create your app (using HTML and JavaScript).

5. Apply native features to your app using PhoneGap and the SDK.

6. Continue with the build as you normally would using the SDK.

See QR Code 2.7 on page 142 for PhoneGap tutorials.

PhoneGap Build (Beta)

While still in beta, the folks at PhoneGap have gone one step further in creating a web-based platform that creates your builds for you called PhoneGap Build[47]. This service presently supports iOS, Android, Blackberry, WebOS, and Symbian.

The process for utilizing PhoneGap Build is as follows:

1. Create your web app using HTML5, CSS3, and JavaScript.

2. Upload the files to PhoneGap Build as a compressed file or by providing a link to the index.html file (see Figure 2.21).

3. Let PhoneGap Build create your build files for you (see Figure 2.22).

4. For the iOS build, you need to provide a certificate that you acquire from your developer account in order to complete the build.

5. Once you have your build files, you can test and upload to the stores.

Figure 2.21,
Figure 2.22:
PhoneGap Build.

appMobi XDK

AppMobi XDK[48] is a web-based service that allows you to use your own HTML documents as the basis for a native app or a web app (see Figure 2.23). They also host your app for you. Though the service and hosting are free, they have affordable add-on services like push notifications and e-commerce solutions you can use to enhance your app.

AppMobi provides more than just the builds for app stores. Using the XDK you can debug your app, view it in a simulator for many different devices, and test your app directly on mobile devices using a wireless connection (see Figure 2.24).

Figure 2.23,
Figure 2.24:
AppMobi
XDK features.

The appMobi XDK is surprisingly easy to use and even integrates with PhoneGap. The platform is shown in Figure 2.25 featuring one of our example HTML5 projects.

Figure 2.25:
AppMobi XDK
in action.

The process for utilizing the appMobi XDK is as follows:

1. Install the Google Chrome browser.
2. Install the XDK on your computer (it only stores a small portion of the XDK software on your computer).
3. Start the XDK (this will launch the platform in the Chrome browser) and create a new app.
4. The XDK will create a project folder on your computer.
5. Copy all of the files for your web app into this folder.
6. The XDK will find your files and simulate them as a mobile app.

QR Code 2.7:
PhoneGap
tutorials[7].

QR Code 2.8:
AppMobi
XDK video
tutorials[8].

7. Make changes to your files as you normally would and the changes will reflect in the XDK.

8. Optionally add features through the XDK like push notifications.

9. Create your builds for iOS and Adroid using the XDK.

Presently, appMobi only creates builds for iOS and Android. The HTML5 example below features the appMobi XDK.

Look in the resource section of this chapter for additional services, books, and other resources that can guide you through the process of using these types of tools to create native apps. See QR Code 2.8 for appMobi XDK video tutorials.

HTML5: One Site to Rule Them All!

Notice a common "HTML5" theme running throughout the book? Does it make you think that HTML5 may be the next big thing in web development? Imagine that you are starting with a clean slate, and you want a web solution that will work across all platforms, dub as a web app, and have the potential to become a native app. Imagine further that you can accomplish this using existing web standards—yes, that's right: HTML5.

Here is how you might create such a presence:

- Create an optimized website using HTML5 (see page 69).
- Use responsive design (see page 62) or other techniques to optimize your site for all platforms (desktop, mobile, tablets, etc.).
- Convert the site to a web app by altering its look using CSS3, and adding app functionality using JavaScript.
- Use a tool to convert the web app into a native app.

Following is a possible scenario you can follow to use an HTML5 site as your mobile site, a web app, and a native app. Read more about HTML5, CSS3, and jQuery on page 133, and about turning web apps into native apps on page 140. For a more thorough tutorial, refer to the resource section of the chapter for further reading.

The Mobile-Optimized Site (HTML5/CSS3)

Figure 2.26, Figure 2.27, Figure 2.28, and Figure 2.29 show the example stand-alone mobile website created for Quill Driver Books on page 69. This site was created using HTML5 and CSS3. This means it is a perfect candidate for conversion to a web app.

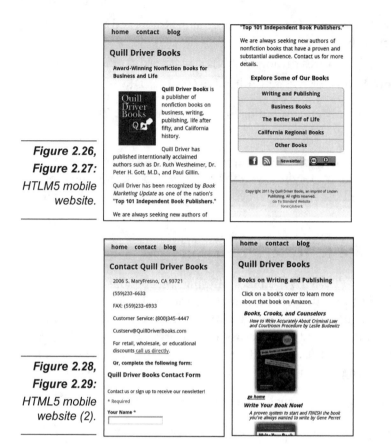

Figure 2.26,

Figure 2.27:

HTLM5 mobile website.

Figure 2.28,

Figure 2.29:

HTML5 mobile website (2).

The Web App (HTML5/CSS3/jQuery)

Figure 2.30, Figure 2.31, and Figure 2.32 show the site after we make some changes to make it act and feel more like a web app, rather than a website. Generally, we want to make the site look more like a web app, and add functionality using JavaScript that can be best utilized within an app.

Figure 2.30,

Figure 2.31,

Figure 2.32:

HTML5 web app.

Quill Driver's site was originally an extension of their existing website, offering a mobile-friendly way for users to browse their books. The web app, however, will be a full-featured catalog, offering bookstores, wholesalers, resellers, and retail buyers an opportunity to browse Quill Driver's catalog, download book excerpts, watch videos, view author event calendars, mark the books they are interested in ordering, and ultimately place an order.

Here are the changes made to the look and feel of the site/app (compare the before and after Figures above):

- Changed the navigation menu to a touch-style navigation bar using CSS3 and jQuery
- Eliminated much of the text from the home page
- Added smartphone-type icons to the bottom navigation bar
- Included a back arrow on each page for easy navigation
- Removed the form from the contact page (this will be replaced by an order form)

Here are the changes made (or that will be made) to the functionality of the site/app:

- Each book now has its own page, with links to a video page, an event page, a download page, and a star for users to mark the book as a favorite (see Figure 2.32).
- From the home page, users can tap the shopping icon to see books they have selected as favorites and place an order via phone or email.
- Ultimately, a check-out page will contain a password-protected form that registered resellers and wholesalers can use to place orders.
- Subsequent features will include a full-featured shopping cart for retail sales and outgoing links to other sales outlets.

To see the changes made to the code, alongside the original code from page 69, access QR Code 2.9.

QR Code 2.9:
Quill Driver web app code and progress[9].

The Native App (appMobi or PhoneGap Build)

Figure 2.33 shows our app on the appMobi platform (see page 141 for more on appMobi). Once it is uploaded and bugs worked out, we can work on adding native features. For our example, we might want to add:

- A shopping solution using appMobi add-on features
- An accelerometer so users can shake to select books as favorites
- Push notifications to inform users when new releases are added

Figure 2.33:
HTML5 native app build; iBuildApp.

Once the native app is ready, we create the builds for Apple and Android and upload the builds to the stores using the proper procedures. See page 132 for more information on development accounts and distribution.

If we want to develop the app for other platforms, we might consider using PhoneGap Build (read more about PhoneGap Build on page 141). Figure 2.34 shows the build results for the same web app uploaded to the PhoneGap Build service.

Figure 2.34:
HTML5 native app build; PhoneGap.

With careful planning, you can have a web presence that is compatible with the web as it is today, and adaptable for the web of tomorrow. Refer to the resource section of the chapter for further reading on this topic.

Creating Mobile Shortcuts

If you have a web app or a mobile-optimized website, you should make sure your website visitors or app users know how to add your site or app as a shortcut on their mobile device's home screen. This can help to keep your website or web app top-of-mind on user's mobile devices.

Adding a Mobile Shortcut

On the iPhone or iPad, the user simply clicks on the "plus" button (or arrow button) when visiting a web page or app in a mobile browser (see Figure 2.35). They can add the site as a shortcut by choosing "Add to Home Screen." See Figure 2.36 and Figure 2.37. An icon that serves as a shortcut to the web page is added to the user's home screen as seen in Figure 2.38.

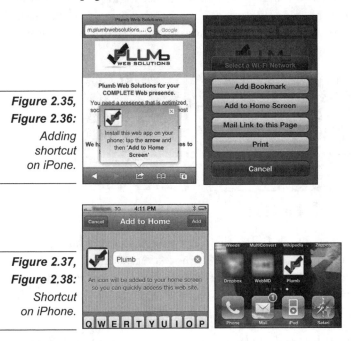

Figure 2.35,
Figure 2.36:
Adding shortcut on iPone.

Figure 2.37,
Figure 2.38:
Shortcut on iPhone.

On an Android device, the process is a little more involved. The user must choose "Add bookmark" from the "more" screen of the main menu as shown in Figure 2.39, Figure 2.40, and Figure 2.41.

QR Code 2.10:
Creating a mobile shortcut video[10].

Figure 2.39,
Figure 2.40,
Figure 2.41:
Adding
shortcut on
Android.

Once the bookmark is added, the user must visit their bookmarks by tapping on the bookmark button (see Figure 2.39), and "holding" the bookmark they want to add to their home screen (see Figure 2.42) until the menu as seen in Figure 2.43 appears. From here, they can "Add shortcut to Home," and the website's icon will show as a shortcut on the user's home screen as seen in Figure 2.44.

Figure 2.42,
Figure 2.43,
Figure 2.44:
Shortcut on
Android.

Creating Your Shortcut Icon

In each of the examples above, the site being saved as a shortcut had its own custom icon that was placed on the user's home screen. This is something you need to plan for by letting the mobile browser know where to find your icon. A mobile browser will add a small screen shot of your website or web app instead of an icon if it is not directed otherwise.

First, create an icon as a .png file that is at least 128px by 128px, name it "apple-touch-icon.png," and place it in the root of your website or web app folder. Many mobile browsers for the iPhone or iPad will search for this file by name and automatically use it. For the other browsers, we need to add some code to the head section of our HTML pages.

Add the following code to the "head" section of each page of your mobile-optimized website or web app:

```
<link rel="apple-touch-icon" href="/apple-touch-icon.png" />
<link rel="apple-touch-icon-precomposed" href="/apple-touch-icon.png" />
```

Once you add this code, the mobile browsers will use your icon as the shortcut icon.

There are tools to help you create custom icons. Figure 2.45 shows the ICONJ iPhone Style Icon Generator[49]. You can upload an image to this generator and it styles the image as a mobile icon. You are given quite a few style choices, but when creating a shortcut icon, be sure to choose "No Glass." Apple devices will automatically add a glassy effect to your icon.

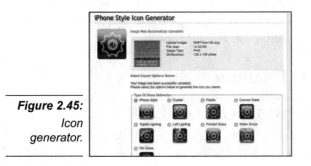

Figure 2.45:
Icon
generator.

Making It Easy for Your Visitors

It may be necessary to give your site visitors some help to encourage them to add your website or web app as a shortcut.

For web apps, add directions within the app instructing users how to add your app as a shortcut. Figure 2.46 demonstrates how the Widgetbox web app service accomplishes this (see the Widgetbox example on page 157). When a user clicks on "Share," they are given the choice to "Install" the web app. Since a web app—unlike a native app—cannot officially be installed on a user's device, the Widgetbox web app instructs the user how to add the app to the user's home screen as a shortcut.

Figure 2.46:
Shortcut
instructions
in app.

For mobile-optimized websites, you could add a button, link, or QR code with instructions on how the user can add your site as a home screen shortcut. You could place a short video on your site to guide them. QR Code 2.10 on page 147 features such a video you can use on your own site.

Automating the Process

In the example on page 148, there is a nifty pop-up that tells the user exactly what to do to add the site as a home screen shortcut. This is accomplished by adding a script to your website or web app. You can find scripts like this for free online, but you should be careful when choosing.

One thing to keep in mind is that you only want this type of pop-up to show up when a user visits your site the first time—otherwise it will annoy your visitors. CUBIQ.org offers just such a script for the iPhone[50]. They are in the process of creating a similar script for Android.

Mobile App Services Examples

▶ **Bootstrapper's Guide** ◀

√ Services can help you create a mobile app affordably and easily.
√ Some only offer web apps, some only native apps, and some both.
√ Research before deciding which to use; see that it can grow with you.
√ Services have their own complexities, but the process is similar.

There are many mobile app services that do not require any programming or HTML experience to use. Some are free, with add-ons that can be purchased; some charge monthly for hosting, and others charge a flat fee. Some services only create native apps; some only create web apps; and some services do both.

We feature a few of these services in this section. Refer to the resource section of the chapter for a list of additional services. Though each service has different levels of complexity and feature offerings, the process is basically the same.

Process for Native App Services:

- Set up your account.
- Choose your app type (iOS, Android, etc.).
- Customize your app.
- Populate your app.
- Complete app setting and upload assets.
- Monetize your app with ads.
- Test your app.
- Associate your developer accounts with the service using certificates.
- Publish your app (create the build file).

- Once you have the build file, you can continue by adding the app to its respective app store (see page 132 for details).
- Repeat for each platform you wish to publish (Android, iOS, etc.).

Process for Web App services:

- Set up your account.
- Customize your app.
- Populate your app.
- Add assets to your app.
- Distribute and promote your app.
- Redirect your app, if applicable.
- Check app analytics.

AppMakr

Native Apps Only
Platforms: iOS, Android, Windows Phone

AppMakr[51] is a service that can help you create a native application, create your build, and help you distribute your app into the app stores, including Apple, Android, and Windows. You can import RSS feeds likes blogs, social media feeds, videos, and image galleries. There is no programming required to create your app, but you can add custom HTML code if you like. See QR Code 2.11 on page 156 to see the AppMakr gallery.

The service is free with ads embedded in your app, or $79/month without ads. AppMakr has add-on features as well, like push notifications if you need them. You can also hire them to publish your app for you.

Setting Up Your Account

Once you have an account, choose the "Create New App" option. Figure 2.47 shows the beginning screen. Enter your first RSS feed here to get started. AppMakr will search for the feed as well as images that may be relevant to the feed (see Figure 2.48).

Figure 2.47,
Figure 2.48:
AppMakr
set up.

App Settings and Assets (part one)

Figure 2.49 shows the next step, which is to enter a short icon name and upload image assets (see page 168 on how to prepare your assets). The icon name is the text that appears under your app's icon on a mobile device's home screen, and should be 11 characters or less. Upload your app's icon and splash screen images next.

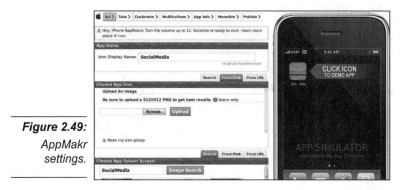

Figure 2.49:

AppMakr settings.

Populating Your App

Clicking on "Tabs" will bring you to the screen shown in Figure 2.50. Here is where you add the tabs (or menu items) for your app. When choosing any of the tab options, you are given a choice of icons to choose from to represent a tab in the bottom navigation (see Figure 2.51).

The app simulator will adjust to show how your app will look on a smartphone as you develop the app. You can see the icons appear at the bottom of the app as you add your tabs (see Figure 2.54 on page 153).

Figure 2.50,

Figure 2.51:

Populating AppMakr.

Figure 2.52 shows the "Add an RSS/Atom Feed" screen. You can import feeds from your blogs, YouTube videos, news sources—any feed you have the right to distribute. Include a style sheet if you want to control the look and feel of the feed, or include some JavaScript code before the feed is displayed. You can also validate the feed before moving on.

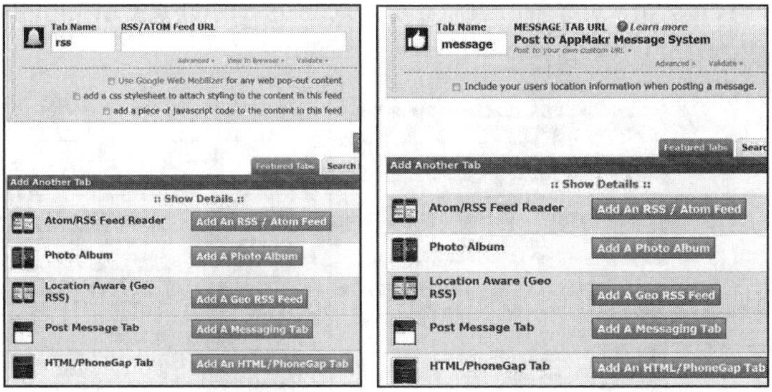

Figure 2.52,
Figure 2.53:

Setting
up feeds.

The "Add a Photo Album" option allows you to enter a feed from Flickr, Picasa, or other image sharing sites. The "Add a Geo RSS Feed" option similarly allows you to enter a feed from Google Maps or other map utility sites that can display a map based on coordinates.

The "Add a Messaging Tab" option allows your app users to send you a message through your app (see Figure 2.53). You can post messages to your own custom URL, or manage them within the AppMakr platform. You can even include a sender's location with the message.

Finally, the "Add a HTLM/PhoneGap Tab" lets you upload custom HTML or PhoneGap code that can act as a custom page or feature within your app. Read more about PhoneGap on page 140. This feature can help you create an app that is more engaging than simply displaying feeds.

Figure 2.54 shows all of the tabs added to our example app. We take advantage of the separate category feeds in our WordPress blog to create separate tabs for tips, resources, and books. We also include tabs for YouTube videos, Flickr photos, and a Twitter feed.

Figure 2.54:
Completed
feeds.

Customizing Your App

The next step is to customize the app. The "Customize" tab screen is shown in Figure 2.55. From here you can upload a header image, control how users can share your content (via Facebook, Twitter, or email), and make it so users must login to access your app.

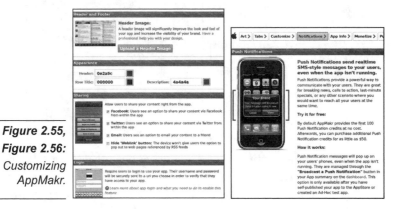

Figure 2.55,

Figure 2.56:

Customizing

AppMakr.

Push Notifications

Next is the "Notifications" tab (see Figure 2.56). AppMakr can help you manage push notifications from within your app (see page 113 for more about push notifications). Your first 100 notifications are free; after that AppMakr charges for them.

App Settings and Assets (part two)

The next tab is the "App Info" tab. This is where you enter the description, website URL, and email address associated with the app (see Figure 2.57). The information entered here is required for the app build. Descriptive text for individual app stores is entered when the app is added to the store.

Figure 2.57,

Figure 2.58:

AppMakr

settings.

Monetizing Your App

From the "Monetize" tab, you can place ads in your app to monetize the content. Choose from several ad serving platforms, or enter custom code as seen on the options on Figure 2.58. Read more about monetizing on page 172.

Testing and Associating Your App

Figure 2.59 shows the options from the "Publish" tab. In this step, you create the "build" file necessary to publish your app to the Apple App Store. Before you can do this, you need to have an Apple developer account[26], and authorize AppMakr to create your build file by uploading a provisional file to the AppMakr platform that you create using your developer account. See page 166 for more details on this process.

Figure 2.59:
Completed
feeds.

Publishing Your App

You can now create the build file for your app. Click on "Create Test App" to get a file to test on your iPhone. Test your app by adding it to iTunes on a Mac computer and synching with your iPhone device (see QR Code 2.12 on page 156 for video instructions). Once you have tested, click on "Create AppStore App."

AppMakr provides an "AQI" score that indicates the likelihood of your app getting approved for the Apple App Store. Figure 2.60 shows some of the reasons an app may not get approved—like not containing enough content, or too few tabs. See a full list of reasons on the AppMakr site[52].

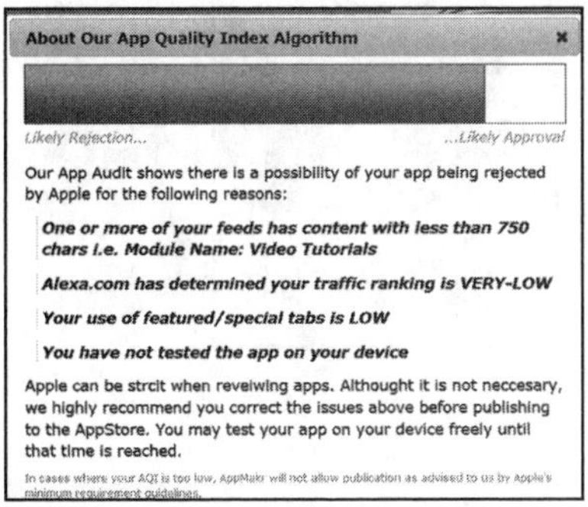

Figure 2.60:
AppMakr
AQI score.

You can now download the binary file necessary to complete the publishing process as outlined on page 132. The iBuildApp example on page 166 demonstrates this process further. See QR Code 2.12 on page 156 for AppMakr tutorials.

Repeat for Android

The process for creating your app for Android is similar. Figure 2.61 shows the Android build page for our example app. From here, we download an ".apk" file and use it to add our app to the Android Market.

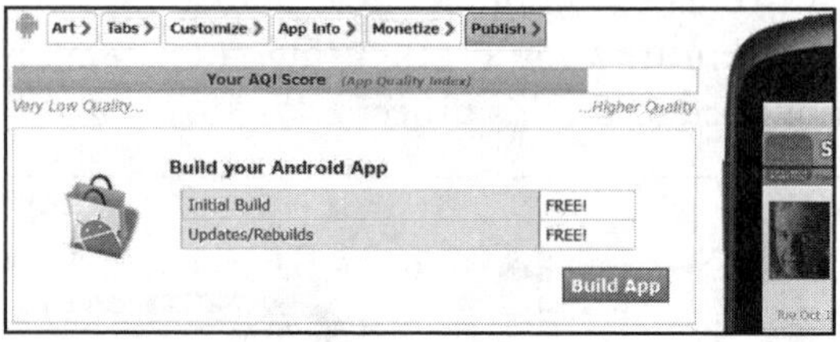

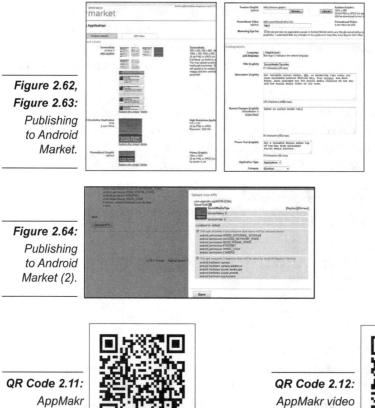

Figure 2.61:
*Publishing
for Android.*

Once we have our build file, we can go to our Android developer account and add a new app by completing the app/product details, uploading our app assets, and uploading the .apk file. Figure 2.62, Figure 2.63, and Figure 2.64 show the process. Read more about adding your app to the Android and Amazon markets on page 132.

**Figure 2.62,
Figure 2.63:**
*Publishing
to Android
Market.*

Figure 2.64:
*Publishing
to Android
Market (2).*

QR Code 2.11:
*AppMakr
gallery[11].*

QR Code 2.12:
*AppMakr video
tutorials[12].*

Widgetbox

Web Apps Only

Widgetbox[53] offers an easy-to-use tool for creating web apps compatible with both iPhone and Android phones. Widgetbox hosts your web app and places it in their app directory for $25/month, with a 14-day free trial. See QR Code 2.13 on page 161 for the Widgetbox gallery.

Setting Up Your Account

Once you have an account with Widgetbox, go to your dashboard to create a mobile app. Figure 2.65 shows the opening screen. Add a title and header image as shown in Figure 2.66.

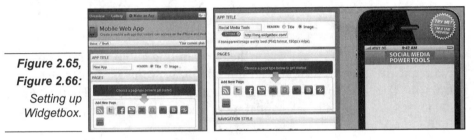

Figure 2.65,
Figure 2.66:

Setting up
Widgetbox.

Adding Pages

Click on an icon to create a new page for your app (see Figure 2.66). You can create pages for your app containing the following types of content:

- Blog feed or other type of RSS feed
- Facebook page updates, Twitter feeds
- YouTube videos
- Image gallery from Flickr, Picasa, or other photo sources
- Polls, maps
- Links for others to share your app
- Custom content created with HTML and CSS

Figure 2.67 shows the process for adding an RSS feed page. In our example, we import specific blog posts from the Social Media Power blog to serve as the main page of the app. Enter your feed URL and set your image and sort preferences. If you want to allow users to view your blog posts in their mobile browser instead of inside the app, and share them with others, choose the "Include view in browser and share buttons" option.

Figure 2.67: Adding pages.

Since the Social Media Power blog is a WordPress blog, each category within the blog has its own RSS feed[54]. We take advantage of this convenient WordPress feature as we create the pages for our example web app. We call the main page of the app "Tips," since it is importing posts from a blog category consisting of social media tips by the contributing authors.

We add another page that consists of social media resources that is pulled from the same blog but using a different category. We call that page "Resources."

One of the goals of this app is for the contributing authors to sell books. Rather than create a custom page for this task, we use a feed category from the Social Media Power blog to list the author's books. Figure 2.68 demonstrates. This will make updating or adding books to the page easier in the future as well.

Figure 2.68: Adding pages (2).

To add a video page to your app, click on the YouTube icon and input the user name of the YouTube account you wish to stream videos from—see Figure 2.69. You can stream videos based on the uploads or favorites of a specific account, or enter a search term to pull videos from the whole of YouTube.

Figure 2.69: Adding pages (3).

The "Share" page allows users to share your app via social networking sites, email, or SMS. This page also includes an option for users to install a shortcut to their mobile device's home screen. See page 147 for more details on mobile app shortcuts.

The last page we add in our example is a custom "About" page. We use some basic HTML and CSS to style a simple page with contributor information and links, as shown in Figure 2.70. Keep in mind that web apps should follow applicable mobile website best practices (see page 16), so pages should be kept simple and uncluttered with images.

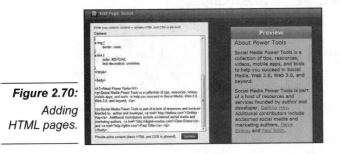

Figure 2.70:
Adding
HTML pages.

Customizing Your App/Adding Assets

Figure 2.71 shows our app dashboard with our pages in place. Once the app is saved, we can customize it by choosing a theme and navigation styles as shown in Figure 2.72. We can further customize by adding assets like an icon and splash (start up) page (see page 168 for information on preparing app assets).

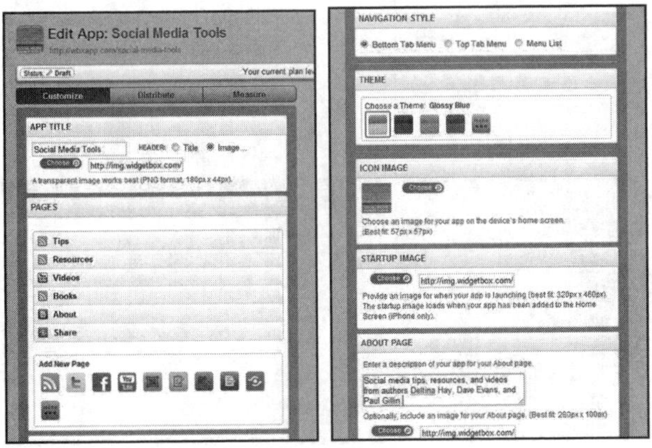

Figure 2.71,
Figure 2.72:
Customizing
Widgetbox.

The "About Page" description and image appear on the app's About page, which is the page visitors see when they click on a link to the app (see Figure 2.73).

Figure 2.73:
Widgetbox
app page.

Distributing and Promoting Your App

Since this is a web app and not a native app, we cannot distribute it through the app stores. Instead, we need to make it available in as many places as possible as a link or QR code. Click on the "Distribute" tab on your Widgetbox app dashboard. Part one of this page, as seen in Figure 2.74, offers a number of ways you can distribute your app:

- The "permalink" is a direct link to your app's About page that you can use to promote the app.
- You can place a QR code on your blog or regular website for mobile device users to scan (see page 186 for more about QR codes).
- Share your app on social networking sites or via email or SMS.

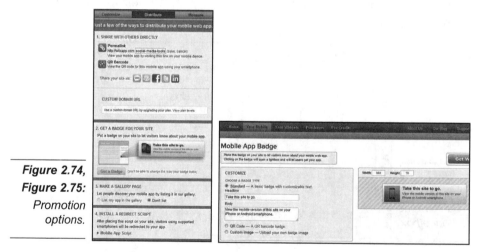

Figure 2.74,
Figure 2.75:
Promotion
options.

Part two of the "Distribute" page offers a badge you can place on a blog or website to promote your app further (see Figure 2.74). Figure 2.75 shows the set-up page for the badge. You can create a custom badge or a QR code badge. When you click "Get Widget" you are provided with code you can

Figure 2.88 shows how we changed the "Home" page to a "Video Feed" page by importing our YouTube channel feed. We subsequently changed the tab icon to read "All Videos" to represent this page more accurately (see Figure 2.88).

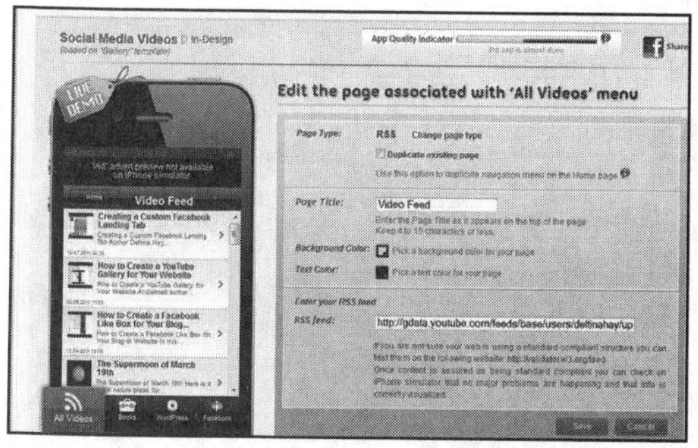

Figure 2.88:
Populating pages.

Our video series includes an entire WordPress tutorial segment, and we want to highlight that segment with its own page. Figure 2.89 shows the page. We choose the "Video Stream" page type for this page so we can feature the videos as a group, and add them one by one rather than with a feed. This page type has its own video player that allows users to view the videos within the app—rather than being directed to YouTube to view them. We change the tab icon for this page to "WordPress," as seen in Figure 2.89.

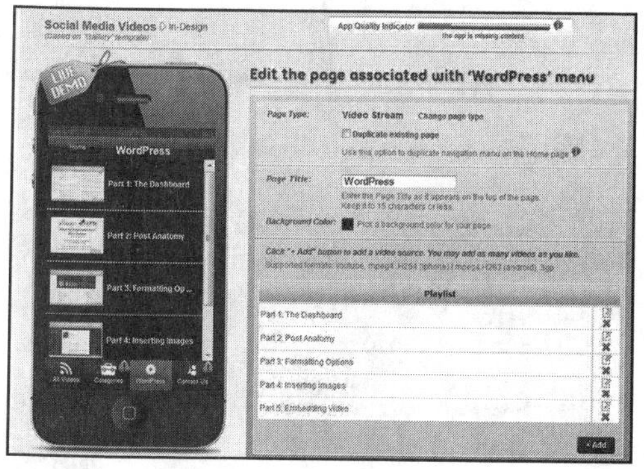

Figure 2.89:
Populating pages (2).

We continue populating pages using the Facebook page type, the Contact page type, and the web page type to display our Facebook page, contact information, and the URL of the author's Amazon author page (see Figure 2.90, Figure 2.91, and Figure 2.92). Figure 2.93 shows our finished app.

copy and subsequently place on your site. See page 100 for instructions on how to place code on a website or blog.

Figure 2.76 shows the QR code badge and the custom badge for our example app on a website. Clicking on the badge or scanning the code produces the screen in Figure 2.77. From here a user can access the app on their iPhone or Android phone.

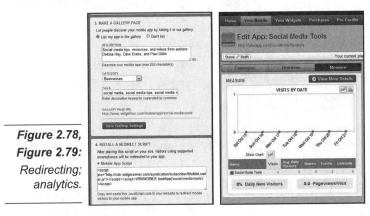

Figure 2.76,
Figure 2.77:
Placing widgets.

Further down the "Distribute" page are two more options to share your web app (see Figure 2.78). You can add it to the Widgetbox gallery, or get a redirect script to place on your website. This type of script detects mobile traffic to your desktop website and redirects it to your mobile web app. Read more about redirecting your app on page 172.

Figure 2.78,
Figure 2.79:
Redirecting; analytics.

Web App Analytics

The "Measure" tab provides numbers on your app visitors, including average daily views, shares, events, and linkouts (see Figure 2.79).

QR Code 2.13:
Widgetbox gallery[13].

ibuildApp

Native Apps and Web Apps
Platforms: iOS for iPhone and iPad, Android, Web Apps

IBuildApp[55] is a free service that lets you create native apps (for iPhone, iPad, or Android) and web apps. They have good tutorials on how to use their service, and on the process of getting your apps in the Apple App Store. See QR Code 2.14 on page 166 to see the iBuildApp gallery.

Setting Up Your Account

Once you have an account, click on "Create App," and you are given the choice of creating a native iPhone/Android app, an iPad app, or a web app (see Figure 2.80 and Figure 2.81).

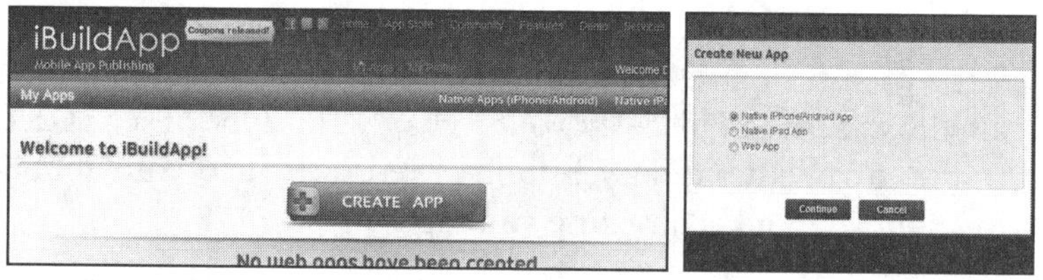

Figure 2.80,
Figure 2.81:
Setting up iBuildApp.

Figure 2.82 shows the next step. From here you can choose from a number of templates based on specific business types. There are also templates for creating ebook apps, galleries, and custom, widget-driven apps. We choose the gallery template for our example. We want to create a native app that features a video tutorial series from YouTube.

Once you choose a theme, give your app a name (using keywords) and choose which platform you wish to create the app for: iOS, Android, or both (see Figure 2.83). We choose iOS for our example app.

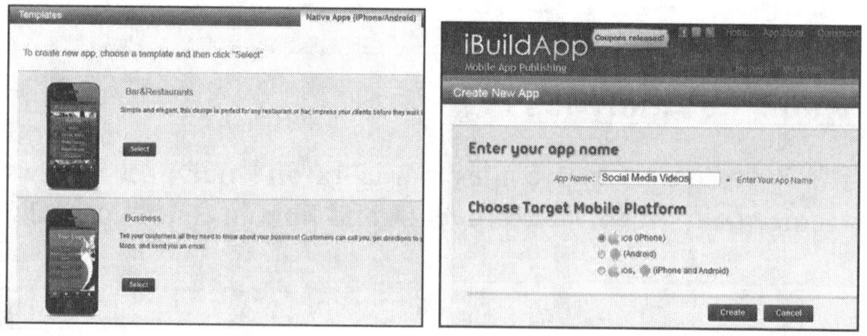

Figure 2.82,
Figure 2.83:
Setting up iBuildApp (2).

Customizing Your App

Customize the theme by changing the background image and header logo, as seen in Figure 2.84. Other customizations will depend on the template

you choose. In our example, we are given home-page text to edit, as well as two main buttons to customize (Gallery and Contact—see Figure 2.84 and Figure 2.85). We can change the name of the buttons as well as upload custom images to use. We can also customize the icons and text for the bottom tabs (see Figure 2.86).

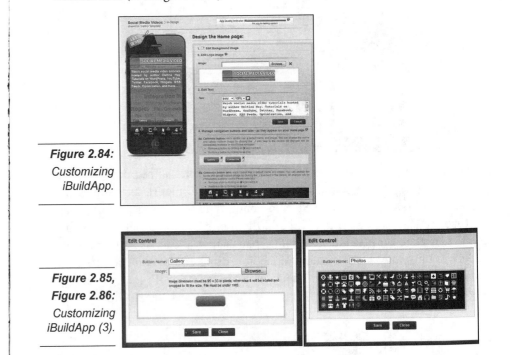

Figure 2.84:
Customizing iBuildApp.

Figure 2.85,
Figure 2.86:
Customizing iBuildApp (3).

Populating Your App

To populate the app with content, click on any of the tabs or buttons to customize and populate the respective page. Each page is customized using "page types." Click on "Change page type" (see Figure 2.88) and you get a lot of options, as shown in Figure 2.87. You can create pages for selling products, offering coupons, importing feeds, displaying maps, and much more. Each page type has its own customization options. (The e-commerce option is not presently available for web apps, but iBuildApp plans to add a PayPal powered feature in the near future.)

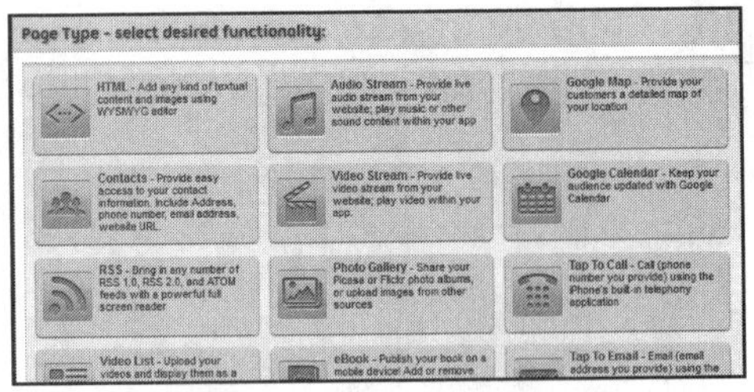

Figure 2.87:
Customizing iBuildApp (3).

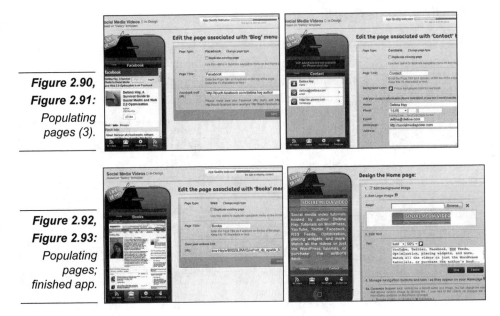

Figure 2.90,

Figure 2.91:

Populating

pages (3).

Figure 2.92,

Figure 2.93:

Populating

pages;

finished app.

Monetizing Your App

IBuildApp does offer in-app purchases for iOS apps. You can also create coupons in iBuildApp through a mobile coupon service (see page 174) or by creating your own. In the next step, you can choose to accept ads on your site. Read more about e-commerce within apps in the "Monetizing Your Mobile App" section.

App Settings and Assets

The next step is the App Settings tab seen in Figure 2.94. From here, choose your target devices (Apple, Android, or both), upload your splash screen image, and choose options for adding ads to your app.

On the "App Info" tab, upload your app icon, and input the description, keywords, and category that best represent your app (see Figure 2.95).

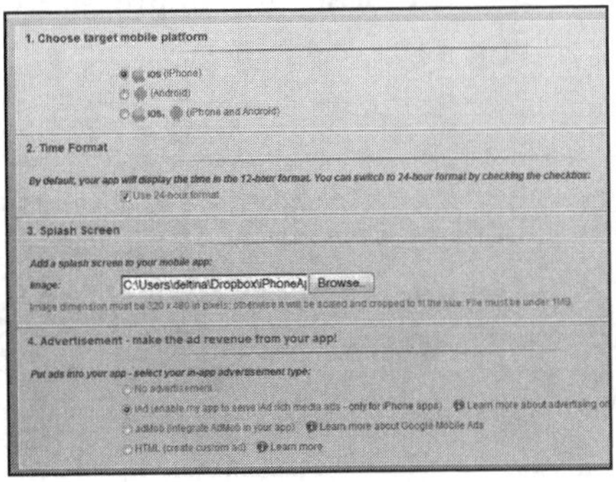

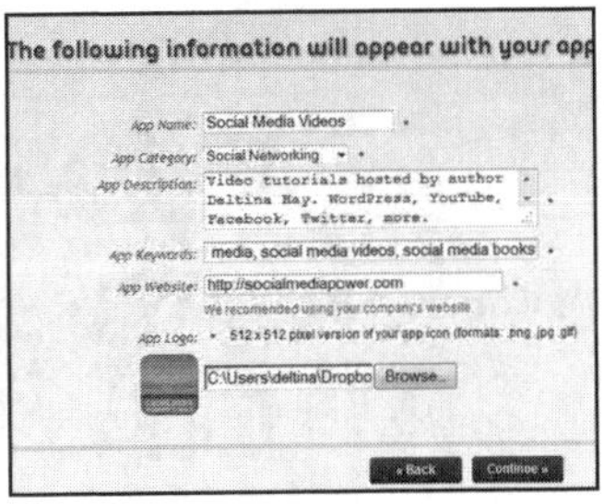

Figure 2.94,

Figure 2.95:

IBuildApp

setings.

Adding Push Notifications

The "Notifications" tab allows you to send push notifications to your app users—even when they are not running your app (see Figure 2.96). IBuildApp does a nice job of explaining the process of setting up push notifications through your Apple and Android developer accounts.

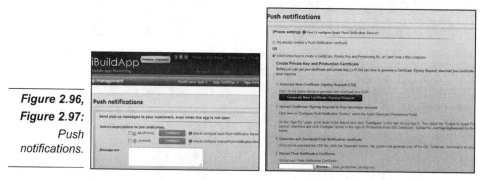

Figure 2.96,
Figure 2.97:
Push
notifications.

Figure 2.97 shows the screen once you click "Configure" next to the iOS icon. In order to send push notifications from an iOS app, you need to have an Apple developer account[26]. IBuild App walks you through the process of allowing iBuildApp to send push notifications for you through your developer account.

Follow their instructions to create the files and complete the other steps necessary for sending push notifications through the iBuildApp platform. The general process is similar to the process in the "Publishing Native Apps" section on the next page. Push notifications are not available for web apps in iBuildApp. See page 113 for more information on push notifications. See QR Code 2.15 for iBuildApp tutorials.

Publishing Native Apps

IBuildApp also does a good job of walking you through the publishing process for your native apps. Figure 2.98 shows the "App Publishing" tab. You can choose to publish the app using your distributor account on your own, or have them do it for you for $199.

QR Code 2.14:
iBuildApp
gallery[14].

QR Code 2.15:
iBuildApp
tutorials[15].

In order to publish an iOS app in the Apple App Store, you need to have an Apple developer account[26]. IBuild App walks you through the process of allowing iBuildApp to create the build file for you through your own developer account.

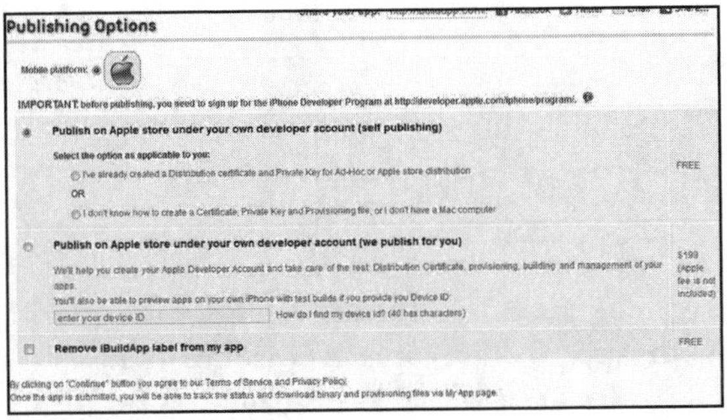

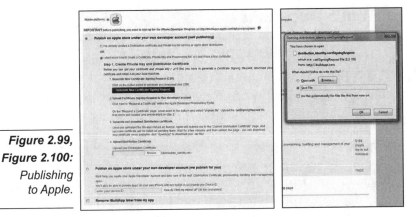

Figure 2.98:
Publishing
options.

IBuildApp even has an option that allows you to go through the publishing process without a Mac computer (see Figure 2.98). Using this option, follow their instructions for creating the files and completing the other steps necessary to publish your app. The general process is:

1. Create a Certificate Signing Request (CSR) File using iBuildApp (see Figure 2.99).
2. Download the CSR file to your computer (see Figure 2.100).
3. Go to your Apple Developer account to "Create iOS Distribution Certificate" (see Figure 2.101).
4. On that page, Apple will ask for the CSR file you just downloaded (see Figure 2.101).
5. Submit the CSR file, and Apple generates a certificate file for you.
6. Download the certificate file Apple created for you (see Figure 2.102).
7. Return to iBuildApp and upload the certificate file (see Figure 2.99).

Figure 2.99,
Figure 2.100:
Publishing
to Apple.

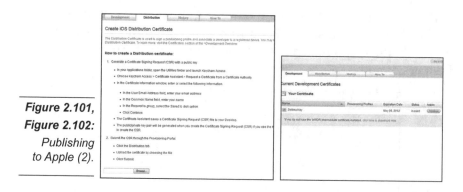

Figure 2.101,

Figure 2.102:

Publishing
to Apple (2).

Once this process is complete, iBuildApp creates your build file that you can use to add your app to the Apple App Store following the process outlined on page 132. See QR Code 2.15 on page 166 for tutorials.

Distributing Web Apps

The publishing options for web apps is shown in Figure 2.103. You can download a QR code (see page 186 for more on QR codes) for the app or a direct URL to promote the app in directories or on your website. IBuildApp also has a gallery you can place your app in by making it public. See the "Promoting Your Mobile App" section on page 175 for more details.

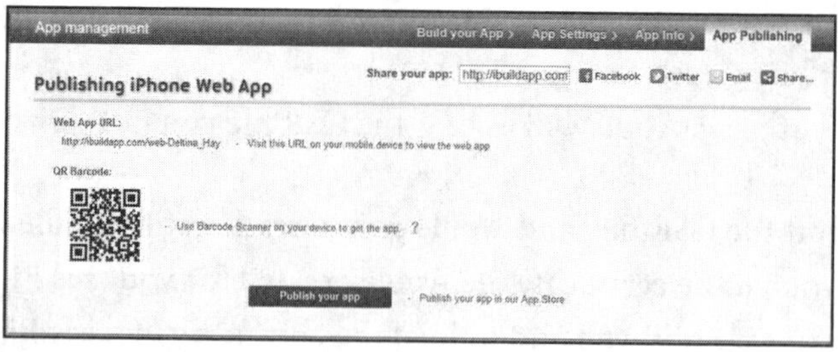

Figure 2.103:

Publishing
web apps.

Preparing Your App Assets

> ### ▶ Bootstrapper's Guide ◀
> ✓ You need specific text and graphics in order to add your app to stores.
> ✓ Prepare and optimize your descriptive text using your best keywords.
> ✓ Graphic assets like icons, thumbnails, and screen shots are required.
> ✓ Each store has their specs for graphic assets, but they are all similar.

You need to prepare descriptive text and graphic assets before you can add your app to mobile app stores. Descriptive text and graphic assets are used to represent your app in the app stores—see Figure 2.104, Figure 2.105, and Figure 2.106—but they can be used wherever you promote your app.

Preparing optimized text and graphics ahead of time can help keep your app presence consistent across all the app stores, directories, galleries, review sites, and other places you plan to feature your app. Access QR Code 2.16 or the resource section of this chapter for a worksheet.

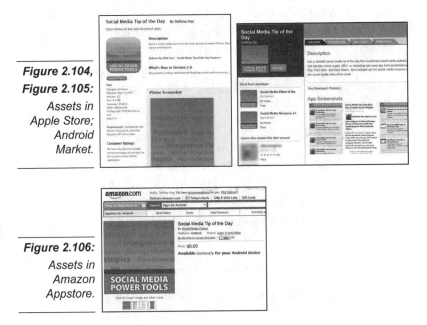

Figure 2.104, Figure 2.105:

Assets in Apple Store; Android Market.

Figure 2.106:

Assets in Amazon Appstore.

Preparing Descriptive Text

When preparing descriptive text, use your best keywords. App store search algorithms put a lot of emphasis on titles, descriptions, and tags when determining placement.

Prepare the following descriptive text items:

- Main App Title: This is the title that shows on the user's home screen, and can only be 11 characters on iOS devices, and 15 on Android devices. Try to include keywords, but not at the expense of clarity.
- Descriptive App Title: Think carefully about your app title. Include your best keywords while keeping clarity. Stores limit your title length to around 30 characters.

QR Code 2.16:

App Assets Prep Sheet[16].

- Descriptions: These can be substantially longer than titles, but get cut off on your main app page and in app store listings—see the examples above. Use your best keywords, but make certain you use the first paragraph of your description to gain the user's attention.

- Categories: You need to choose categories for your apps in most of the stores. Research the types of apps in a store's categories to make sure you choose the appropriate categories for your apps.

- Tags: Some stores allow you to add your own tags to describe your app. Use your best one, two, and three-word key terms as tags. Make certain the tags are also contained within your title and/or description.

Preparing Graphic Assets

Mobile app graphic assets are images and video that you submit along with your app build and descriptive text when adding your app to app stores. Though the types of images are fairly consistent, the size and resolution can fluctuate. Always check with a store's asset guidelines before attempting to upload assets.

Usually, the following types of assets are required:

- App Icon: This is the small icon that represents your app in the app stores as well as on the home screen of the user. Apple adds a glassy effect to your icon automatically, so do not add that yourself.

- Thumbnail Image: This is a larger version of your icon that is used on many of your app store pages.

- Screen Shots: These are actual screen shots of your app that give users an idea of what they can expect to find within your app. The Apple store uses the first screen shot you upload as the graphic for your app store page as well as for the splash screen of your app (a splash screen is the screen a user sees when the app is initially loading).

- Promotional Graphic: This is the graphic that is used to represent your app in the listings of the app stores.

- Featured Graphic: This is a graphic used by the Android Market for featuring apps on their feature pages.

- Video: App videos should be short (from 30 seconds to two minutes) videos that show a glimpse into what a user might experience when using your app. Some app stores let you upload video, while others let you link to YouTube videos.

Following are the general requirements of the Apple App Store[28], the Google Android Market[56], and the Amazon Appstore[57] to give you an idea of their expectations. Note that these specs may have changed; you should always check the asset requirements of a store before preparing your assets. This table only shows specs for portrait screen shots (px stands for pixels).

Asset Type	Apple App Store	Android Market	Amazon Appstore
App Icon	57 x 57 px 24 bit PNG	96 x 96 px 32 bit PNG	114 x 114 px PNG
Thumbnail Image	512 x 512 px JPEG or 24 bit PNG	512 x 512 px 32 bit PNG or JPEG	512 x 512 px PNG
Screen Shots R=Required A=Allowed	R: 1, A: 3 From: 320 x 460 px To: 640 x 960 px	R: 2, A: 8 From 320 x 480 px To: 480 x 854 px 24 bit PNG or JPEG	R: 3, A: 10 480 x 854 px 24 bit PNG or JPEG
Promotional Graphic	N/A	180 x 120 px 24 bit PNG or JPEG	512 x 512 px PNG, JPEG, or GIF
Featured Graphic	N/A	1024 x 500 px 24 bit PNG or JPEG	N/A
Video	N/A	Link to YouTube video	Up to 5. At least 720 px wide, 30 mb max, MPEG, AVI, more...

Figure 2.107, Figure 2.108, and Figure 2.109 show the icon, thumbnail, and promo graphic assets for the AppMakr example on page 151. Figure 2.110, Figure 2.111, and Figure 2.112 show some of the screen shots for our example. Note that the screen shots do not contain the status bars, navigation, or any other element of the mobile device. Images will be rejected if they contain anything other than pure screen shots of your app.

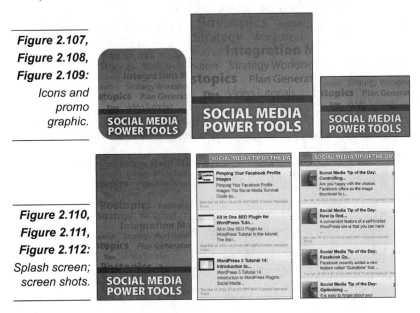

Figure 2.107,
Figure 2.108,
Figure 2.109:
Icons and promo graphic.

Figure 2.110,
Figure 2.111,
Figure 2.112:
Splash screen; screen shots.

Redirection Issues

> ### ► Bootstrapper's Guide ◄
>
> √ If you plan to have an app but no mobile website, think about redirecting mobile traffic from your standard website to your mobile app.
> √ Make sure to only redirect devices that are compatible with your app.
> √ Mobile app landing pages may encourage users to download your app.

If you plan to create a mobile app, but do not plan to create a mobile version of your website, you should address how to manage the mobile traffic coming to your website.

One option is to use a redirect script. As discussed in the "Detection and Redirection" section of the "Mobile Websites" chapter on page 81, these are scripts that redirect mobile-device traffic to the mobile version of your website. The same method can be applied to redirecting mobile traffic to your mobile app, but some precautions should be taken.

Since mobile apps are designed to work on smartphones and tablets, you should be careful to specifically redirect smartphone and tablet traffic to your mobile app, and find another alternative for feature phone traffic. If you are redirecting to a native app, make certain you only redirect traffic from platforms your app will work on, like iOS or Android.

Another concern with the redirect script method is that there is no guarantee that users will want to download an app in the middle of a mobile web browsing experience. One possible workaround to this problem is to create a mobile app landing page that offers users a choice to remain on your standard website or download/bookmark your mobile app instead. Read more about mobile app landing pages on page 177.

Monetizing Your Mobile App

> ### ► Bootstrapper's Guide ◄
>
> √ In-app purchases help sell add-ons and subscriptions from your app.
> √ You have options when selling products in apps, but follow guidelines.
> √ Mobile coupons can drive traffic to a location, or sell products in apps.
> √ Utilizing ad networks like AdMob in your app can help defray costs.

You have some choices for monetizing your app beyond charging your users for it. You can take advantage of in-app purchases offered by Apple's App Store and the Google Market if you have native apps in those stores.

You can sell products within your app; you can offer coupons; or you can join ad networks that place ads in your app and pay you for click-throughs.

In-App Purchases

In-app purchases are purchases made within your app that are *used in your app*. For instance, users can purchase game enhancements (like extra lives, game tokens, etc.), buy upgraded features of an app (like enhanced maps or access to exclusive rewards), buy one-time subscriptions to specific features of an app, or purchase monthly subscriptions to news sources or magazines.

In-app purchases for native apps are managed within your developer account for each respective app store. For example, iOS in-app purchases are managed from your iTune's Connect account[58], and in-app purchases for the Google Android Market are managed from your Google Android Developer account[59].

Users are required to use each store's built-in billing system: iTunes for the Apple store and Google Checkout for the Android market. This allows the store to take a cut of each purchase.

Selling Products

Selling within mobile apps is not as convenient as selling from a website. This is mostly due to the user's reluctance to exit the app to make a purchase. If you use a shopping solution that offers a mobile app version, like the e-commerce solution Magento[60], then you can offer the user a seamless shopping experience within your app. Some mobile app services, like appMobi, offer shopping solutions as well.

If you have a web app or the mobile solution you choose has a built-in browser, then there are other options available. Both PayPal[61] and Google Checkout[62] have mobile-optimized solutions you can use to sell products from a mobile browser. See the resource section of this chapter for more mobile e-commerce solutions.

You can always link to other sources where your users can purchase your products. In the iBuildApp example on page 162, we send the user to the author's Amazon Author Central page[63] where the user can buy any one of the author's books. Google Product Search[64] is another good choice. Figure 2.113 shows a specific Google Product page on a mobile device. This solution shows the user options for purchasing the product, as well as a list of nearby stores where the user can find the product (see Figure 2.114).

Figure 2.113, Figure 2.114:

Google Product Search example.

If you are offering native apps in the leading app stores like the Apple App Store or the Google Android Market, check your developer agreement to make sure your e-commerce solution does not violate the terms of use.

Mobile Coupons

You can offer coupons within your mobile apps or mobile websites by creating your own or using a service. Figure 2.115 shows the types of coupons you can create using the MobileCoupons.com[65] service. Embedding coupons like this into your mobile apps can encourage users to visit your location or purchase products outside of your mobile app. See the resource section of this chapter for additional mobile coupon services.

Figure 2.115:

Mobilecoupon. com.

Ad Networks

Ad networks offer you a way to monetize your mobile apps using ads. Once you are registered with an ad network, you can make your apps available to display ads from the network. You subsequently get paid for each click-through on an ad.

Google's ad network, Adsense[66], now extends to mobile-optimized web pages. You could use this network on your mobile-optimized website or inside of mobile web apps (since web apps run in mobile browsers).

Google Mobile Ads[67] is an ad network specifically for mobile apps. Using a special SDK (software development kit), you can prepare your mobile app for mobile-ready ads like rich media ads (see page 100), full-screen tablet ads, and custom search ads. Custom search ads can be especially profitable if your app offers local or regional search capabilities. You can offer Google Mobile Ads in your Android, iOS, WebOS, or Windows Phone apps.

Apple offers its own ad network for iOS apps distributed through the Apple App Store called the iAd Network[68]. You register for iAd from your iTunes Connect account[26], and enable each of your apps individually for the iAd network. Look in the resource section of this chapter for a list of other ad networks.

Promoting Your Mobile App

▶ Bootstrapper's Guide ◀

√ Place your app in directories and stores, and submit to review sites.
√ Google Adwords has special ads for mobile apps that you can utilize.
√ Mobile app landing pages can make a good first impression on users.
√ Optimize your app store entries for good placement in searches.

Refer to the "Promoting Your Mobile Site" section on page 100 for promotion tactics that can also be applied to mobile apps, tactics such as promoting on your standard and mobile websites, promoting on social networking sites, and using QR codes. Also refer to the "Mobile Marketing Tactics" chapter on page 186 for additional tactics and a more thorough discussion of marketing with QR codes.

Beyond the areas of the book mentioned above, this section addresses some specific tactics you can use to promote your mobile apps.

Mobile App Directories

There are different types of app directories. One type only features apps that are listed in the leading app stores, like Apple's App Store or the Google Android Market. If you have a native app in one of the leading stores, your app will also appear in this type of directory. Appolicious[69] is an example of this type of directory.

Another type of directory has listings of both native and web apps. These directories pull native apps from the leading app stores *and* accept submissions for web apps. If you have a web app or a native app that is not listed in the leading stores, you should submit your app to these directories. If you have a native app, you should *claim* your app in these directories. Open Mobile Application Directory (OMAD)[70] is a directory that lets you claim your apps, submit apps, and use tools to track apps.

There are even some innovative sites that add something extra to the directory experience. AppMatcher[71] is a directory that matches business apps to its target audience. See the resource section of this chapter for a list of additional mobile app directories.

Mobile App Review Sites and Blogs

Review sites like appstorm[72] and makeuseof[73] can get your app a lot of exposure. Look for review sites like Appolicious as well as directory sites that also do reviews. See the resource section of this chapter for more app review sites.

Reach out to bloggers who review mobile apps. Search Technorati[74] or Google Blog Search[75] to find relevant bloggers, and always use best practices when pitching to bloggers[76].

Independent App Stores

If you have a web app or your native app is not available in the leading app stores, you should add your app to as many relevant independent app stores as you can. There are quite a few independent app stores out there. The best way to decide whether one is relevant to your app is to determine if their audience aligns with your target market. Some popular independent app stores are GetJar[77], hangango[78], and ZeeWe[79]. Look in the resource section of this chapter for more independent app stores.

Mobile Advertising

In-App Ads

In the previous section we looked at ways to monetize your mobile apps, including placing ads within your apps using ad networks like Apple's iAd and Google's Mobile Ads. You can take advantage of those same tactics when promoting your site.

Apple's iAd Network encourages developers[80] to advertise their apps within the network; however, if the cost is anything like the regular iAd network, it is likely very expensive.

Google Mobile Ads[81] offer developers affordable options for advertising within other apps, as well as free "house ads" that allow you to cross-promote your apps within the other apps in your portfolio.

Adwords

We discuss Adwords in more detail on page 202, but there is one feature that is specific to mobile app advertising. Google AdWord[82] ads linking to mobile app downloads will appear only on devices that offer those apps. The ad will also include a "Download" link instead of a URL, so the user can automatically download an app when they click on the ad.

To make this feature work, you need to use the URL that points directly to your app in the leading app store, like "itunes.apple.com/nameofapp" or "market.android.com/nameofapp." See Figure 2.116.

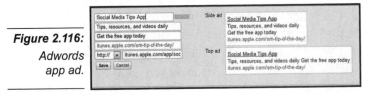

Figure 2.116:
Adwords app ad.

Mobile App Landing Pages

If you plan to launch ad campaigns for your mobile apps, you might want to include a mobile app landing page. App descriptions and assets in the app stores may give users a limited understanding of your app. A landing page can also provide a place to link to all versions of your app—in the iOS store, the Android store, the Blackberry market, etc..

Other items you might include on a mobile app landing page, include:

- Screen shots of your app on all platforms (iOS, Android, etc.)
- App videos or slide presentations
- App upgrades and changes over time
- Bulleted list of app features
- User reviews and other accolades
- Support and contact information

Figure 2.117 and Figure 2.118 show some stylish and functional mobile app landing pages that may inspire you from the apps Tea Round[83] and Bills on Your Table[84]. Six Revisions[85] has a post that features many more.

Figure 2.117,
Figure 2.118:
Mobile app landing page examples.

Improving Your Placement in App Stores

In addition to promotional tactics, you should apply some tactics for improving your placement in the leading and independent app stores. Here are some things you can do to improve your placement and popularity in these stores:

- Use your best keywords in the title of your app, your app description, and any other place you can squeeze them in.

- Create videos for your apps and upload or link to them from the app stores.

- Creating attractive icons and representative screen shots can leave a good first impression.

- Encourage your users to review your app—send push notifications to ask for reviews.

Supporting, Tracking, and Testing Your Mobile App

▶ Bootstrapper's Guide ◀

√ Provide support for your app with a form or by using a CRM service.
√ There are analytics tools designed to track and analyze mobile apps.
√ Test native apps using the SDK, an app service, or a testing tool.
√ Use similar testing tactics for mobile apps as for mobile websites.

Supporting Your Mobile App

Providing support for your app is important to your reputation. You should have some way for users to report problems, suggest features, or contact you with other issues relating to your app. This could be a simple form, as in Figure 2.119, or a robust CRM (customer relations manager) like Salesforce[86]. There are affordable solutions in between as well, like Get Satisfaction[87] (see Figure 2.120 for Tea Round's Get Satisfaction page).

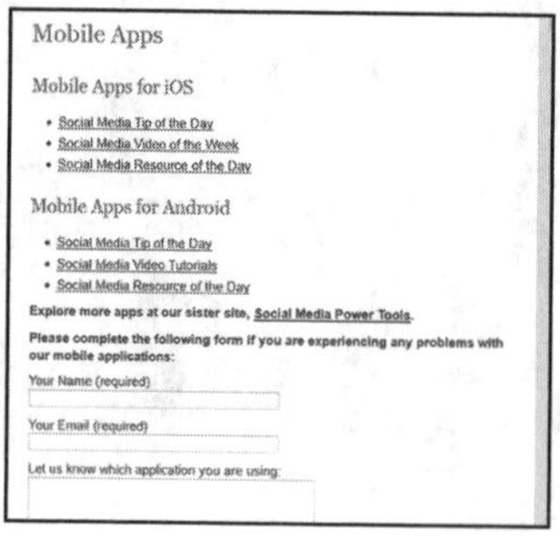

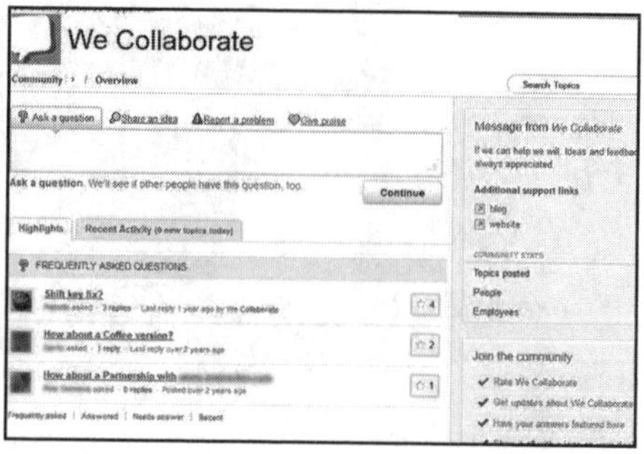

Figure 2.119,
Figure 2.120:
Support form, Get Satisfaction.

Mobile Analytics Tools

There are analytics tools specific to mobile apps. Google Analytics has a special SDK[88] you can use to embed an analytics code to track user engagement within Android and iOS apps. If you have an Android Developer account, this tool can also help you track ads placed in your Android apps.

There are other mobile-app-specific analytics tools as well, like Localytics[89]. Localytics helps you gain real-time insight into your iOS, Android, Blackberry, and Windows Phone apps. App directories like OMAD also offer analytics features.

See the resource section of this chapter for more mobile analytics tools.

Testing Your Mobile App

The testing strategy you use depends on whether you create a native app or a web app.

Testing Native Apps

If you are using a good build tool or native app service, they will have built-in features for testing your apps. If you are using the SDKs to build your apps, they also have built-in functions to help test your apps, including builds that have debugging information to help troubleshoot issues.

Testing Web Apps

If you use a service to create your web app, they will have built-in tools for you to test your app. If you create your app using HTML5, refer to the "Testing Your Mobile Website" section on page 90 for testing tactics and emulators that can help you test and troubleshoot issues.

Another tactic you can use to test your HTML5 apps is to use a build tool like appMobi. Even if you do not plan to use the tool to ultimately build a native app, you can take advantage of the live testing features it provides.

Testing Services

There are some services and tools you can use to help test your mobile apps as well. Services like Device Anywhere[90] are designed for enterprise-class apps, and tend to be quite expensive. Other services, like uTest[91], provide pricing on an individual app basis.

See the resource section of this chapter for more mobile testing services and tools.

Endnotes

1. Trademarkia.com. "THERES AN APP FOR THAT." http://www.trademarkia.com/theres-an-app-for-that-77980556.html

2. ABI Research. "Android Overtakes Apple with 44% Worldwide Share of Mobile App Downloads, Says ABI Research." http://www.businesswire.com/news/home/20111024006574/en/Android-Overtakes-Apple-44-Worldwide-Share-Mobile

3. Flurry. "Mobile App Usage Further Dominates Web, Spurred by Facebook." http://blog.flurry.com/bid/80241/Mobile-App-Usage-Further-Dominates-Web-Spurred-by-Facebook

4. Wikipedia. "List of digital distribution platforms for mobile devices." http://en.wikipedia.org/wiki/List_of_digital_distribution_platforms_for_mobile_devices

5. Apple iTunes App Store. http://itunes.apple.com/us/genre/ios/id36?mt=

6. Android Market. https://market.android.com

7. Nokia OVI. http://store.ovi.com/applications

8. Blackberry App World. http://us.blackberry.com/apps-software/appworld

9. Windows Phone Marketplace. http://www.windowsphone.com/en-US/marketplace

10. Amazon App Store. http://www.amazon.com/mobile-apps/b?ie=UTF8&node=2350149011

11. Nielsen. "Mobile Games Most Popular Mobile App Category in US." http://blog.nielsen.com/nielsenwire/online_mobile/games-most-popular-mobile-app-category

12. W3C. "Web Notification Working Group Charter." http://www.w3.org/2010/06/notification-charter

13. Apple Web Apps. http://www.apple.com/webapps

14. MobiUS. http://www.appmobi.com/?q=node

15. useit. "Mobile Sites vs. Apps: The Coming Strategy Shift." http://www.useit.com/alertbox/mobile-sites-apps.html

16. Sawaya Consulting. http://www.slideshare.net/sawayaconsulting/why-build-a-mobile-app

17. Localytics. "First Impressions Matter! 26% of Apps Downloaded in 2010 Were Used Just Once." http://www.localytics.com/blog/2011/first-impressions-matter-26-percent-of-apps-downloaded-used-just-once

18. Mashable. http://mashable.com/2011/02/24/mobile-app-dev-cost

19. Amazon Web Services. http://aws.amazon.com/iphone-application-hosting

20. Elance. http://elance.com

21. Eclipse IDE. http://www.eclipse.org/downloads/

22. Android SDK. http://developer.android.com/index.html

23. Apple SDK. http://developer.apple.com/ipad/sdk/index.html

24. Blackberry SDK. http://us.blackberry.com/developers/javaappdev

25. Windows Phone SDK. http://www.microsoft.com/download/en/details. aspx?id=27570

26. Apple Developer Account. http://developer.apple.com/devcenter/ios/index.action

27. Objective C Primer. http://developer.apple.com/library/ios/#referencelibrary/ GettingStarted/Learning_Objective-C_A_Primer/_index.html

28. iTunes Connect Developer Guide. https://itunesconnect.apple.com/docs/ iTunesConnect_DeveloperGuide.pdf

29. iOS Developer Library. http://developer.apple.com/library/ios/navigation

30. Android Developer Account. http://market.android.com/publish

31. Amazon Developer Account. https://developer.amazon.com

32. Android Developer Guide. "Publishing on Android Market" http://developer. android.com/guide/publishing/preparing.html

33. Android Developer's Guide. "Preparing for Release" http://developer.android.com/ guide/publishing/publishing.html

34. WebKit. http://www.webkit.org

35. mobile tuts+. http://mobile.tutsplus.com/tutorials/iphone/ iphone-web-app-meta-tags

36. jQuery. http://jquery.com

37. jQTouch. http://jqtouch.com

38. W3C. http://www.w3.org/TR/mwabp

39. Modernizr. http://www.modernizr.com

40. HTML5 Rocks. "Feature, Browser, and Form Factor Detection: It's Good for the Environment." http://www.html5rocks.com/en/tutorials/detection/index.html

41. HTML5 Rocks. "HTML5 Techniques for Optimizing Mobile Performance." http:// www.html5rocks.com/en/mobile/optimization-and-performance.html

42. W3C. "Standards for Web Applications on Mobile: February 2011 current state and roadmap." http://www.w3.org/2011/02/mobile-web-app-state.html

43. Sencha Touch. http://www.sencha.com/products/touch

44. jQuery Mobile. http://jquerymobile.com

45. Tiggzi. http://tiggzi.com

46. PhoneGap. http://phonegap.com

47. PhoneGap Build. http://build.phonegap.com

48. appMobi XDK. http://appmobi.com/index.php?q=node/27

49. ICONJ. http://www.iconj.com/iphone_style_icon_generator.php

50. CUBIQ.org. http://cubiq.org/add-to-home-screen

51. AppMakr. http://www.appmakr.com

52. AppMakr AQI. "What do the AQI audit responses actually mean?" http://help.appmakr.com/entries/178545-possible-responses-from-aqi-and-what-they-mean

53. Widgetbox. http://www.widgetbox.com

54. WordPress Feeds. http://codex.wordpress.org/WordPress_Feeds

55. iBuildApp. http://ibuildapp.com

56. Android Market Assets. http://www.google.com/support/androidmarket/developer/bin/answer.py?answer=1078870

57. Amazon Appstore Assets. https://developer.amazon.com/help/faq.html#Submitting%20Apps%20App%20Details

58. Apple In-app Purchases. http://support.apple.com/kb/ht4009

59. Google Billing. "Administering In-app Billing." http://developer.android.com/guide/market/billing/billing_admin.html

60. Magento Mobile. http://www.magentocommerce.com/product/mobile

61. PayPal Mobile. https://cms.paypal.com/us/cgi-bin/?cmd=_render-content&content_ID=developer/e_howto_api_ECOnMobileDevices

62. Google Checkout Mobile. http://checkout.google.com/seller/mobile/index.html

63. Amazon Author Central. https://authorcentral.amazon.com

64. Google Product Search. http://www.google.com/prdhp

65. MobileCoupons.com. http://mobilecoupons.com

66. Adsense for Mobile. http://www.google.com/adsense/support/bin/answer.py?hl=en&answer=68724&ctx=as2&rd=1

67. Google Mobile Ads. http://www.google.com/ads/mobile/publishers/app-developers.html

68. iAd Network. http://developer.apple.com/support/ios/iad-network.html

69. Appolicious. http://www.appolicious.com

70. OMAD. http://www.openmobileapp.com/homepage.html

71. AppMatcher https://www.appmatcher.com

72. appstorm. http://web.appstorm.net/about/submit-an-app-for-review

73. makeuseof. http://www.makeuseof.com

74. Technorati. http://technorati.com

75. Google Blog Search. http://www.google.com/blogsearch

76. Ignite Social Media. "Tips for Agencies Pitching to Bloggers." http://www.ignitesocialmedia.com/blogger-outreach/tips-for-agencies-pitching-to-bloggers

77. GetJar for Developers. http://developer.getjar.com

78. handango. http://www.handango.com/homepage/Homepage.jsp?storeId=2218

79. ZeeWe for Developers. http://www.zeewe.com/zeewe/web/developers

80. Ad Network for Developers. http://advertising.apple.com/developers

81. Google Mobile Ads for Developers. http://www.google.com/ads/mobile/publishers/app-developers.html

82. Google AdWords. "Go Mobile! Series: New targeting options for mobile ads." http://adwords.blogspot.com/2010/01/new-targeting-options-for-mobile-ads.html

83. Tea Round. http://www.tearoundapp.com

84. Bills on Your Table. http://www.billsonyourtable.com

85. Six Revisions. "35 Beautiful iPhone App Website Designs." http://sixrevisions.com/design-showcase-inspiration/35-beautiful-iphone-app-website-designs

86. Salesforce. http://salesforce.com

87. Get Satisfaction. http://getsatisfaction.com

88. Google Analytics for Mobile Apps. http://code.google.com/mobile/analytics/docs

89. Localytics. http://www.localytics.com

90. Device Anywhere. http://www.deviceanywhere.com

91. uTest. http://www.utest.com

QR Code Notes

1. Mobile App Strategy Worksheet. http://goo.by/wJWYGw/bgmw2-1

2. Mobile App Strategy Examples. http://goo.by/wq06JN/bgmw2-2

3. Publishing an Apple App Presentation. http://goo.by/w2BYPT/bgmw2-3

4. Publishing an Android App Presentation. http://goo.by/w3BwSn/bgmw2-4

5. Tiggzi Tutorials. http://goo.by/wmQ3qa/bgmw2-5

6. Bootee Catcher App Progress. http://goo.by/wjkPEK/bgmw2-6

7. PhoneGap Tutorials. http://goo.by/wrFxog/bgmw2-7

8. appMobi XDK Video Tutorials. http://goo.by/wyxJzY/bgmw2-8

9. Quill Driver Books App Code. http://goo.by/w3J9cG/bgmw2-9

10. Creating Mobile Shortcuts Video. http://goo.by/w9fOtj/bgmw2-10

11. AppMakr Gallery. http://goo.by/wX6fbo/bgmw2-11

12. AppMakr Video Tutorials. http://goo.by/wCSa1F/bgmw2-12

13. Widgetbox Gallery. http://goo.by/wSJEG9/bgmw2-13

14. iBuildApp Gallery. http://goo.by/wXI7n0/bgmw2-14

15. iBuildApp Tutorials. http://goo.by/wDJ194/bgmw2-15

16. App Assets Preparation Worksheet. http://goo.by/wI7E06/bgmw2-16

17. Chapter Two Resources. http://goo.by/wJniwm/bgmw2-17

Additional Resources

Resources for the topics covered in this chapter can be found at TheBootstrappersGuide.com under the categories listed below. Additional resources and examples are added to the website on a regular basis.

Mobile App Resources

- Mobile App Stores
- Independent Mobile App Stores
- Mobile App Creation Services
- Finding App Developers
- Mobile App Development Tools and Resources
- HTML5 Mobile App Frameworks and Resources
- HTML5, CSS3, JavaScript Tutorials
- Mobile E-Commerce Solutions
- Mobile Coupon Services
- Mobile Ad Networks
- Mobile App Directories & Review Sites
- Mobile App Store Submission Links
- Mobile App Advertising Resources
- Mobile App Support Tools
- Mobile Testing Tools
- Mobile Analytics Tools

Mobile Application Worksheets

- Mobile App Strategy Worksheet
- Mobile App Assets Preparation Worksheet

Mobile App Examples

Mobile App Strategy Examples

- Content-Driven, multimedia
- Branded utility, just for fun, more

Mobile App Tool Examples

- Mippin
- More...

QR Code 2.17:
Chapter two resources[17].

3 Mobile Marketing Tactics

"By 2013, mobile phones will overtake PCs as the most common Web access device worldwide." —Gartner[1]

In This Chapter

Quick Response (QR) Codes

Location-Based Marketing

Mobile Advertising Campaigns

Mobile Optimized Landing Pages

SMS Marketing

Social Media Diligence

Augmented Reality

Near Field Communication (NFC)

On Being Context Aware

Bootstrapper's Guide

I want to increase traffic to my store or event: See pages 186 and 195

I want to reach customers through their smartphones: See page 208

I want to optimize my landing pages for the mobile web: See page 205

I need to drive mobile traffic to my website: See pages 186 and 201

I want to add mobile sites and apps to my ad campaigns: See page 201

Help me improve placement in mobile search engines: See page 214

Show me the future so I can plan for it now: Skip to page 210

Mobile Marketing Tactics

Mobile optimized websites and mobile applications are not the only way you can leverage the mobile web. In this chapter we discuss other tactics and tools you can apply to your overall mobile web strategy. We introduce some new technology and tools that are specific to the mobile web, as well as time-honored tactics that may require some tweaking to work effectively in a mobile environment.

QR Codes

> ▶ **Bootstrapper's Guide** ◀
>
> √ QR codes are small barcodes you can place on print and online media.
> √ They bridge the gap between the physical world and the digital world.
> √ Users scan contact info, URLs, maps, and more with mobile devices.
> √ Use QR codes for marketing, business cards, links to your mobile site.

It seems as though they are everywhere nowadays—in magazines, on billboards, on websites, in books. Quick response codes (QR codes*) are appropriately referred to as paper-based hyperlinks. They are bar codes that, when scanned by a mobile device, redirect the user to a URL or perform some other function.

Think of QR codes as a way of bridging the gap between the physical world and the digital world. People scan QR codes that are printed or placed on business cards, advertisements, websites—anywhere an image can be placed in print or online—and are given an opportunity to interact with your content via the QR code through their mobile device.

*The term "QR Code" is a registered trademark of Denso Wave Incorporated.

Deciphering QR Codes

In order to "read" a QR code, the mobile device user needs a QR code (or bar code) scanner application. Look in the resource section of this chapter for a list of popular QR code scanning apps for your mobile device. The scanner apps work like a camera, where the user gets the code "in focus" with their mobile device. The scanner decodes the QR code and performs the embedded function, like taking the user to a URL, playing a video, or serving up contact information.

Figure 3.1 shows the process of a smartphone scanning a QR code from a business card. When the QR code is decoded by the scanner app, it reveals contact information that the user can store in their contact database. They might also be able to see a map of the physical address, dial the contact's phone number, or send the contact an email message. Tapping on "Add Contact," in this case, allows the user to save the contact information to one of their databases.

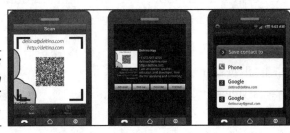

Figure 3.1:
QR code scan
example:
contact info.

Figure 3.2 shows the process of a smartphone scanning a QR code from a website. In this instance, a URL to a mobile application is embedded in the code. When the code is decoded, the scanner app asks if the user would like to go to the URL, or share it with someone else via email or SMS (text message). Tapping on "Open Browser" in this case brings the user to the mobile application.

Figure 3.2:
QR code scan
example:
URL redirect.

What to Do with QR Codes

In this book, we demonstrate how to use QR codes to promote your mobile website (page 100), promote mobile applications, and to spice up your profiles on location social networking sites (page 198). These are just a few ways you can utilize QR codes in your overall marketing campaign—here are some ideas for more...

Types of information you might embed into a QR code include:

- URL to a website, social networking site, mobile application, etc.
- URL to a custom landing page with special offers or contests
- Personal or company contact information in a MeCard or vCard (MeCard and vCard are standardized contact formats that can be recognized easily and stored by mobile devices)

- A phone number which can be dialed by the mobile device
- Product specifications, nutritional information, exclusive offers
- RSS feeds, blogs, or tweets, URL to a video
- Text messages, short promotional blurbs, buy now buttons
- Calendar events with description, date, time, and location
- A physical address with location coordinates

Where you might place a QR code:

- Business cards, flyers, brochures
- Email messages, newsletters, email signatures
- Websites and landing pages
- Social media profiles, social networking status updates
- Print, billboard, banner ads
- Product labels, invitations, greeting cards
- Event swag like bags, badges, t-shirts
- Print books and e-books
- Retail window/counter, coupons, sales receipts

You are limited only by your imagination when thinking of ways to utilize QR codes (see Figure 3.3 from QR Stuff[2]). There are also links to more examples in the resource section of the chapter if you want to see how other organizations are using QR codes.

Figure 3.3:
QR code
examples.

Diversity of QR Codes

Out of the box, a QR code looks like a square version of a black and white bar code symbol you might see on the back of a book. As seen in Figure 3.4 and Figure 3.5, the density of the QR code design can vary greatly. This density is determined by the amount of information embedded into the QR code. There are other factors that can affect the look of a QR code, as we will discover later in the chapter.

**Figure 3.4,
Figure 3.5:**

*QR code
diversity.*

There is no need to settle for the squared-off, black and white look of a typical QR code. QR codes can be customized to reflect your branding. Figure 3.6[3] and Figure 3.7 (by Craig Sullender[4]) show examples of branded (or custom) QR codes.

**Figure 3.6,
Figure 3.7:**

*Custom
QR code
examples.*

The process of branding QR codes needs to be done carefully to keep from disrupting the embedded information. You can attempt this process yourself or use a service. See the resource section of this chapter for links to tutorials and services. Follow QR Code 3.2 to see a custom QR code gallery.

Creating QR Codes

One of the things that makes QR codes so popular is how easy they are to create. You have a few choices for creating your QR codes:

- Create the code from scratch using a tutorial
- Use QR code software to create the codes yourself
- Use a QR code generator service or tool

If you are feeling adventurous, there are tutorials listed in the resource section on how to create and brand QR codes from scratch, as well as links to QR code software. Otherwise, there are online tools to help you create QR codes. Refer to the resource section for a list of services and tools.

You should be selective when choosing a service or a tool to create your QR codes. It can be frustrating to invest time and money into a QR code campaign only to have your codes become untrackable, defective, or even expire.

Here are some things to look for when choosing a QR code service or tool:

Limitations

Always check the limitations of a free service. Free services may embed ads in your codes, attach expiration dates, or limit the number of scans your codes can receive. By upgrading to the paid version of a service, you can usually avoid such limitations.

Features

Here are some questions to ask about the features of a QR code service:

- Can you track—or get analytics on—your QR codes?
- Can you create full blown QR code campaigns?
- Can you change your codes once they are published?
- Can you create QR codes in batches?
- Can you download your QR code in many different file types, including vector files and print-ready file formats?
- Does the service offer mobile landing pages in case you do not have your own?

Compliance

QR code standards are maintained by the International Organization for Standardization (ISO)[5]. A reputable QR code service or generator should adhere to these standards. If they do adhere, they will typically tout the fact on their website. If you are not sure, you should ask.

Reputation

Find out what others are saying about a service on Twitter, Facebook, or on the service's own wiki, blog, or support pages. Check the service's feedback or support site to see how well they interact with their customers.

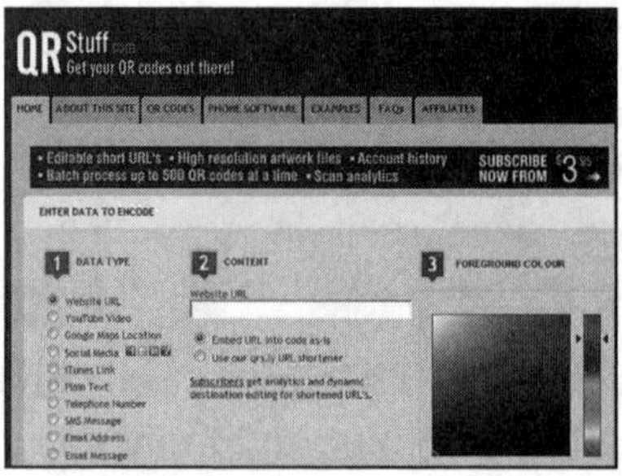

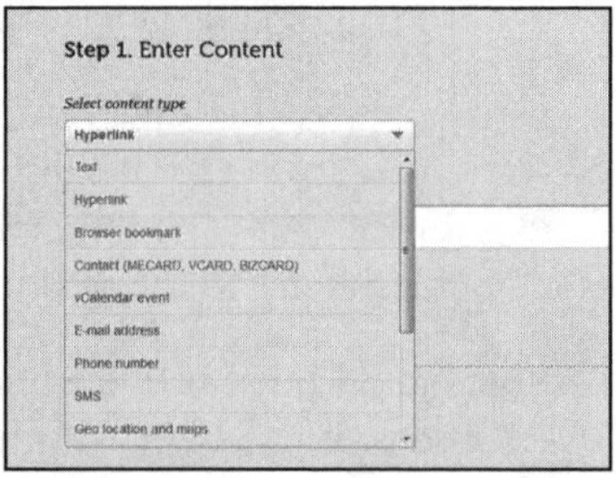

Figure 3.8,
Figure 3.9:
QR code
generators.

Figure 3.8 and Figure 3.9 demonstrate two QR code generators from Esponce[6] and QRStuff[2]. Each tool looks a little different, but the general process for creating your QR code is similar:

- Choose your "content type"—a hyperlink (URL) to a website, a vCard containing contact information, coordinates for a map, etc.
- Input the information you want to embed in your QR code—this will differ depending on your content type.
- Configure your code according to the tool you are using—you can usually configure size, density, padding, and other settings (see example below).
- Enter tracking information if applicable.
- Customize your code by changing colors or embedding a logo, depending on the tool.
- Test your code with a QR code scanner before publishing.
- Download your QR code in the file format you need for the web or for print. (The generator creates your code in a number of file formats.)
- Place your code on your website, on your print media, or wherever you plan to launch your campaign.
- Track your QR code to see how many views it has received.
- Continue to test the code for stability.
- Change the code as needed over time, if applicable.

QR Code Service Example

Figure 3.10 shows the Esponce QR code generator[6] when we choose Hyperlink as our QR code content type. You can create free QR codes using this service, but they have an expiration date of one year. The upgrade for unlimited expiration dates and other features is around $12/month.

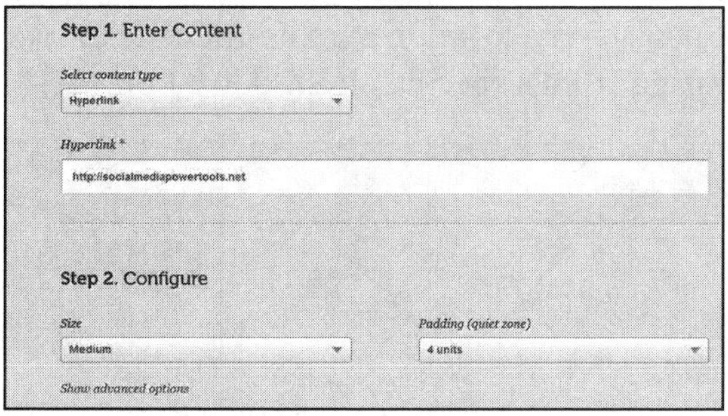

Figure 3.10: Creating a QR Code (1).

We enter the URL (Hyperlink) where we want the user directed once they scan our code in Step 1. In the second step we configure our QR code by clicking on "Show Advanced Options" (see Figure 3.11).

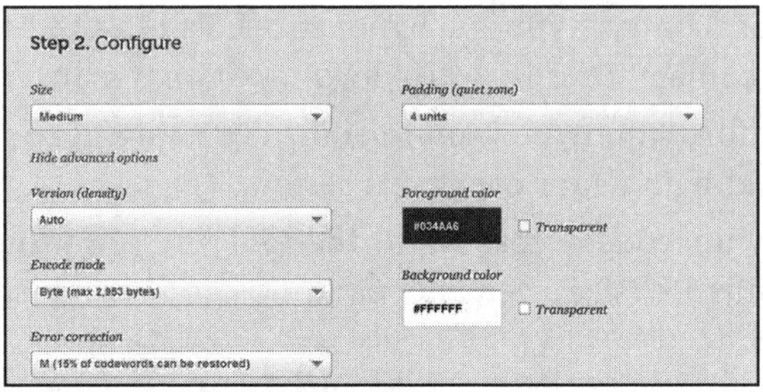

Figure 3.11:

Creating a QR Code (2).

In this step we set the following configurations:

- Size: Choose small or medium if you only plan to use your code online; choose large if you plan to use the code on print materials.
- Padding (quiet zone): This is the buffer space around the entire image to keep other images from interfering with the code.
- Version (Density): Controls the density of the QR code. See page 188 for an example.
- Encode Mode: This mode can be Byte, Numeric, or Alphanumeric. It is set by the tool depending on content type, but can be overridden.
- Error-correction: This is a range from 7% to 30% that gauges how much of the image can be damaged before the code is no longer readable. If you plan to place a code on something that will likely be handled a lot, use a higher rate.
- Colors: Control the background and foreground colors of the code.

The next step, shown in Figure 3.12 and Figure 3.13, is to set the short URL to something more descriptive and give this code a name so we can track it more easily. We can also set a location for this QR code in case we want to launch a QR campaign from a specific physical location.

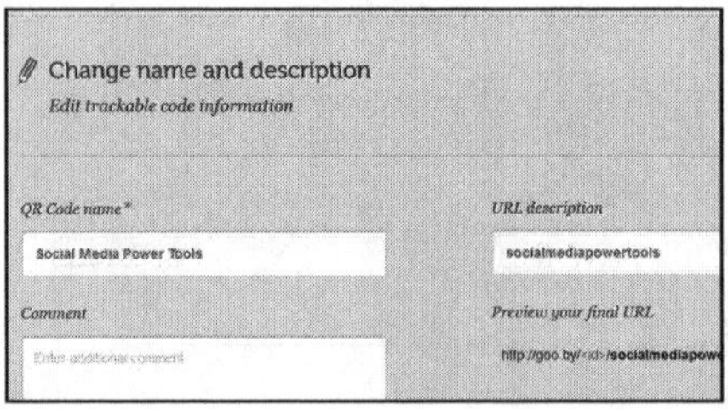

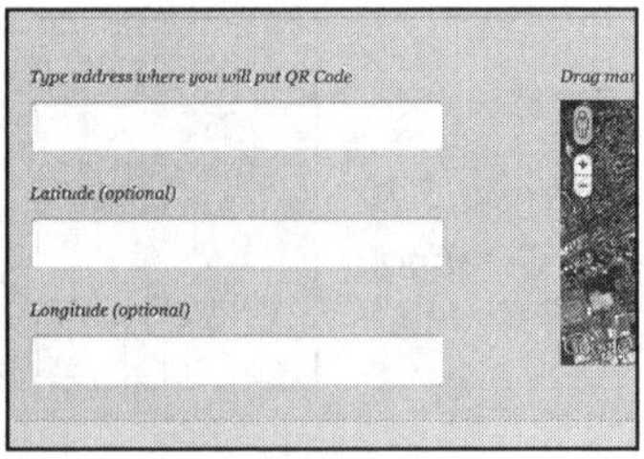

Figure 3.12,

Figure 3.13:

Creating a QR Code (3).

The next step allows us to place a logo or other image on our code to brand it. Figure 3.14 shows the logo image centered on the code when we upload it. We can then move and expand the code to our liking. The tool will let us know if the position or size of the image disrupts the readability of the code (see Figure 3.15).

Figure 3.14,
Figure 3.15:
Customizing
a QR Code.

We can now download the QR code image and place it on our website, business card, advertisement, or wherever we plan to display it. There are a number of file formats available. We can also track how many views the code receives using the Esponce tool's tracking function. See Figure 3.16 and Figure 3.17.

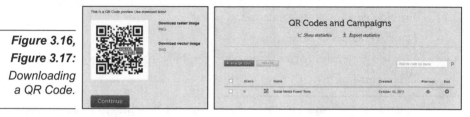

Figure 3.16,
Figure 3.17:
Downloading
a QR Code.

This tool also allows us to change our QR code, if needed. QR codes that can be changed in this way are referred to as dynamic QR codes. The advantage to dynamic codes is that you can keep the content fresh no matter how old the code gets. You don't necessarily need to use a *dynamic* QR code to accomplish this, however, as you could just as easily point the code to a landing page that changes over time.

The steps are similar for other types of QR codes, like contact information or maps. The main difference is the information we enter that will be embedded in the code.

Planning Your QR Code Campaign

Using QR codes in your marketing campaigns can be beneficial, but they can prove disastrous if used improperly. Go forth with a good plan that follows best practices and you can reap the benefits and avoid common mistakes. See QR Code 3.2 or the resource section of this chapter for a worksheet to help you plan.

Create Reliable Codes

Choose a reputable service or firm to create and manage your codes. See page 190 for a list of criteria. Always test your codes before publishing! If you plan to run your campaign for a long period of time, scan the code periodically to test its continued validity.

Plan for Your Target Audience

If your target audience is not tech savvy, you should provide instructions on how they can scan your QR codes.

Know Your Goals

What do you wish to accomplish with your QR code campaign:

- Drive traffic to your mobile website?
- Sell more products?
- Increase awareness of a product or service?
- Grow your mailing list or newsletter subscribers?
- Increase your Facebook fans, Twitter followers, or blog subscribers?
- Provide product information?
- Improve customer relations?
- Provide general information about you or your business?
- Offer more information on a topic?

Be very clear about your objectives so you have a baseline to measure your results against.

Use Best Practices

Deliver what your campaign claims—direct users to a landing page or deliver a function that is relevant to the campaign.

Don't let a link die—if a campaign is over, maintain a landing page that states as much.

QR Code 3.1:
Custom QR
code gallery[1].

QR Code 3.2:
QR Code
campaign
worksheet[2].

Test your codes by scanning them on as many different mobile devices as possible, and test on the actual print or online media where you plan to publish them, at the size they will be published.

Make certain your codes direct users to a mobile-friendly website (see page 16) or a mobile optimized landing page (see page 205), where applicable.

Always let a user know what a code does, or where it will redirect them.

Try to use short URLs when possible, but make sure users know where the link is taking them by offering a description within the short code (like http://goo.by/name-of-site).

QR Code Examples

QR Code 3.1 on page 194 leads to examples of QR codes in the real world. More examples are referenced in the resource section of this chapter. Of course, the QR code enhanced book you are reading right now is an example in the flesh!

Location-Based Marketing

▶ Bootstrapper's Guide ◀

✔ Location services help drive traffic to local businesses through sharing.
✔ Use the services popular in your region and with your target market.
✔ Create campaigns with services to encourage customers to "check in."
✔ Leverage your customer base by rewarding when they "check in."

As we have discovered throughout this book, mobile device users think locally. Statistics show that most searches from mobile devices are for local services (see page 10). Equally popular are mobile applications that focus on local news and activities.

Combine the above with the popularity of social networking and you get a culture of mobile users who love to "check in" from local venues and stores and who aren't afraid to voice their opinions. Location-based services (LBS) allow them the outlet to do so.

Location-based services, similar to social networking sites, offer people a way to connect around a particular location, whether it be a café, a theater, or a park—any place where people can gather. Users check in (letting others in their network know where they are) from that location and comment, leave reviews, play games, and even reap rewards from within the service. The most popular LBSs offer mobile apps so users can check in right from their smartphones.

Business owners can tap into this mobile gold mine by offering deals, rewards, discounts, and other incentives to encourage people to check in from their location. If you have a local business, you should be engaging in location-based marketing. If you don't have a local business, you can still take advantage of LBS platforms.

Mobile users are listing and reviewing your business whether you are engaging or not, so if nothing else, make certain your business is listed properly on the most popular LBSs.

Location-Based Service Examples

There are a lot of LBS sites out there, and you could go nuts trying to establish a presence on all of them, but, with some research, you can discover which ones are the most popular in your city—and within your target market— and go from there (see the "Creating a Location-Based Marketing Plan" on page 198). Only a few of the services are featured here, but you can find a host of services listed in the resource section of this chapter.

foursquare

Foursquare[7] is probably the most popular LBS. Their platform is straightforward, offering users a way to check in and engage with their friends from different venues around the globe (see Figure 3.18). Foursquare can also be linked with Facebook and Twitter.

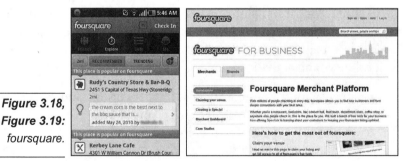

Figure 3.18,
Figure 3.19:

foursquare.

Foursquare offers merchants a way to "claim" their venue and verifies this claim via mail or telephone. As an established merchant, you can create "specials" for free (see Figure 3.19). Specials can be free offers, discounts, special treatment, or rewards. You can even target specials to specific users, such as established customers or newcomers.

Brands and other businesses without a physical location can create foursquare pages as well, which allows them to engage with consumers using the foursquare platform. Go to the foursquare For Business page[8] for more information.

Google Places

Google Places[9] is built into Google's mobile search engine (see Figure 3.20). As a result, it is especially important to verify your information in this LBS.

Figure 3.20,
Figure 3.21:

Google
Places.

Google offers businesses a way to upload photos and videos, engage with customers, and post special promotions for free (see Figure 3.21). They also link your Places account to Adwords Express, which is a simplified version of Google's advertising service. Refer to page 202 for more information on Adword campaigns.

Even businesses without a shingle can be on Google Places. Google allows online or home-based businesses to claim a "service region" and hide their physical address. See Google Places for business[10] for more information.

Yelp

Yelp[11] is a very popular LBS that shows up consistently at the top of search engine results. With the Yelp mobile app (see Figure 3.22), users can search for nearby businesses and deals, check in, and see where their friends are.

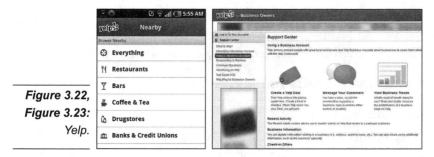

Figure 3.22,
Figure 3.23:

Yelp.

Businesses can offer "deals" in Yelp, engage with customers, upload photos and other information, and recommend other businesses (see Figure 3.23). Yelp also allows business owners the opportunity to reply to reviews publicly or privately. Go to the Yelp business support page for more information[12].

SCVNGR

SCVNGR[13] is a unique take on location-based services. The SCVNGR platform turns the "check in" into a game. Users check in, complete challenges, and reap rewards. See Figure 3.24.

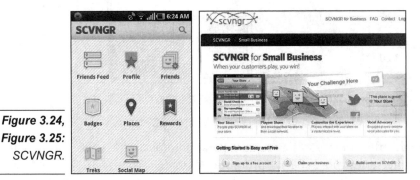

Figure 3.24,
Figure 3.25:
SCVNGR.

Businesses can create profiles, link their profile to their Facebook account, and check analytics. Businesses can also become part of the SCVNGR game by building challenges, treks, and rewards of their own. See Figure 3.25. Go to SCVNGR Small Business[14] for more information.

Facebook Places

Facebook offers a way for users to include a "place" as part of their regular status updates. Businesses should verify through Facebook that a "place" is their own. Once verified (usually through a telephone call), a business or brand can merge their place with their Facebook page to encourage more fan engagement[15].

Other popular LBSs include Gowalla, Loopt, Brightkite, MyTown, UrbanSpoon, and Twitter. Refer to the resource section of this chapter for a list of more location-based services. See QR Code 3.4 for a presentation.

Creating a Location-Based Marketing Plan

Preliminary Steps

Check your business listing within every LBS used in your region, even the ones you do not plan to develop. Update errors and contact the service's support team if you cannot figure out how to fix discrepancies.

Update the "places" options in the social media platforms where you already have a presence, like Facebook and Twitter. Link your Facebook Places with your Facebook business page (above).

As discussed before, not every LBS is going to be a good fit for your business or region. Research the tools that are most popular in your market region and for your target market. You may need to get creative and perform your own local searches within each tool to get a clear picture. Based on this research, choose the tools to include in your plan.

Prepare your content using edited business descriptions that include your best keywords, accurate contact information, and updated hours of operation. Prepare photos, videos, and QR codes to upload to the services you want to use. See QR Code 3.3 or the resource section of this chapter for a worksheet to use for planning.

Determine Your Resources

As in social media, you do not want to over-extend your resources. Take a look at the resources you have to put toward location marketing, and base your initial plans on that assessment, prioritizing services as you go.

Outline Your Goals

What do you want to achieve with location-based marketing?

Do you want:

- To drive traffic to your location in general?
- Drive more traffic during a particular time of day?
- Sell more of a specific product?
- Increase customer loyalty?
- Improve customer relations?
- Target new customers or established patrons?

Answering these questions will accomplish two things: help you focus your efforts and allow you to establish a baseline for measuring success.

QR Code 3.3:
Location-based marketing plan worksheet[3].

QR Code 3.4:
Location-based marketing presentation[4].

Create Your Optimized Presence

For each tool you decide to develop, create an optimized presence as follows:

- Fill out your business profile or page completely.
- Use edited descriptions that include your best keywords.
- Properly categorize your business, where applicable, so it places well in searches.
- Upload custom logos or banners where applicable.
- Integrate your other social media tools—like blogs, Twitter, and Facebook, where applicable.
- Take advantage of any "extras" a service offers, like uploading or linking to promotional videos and photos, or placing QR codes on your page or profile.

Each tool will be different, but most of them have ways for you to stand out in the crowd.

Offer Incentives, Promote, and Engage

Once you have updated and optimized your profile within a service, start looking into ways you can utilize the service to drive traffic to your business or fulfill other established goals.

Some popular incentives include:

- Offering "digital punch cards"—like "get a free cup of coffee with every tenth check-in"
- Providing deals, specials, and rewards specific to individual services
- Offering raffles—where each check-in is entered to win a prize
- Providing "mayorships" to the customer who checks in most often, and giving them special privileges
- Creating rewards for regular customers and discounts for newcomers
- Offering challenges and treks in specialty services like SCVNGR

Research how your competitors are leveraging these services for more ideas.

Let your customers know in which services you are offering deals or other incentives. Provide table tents or other promotional material in your store or venue making your mobile information available, so they can find you on their LBS of choice.

And don't forget to engage your customers. Responding to customer reviews and acknowledging concerns lets your customers know you are listening and improves customer loyalty. Engagement is a key factor to success in any type of social media marketing campaign.

Track Your Results

Many location-based services provide analytics dashboards so you can see how well your page or a specific campaign is doing. In addition to these tools, measure your success using the goals you set for your campaign.

Where to Go from Here

This section is meant to be an introduction to location-based marketing. If you have a local business, you should pursue these marketing techniques further. There are a number of good books and articles in the resource section of the chapter that can help you create and maintain a more developed location-based marketing plan.

Mobile Advertising Campaigns

▶ **Bootstrapper's Guide** ◀

✔ Adwords for mobile is hot right now, but has different requirements.
✔ Create separate mobile campaigns from regular Adwords campaigns.
✔ Advertising in mobile apps offer rich media opportunities.
✔ Mobile-optimized landing pages are vital to good ad conversions.

While many people have become desensitized to ads when browsing the Internet on desktop computers, studies show that mobile device users are much more likely to respond to mobile ads.

In a study from Google conducted by Ipsos OTX[16]:

- 71% of smartphone users search because of an ad they've seen either online or offline.
- 82% of smartphone users notice mobile ads.
- 74% of smartphone shoppers make a purchase as a result of using their smartphones to help with shopping.
- 88% of those who look for local information on their smartphones take action within a day.

There are many ways you can tap into mobile advertising at very little cost. In this section we provide an introduction to pay-per-click advertising,

advertising in mobile applications, and the importance of mobile-friendly landing pages.

Google Adwords for Mobile

Pay-per-click advertising (PPC) is a common type of Internet advertising. The advertiser places an ad on a website—usually a search engine—and pays a small fee every time the ad is clicked. The process can get more complicated, but that is it in a nutshell.

Adwords is Google's solution to PPC advertising. Using Google Adwords[17], you create an ad campaign containing as many individual ads as you like, and assign relevant keywords to the entire campaign. When your keywords are relevant to a user's Google search (and your "bid" is high enough), your ad appears on the page along with the search results.

If you are not familiar with this form of advertising, you should learn as much as possible before jumping in. There are many good tutorials and books on creating successful PPC ad campaigns. Refer to the resource section of this chapter for recommended readings. The remainder of this section assumes that the reader has a working knowledge of Google Adword campaigns.

First, do not assume that your existing Google Adword campaigns are running on Google's mobile search engine! Google has special requirements for the ads it places on its mobile engine. This means that you are missing out on a lot of potential customers if your ads do not comply. Read more about Google's mobile search engine on page 84.

Rather than adding mobile ads to existing campaigns, create a separate campaign for your mobile ads. Figure 3.26 shows how to create a campaign targeted at mobile devices. Choosing the "Mobile and tablet devices only" option means that the ads in your campaign will target those specific mobile devices. Another reason to create a separate mobile campaign is to target a campaign's keyword list by using shorter terms more conducive to mobile search (read more about choosing keywords on page 85).

Figure 3.26:
Creating a
mobile ad
campaign.

Every ad within this "mobile" campaign will be targeted to mobile devices like smartphones and tablets, but if you want your ads to also target feature phones, you need to create ads specifically to do so. When creating that type of ad, choose "WAP mobile ad" as the ad type (see Figure 3.27).

Figure 3.27:

Creating a
WAP ad.

You are given additional options when creating a WAP mobile ad, such as including a phone number mobile device users can dial from within the ad, or a physical address the user can use to access a map (see Figure 3.28).

One requirement for creating a mobile Adwords ad is that your ad links to a mobile-ready landing page. Google may disapprove your mobile ad if your landing page cannot be viewed properly on mobile devices. The "Mobile Optimized Landing Pages" section on page 205 can walk you through how to create a landing page that will qualify.

Figure 3.28 demonstrates another requirement of a WAP mobile ad: choosing the markup language of your landing page. Google uses this information to determine on which devices to place your ad. If your page is optimized for smartphones only, choose WAP 2.x; if your page is optimized for feature phones as well, choose WAP 1.x also. Refer to the "Testing Your Mobile Website" section on page 90 for more details on markup languages.

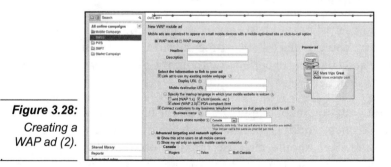

Figure 3.28:

Creating a
WAP ad (2).

Adword WAP ads have more limitations than desktop ads, especially when it comes to text length. Figure 3.29 shows an Adwords WAP text ad set up page. There is only room for 18 characters in the header and description fields for the ad, and the display URL can only be 20 characters. Figure 3.30 shows the size limitations for WAP image ads.

Figure 3.29,
Figure 3.30:
Creating a
WAP ad (3).

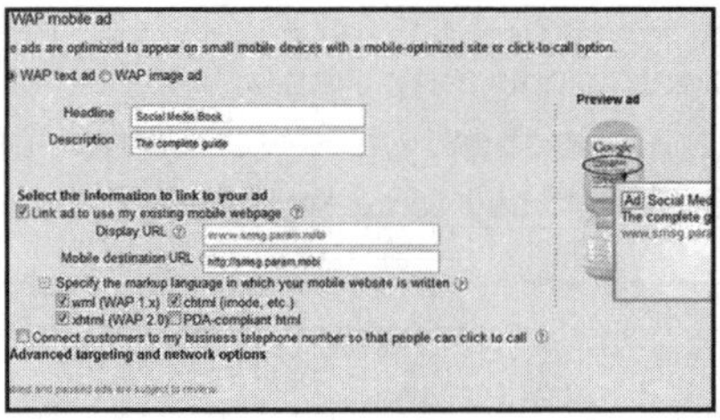

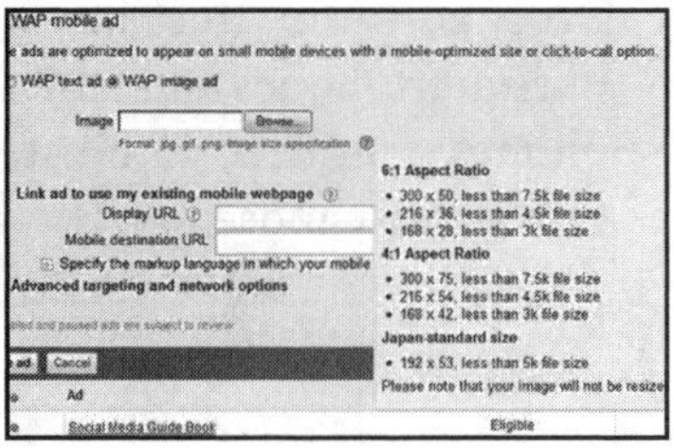

Rich Media Ads

Tablet computer and smartphone users tend to respond better to ads that encourage interactivity or that take advantage of the native features of their devices. These types of ads are referred to as "rich media" ads, and include formats such as:

- Click-to-interactive video: The user chooses to click on an ad to watch a video on their mobile device.
- Animated banners: This type of banner ad takes advantage of tablet computer media capabilities like simple animation or audio.
- Expandable banners: This is a banner ad that expands to the width of the device when clicked.

You can place rich media ads in Google and other ad networks. See the resource section of the chapter for more sources.

Mobile App Advertising

In addition to mobile ad campaigns that target websites and search engines as discussed above, you can place ads within mobile applications (read more about mobile applications on page 109).

Mobile app ad campaigns are best served as rich media so they can fully engage the user. You can place static banner ads in apps, but offering users an interactive and engaging experience without the need to leave the active app will likely yield better results.

When creating ads for mobile apps, be mindful of load times. This can be challenging when working with rich media, but it is essential to good conversion rates. You should also use mobile-optimized landing pages when applicable. Never send a user to a landing page or a website that is not compatible with their device. See page 205 for more details.

The two biggest players in the mobile app ad market are Google's Admob[18] and Apple's iAd[19]. Visit these sites to learn more about mobile app ad campaigns.

Custom Search Ads, Proximity, and Beyond

Google recently developed a way to bring its Adword search ads to mobile apps. Google's "Custom Search Ads"[20] are designed for mobile apps that offer search capabilities. Google provides a way for app developers to display ads within their apps relevant to what users are searching for.

"Mobile App Extensions" is a Google ad feature still in beta, where users can be directed to one app from another app installed on their device based on their search results within the first app. For example, if someone searches for a specific book on a mobile device, they might see an ad that takes them to a relevant page on a shopping app they already have installed on their device.

Since "local" is such an important element of mobile search, Google now uses what it calls "proximity as a factor in mobile search ads ranking." This means that Adword ads for businesses with a closer proximity to a mobile device user will have a better chance of appearing at the top of search results during a relevant Google search.

These are just a few of the trends popping up in the mobile ad world. Since mobile device and mobile app advertising is relatively new, there is no telling where it will go. Keeping abreast of the latest trends is worth the effort if you do—or plan to do—a lot of online advertising. Keep up with these and other trends at the Google Mobile Ads Blog[21].

Mobile Optimized Landing Pages

A landing page is the page a user is directed to once they click on an ad, like the pay-per-click and mobile app ads we discussed in the previous sections. To maximize the conversion rate (the rate at which the ad's call-to-action is acted upon) of an ad campaign, landing pages should follow certain best practices. Here are a few important guidelines to follow for creating successful landing pages:

- A landing page should be relevant to the ad that sent the user there in the first place—you should create a different landing page for every campaign.
- Get to the point in as few words as possible—you only have seconds to make a conversion.
- Make your call-to-action very clear—use large links or buttons for emphasis.
- Do not make the user scroll—if it cannot be helped, make certain your call-to-action is above the fold.

- Require as little as possible from the user—keep forms short and clicks to a minimum.

This is only a partial list of landing page best practices. Refer to the resource section of the chapter for suggestions for further reading.

In addition to the elements that make a good landing page in general, there are additional considerations when creating a mobile optimized landing page.

First, your landing page must be mobile ready and compliant. As we discovered in the previous section, Google may even disapprove your mobile ad if it does not go to a mobile ready page. Refer to the "Mobile Websites" chapter for a complete guide to creating mobile-friendly and optimized websites and pages.

Next, more than any other type of mobile web page you create, mobile landing pages should not force the user to scroll. You need to make your point and invoke a call-to-action in seconds—forced scrolling can kill that process fast.

Finally, every page in the conversion process needs to be mobile optimized. Providing a mobile optimized landing page that sends the user to a product page or an opt-in form that displays poorly (or not at all) on the user's mobile device can quickly end a conversion. Make every page in the conversion process fast loading, easy to read, and easy for the user to enter information. See QR Code 3.5 for a video on creating landing pages.

Landing Page Examples

Figure 3.31, Figure 3.32, and Figure 3.33 show the process from a Google Adwords ad to the final conversion page in a mobile campaign for Plumb Web Solutions. The goal is to increase the company's mailing list. The call-to-action is for the user to subscribe to the company's newsletter.

QR Code 3.5:
Mobile landing
page video[5].

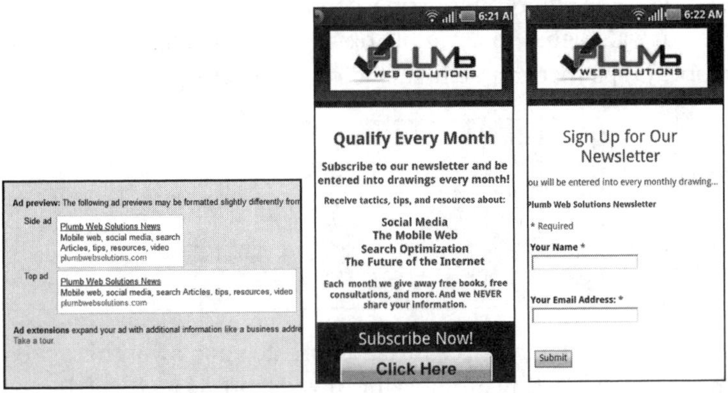

Figure 3.31,

Figure 3.32,

Figure 3.33:

Mobile landing page example.

The mobile landing page was created using Google Sites. The page is mobile ready, mobile compliant, and does not force the user to scroll to see the call-to-action button. Once the call-to-action button is pressed, another mobile optimized page appears with a minimum of required information.

Figure 3.34, Figure 3.35, and Figure 3.36 show the conversion process for a mobile sales campaign for the book, *The Social Media Survival Guide*. This landing page was created using the hosting service mobiSiteGalore (see page 40). This site is a little different since it has a couple of menu choices that direct the user to buy the book from Amazon or from Barnes & Noble (a landing page like this is often called a "micro site").

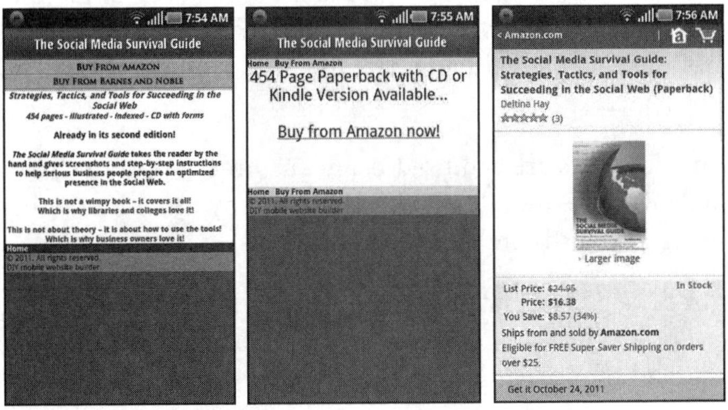

Figure 3.34,

Figure 3.35,

Figure 3.36:

Mobile landing page example (2).

Every page of the micro site is mobile optimized. Since Amazon has a mobile version of their site that detects mobile devices, the user has a mobile optimized experience throughout the entire process.

Figure 3.37 shows an Adwords ad for Social Media Power Tools. Since the Power Tools site is a responsive website (see page 62), they can safely direct mobile users right to a page on their site. Though this direct approach may not be recommended for landing pages, we can be assured that the page will render properly on mobile devices, and that each link on the page also goes to a mobile optimized page. Specifically, the links go to mobile apps that can be installed on the user's phone.

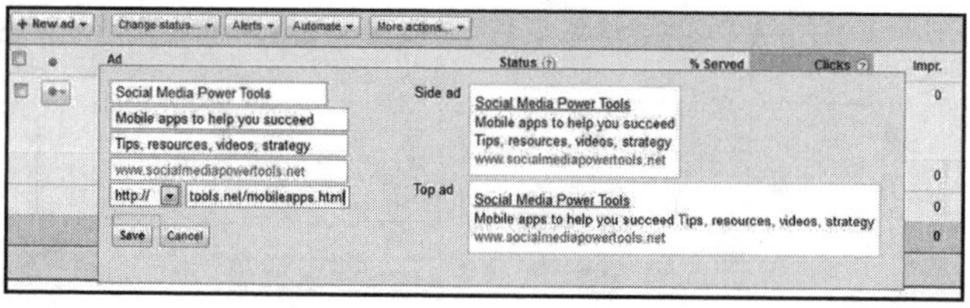

Figure 3.37:
Mobile landing page example (3).

If you do not have the resources to create your own, there are services that specialize in creating mobile-optimized landing pages. Refer to the resource section of this chapter for more information

SMS Marketing

> **▶ Bootstrapper's Guide ◀**
>
> ✓ SMS is like email marketing, using text messages to send campaigns.
> ✓ A short code is a short telephone number to use for your campaigns.
> ✓ Using mobile-optimized landing pages is vital to good conversion.
> ✓ Use ethical practices like you would for email marketing campaigns.

Similar to email marketing, SMS marketing uses SMS (Short Message Service) text messaging to send updates, offers, coupons, and other promotions and advertising via the text messaging functionality of a mobile device.

SMS mailing lists are acquired using customer opt-in techniques through a mobile website, mobile applications, and by using marketing campaigns involving keywords and short codes.

A short code is a special telephone number that is only 5 to 6 digits long. A campaign encouraging a person to take an action using a short code may look something like this:

"Text JOIN to 12345 to join our mailing list" or "JOIN@12345 to join our mailing list"

Short codes are managed by the Common Short Code Administration[22], and can be acquired for a hefty monthly fee. Alternatively, there are services that lease short codes as well as manage your campaigns and databases, similar to how email marketing services like Constant Contact operate.

Just like email marketing, SMS marketing is abused by spammers. It is important to use a reputable SMS service that prohibits spamming by requiring your lists to be opt-in only. This allows you to protect your business' reputation and avoid inadvertently spamming potential customers. Refer to the Mobile Marketing Association's code of conduct[23] for best practices when using SMS marketing.

Three services that support the MMA's codes of conduct are mobileStorm[24], Texages[25], and TextMarks[26].

SMS marketing campaigns can be useful for:

- Acquiring numbers and email addresses for mailing lists
- Sending coupons and special offers
- Administering polls and quizzes
- Sending news and RSS feed updates
- Sending event or meeting reminders
- Promoting social media accounts
- Promoting mobile websites and applications
- Location marketing campaigns

Keep in mind that SMS is *mobile* marketing. The calls-to-action within your SMS campaigns should be mobile-friendly. Any functionality within your messages should be designed for mobile devices, and links should only go to mobile-ready websites or mobile-optimized landing pages (see page 205).

Social Media Diligence

> ▶ **Bootstrapper's Guide** ◀
>
> ✔ Social media is a big part of the mobile web; use it in your strategy.
> ✔ Use QR codes and location-based strategies in social media accounts.
> ✔ Link to social media in your mobile web campaigns and sites.
> ✔ Learn how your audience uses social media tools on mobile devices.

Most of the mobile web tools discussed in this book affect how people use social media in one way or another. The mobile web, like social media, is about interacting and engaging. Your mobile web strategy should be an extension of your social media strategy and an opportunity to make a new commitment to a strong social media presence.

Here are some places to start:

- Use location-based services (LBS) to engage with your customers and integrate them into your existing social media strategy.
- Use mobile app versions of your favorite social media tools like Facebook and Twitter—this can give you firsthand knowledge of how your customers are using social media on their mobile devices.
- Use social media tools like Flipboard[27] to get a feel for how people access social media sites on tablet computers.
- Learn how to utilize SMS with your social media accounts and blogs—for example, you can interact with your WordPress blog, send Tweets, or make Facebook updates using text messaging.
- Use QR codes to drive mobile traffic to your social media accounts from your website, other social media accounts, and print media.
- Make your social media presence known throughout your entire mobile web presence—place social media badges and links wherever you can.

These tactics can help you rethink, reposition, and even revitalize your social media presence. For information on creating an optimized presence in the social web, read the author's book, *The Social Media Survival Guide*. There are other suggested readings in the resource section of this chapter.

Mobile Trends to Watch Closely

> ▶ **Bootstrapper's Guide** ◀
>
> √ Augmented reality and object recognition can benefit local businesses.
> √ Become familiar with mobile search apps and browsers for good SEO.
> √ Near field communication is the future of mobile payments and more.
> √ Context awareness is the new SEO—leverage this now to stay ahead.

Augmented Reality

Augmented reality (AR) and object recognition are terms used to describe mobile apps and other types of software that "recognize" objects (usually through a smartphone camera) from the "real world" and provide information about the object or its surroundings to the user. See QR Code 3.6 for an augmented reality presentation.

If an object is recognized by the AR app, the user might be offered additional information about the object or about other items or businesses in the object's proximity, given advanced search options based on the object or geographic area, or provided with an interactive experience based on the object. Popular AR mobile browsers like Wikitude[28] combine augmented reality with location-based services to provide an interactive experience for the user (see Figure 3.38).

Figure 3.38:
wikitude.

This type of technology is clearly beneficial for local businesses, but can also be useful for promoting tangible goods. The object recognition app Google Goggles[29] offers mobile device users a way to scan any object and receive information about that object. If the object is a product or book that is in the Google Product Search directory[30] or the Google Books database[31], then the user is directed accordingly.

Figure 3.39 and Figure 3.40 show the results when a book cover is scanned using Google Goggles. Since this book is in both the Google Product Search directory and the Google Books database, the user is given the option to find the book using one of these options, or perform a traditional web search using the book title.

Figure 3.39,
Figure 3.40:

Google
Goggles
example.

Figure 3.41 shows the other types of items and objects you can scan with Goggles, including landmarks, art, logos, even translation services. Goggles also allows users to contribute to the Goggles project by offering their own

QR Code 3.6:
Augmented
reality
presentation[6].

information on an object if it cannot be found in the existing database or is misrepresented.

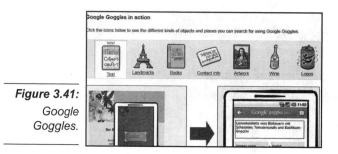

Figure 3.41:
Google
Goggles.

At this time, the best way to leverage AR and object recognition applications is to become familiar with the most popular apps and take measures to ensure your business and products are represented accurately within them. You can also brainstorm ways to get your name or your business name to show up on popular landmarks. Refer to the resource section of this chapter for a list of popular apps.

Search Apps

Like the AR browser apps discussed earlier, there are other popular search applications that mobile device users turn to for a more specialized search experience. UrbanSpoon[32] is a search app that only searches for information related to restaurants and food in general. RedLaser[33] is a search app that allows users to scan bar codes from products to find out where the best deals are.

You should investigate apps that your target market may be using to find your business or products, and research ways of getting good placement within the apps. Recall that the Google Adwords platform offers mobile search app developers ways to feature Adword ads directly in their apps (see page 205). This could be an easy and affordable way to get your products or business into these search apps.

Look in the resource section of this chapter for a list of more search apps you may want to research.

Near Field Communication

Near Field Communication (NFC) is a technology that allows devices a way to transmit small bits of data when they are in close proximity to each other. NFC can be used to transmit credit card information, ticket purchase information, contact information, etc. And when we say "close," we mean the devices need to be very close—like almost touching—and transactions are controlled using PIN numbers like a debit transaction. This makes the technology more secure, and that is a good thing since it is the technology that powers what is referred to as "contactless pay." See QR Code 3.7 for a presentation on NFC.

Google Wallet[34] is the most prevalent contactless pay mobile application at this time. It can be used to make small purchases using a mobile device and the Google Wallet app for Android. Users "swipe" their phone along a reader the same way they might swipe a credit card. The app is only available on certain phones using specific plans, but its usage is growing steadily. If you want to become an early adopter, go to the Google Wallet[35] merchant's page to apply. PayPal also has an NFC app only available in the Android market as of March 2012.

One reason Wallet is only offered on certain phones is because each device in a transaction must have an NFC chip. Though the number of phones in use with NFC chips—as of this writing—is low, every new smartphone coming to the market in 2012 will most likely have NFC chips embedded. And with both Google and the major credit card companies backing the technology, NFC usage is expected to skyrocket.

Beyond contactless pay, NFC can be used to transmit information between individual mobile devices by "bumping" them together, or from products and media with NFC tags attached—similar to how QR codes are used. Unlike QR codes, NFC tags are communication chips (more akin to Bluetooth), so scanning a NFC tag creates a two-way connection between the tag and the mobile device.

NFC technology is expected to bring mobile device usage to a new level of engagement with the real world. Some of the ways we might use NFC technology include:

- Bumping phones with friends to instantly share music, video, or image files
- Bumping phones with colleagues and clients to exchange contact information
- Purchasing tickets and checking in at airline kiosks and terminals

QR Code 3.7:
Near field communication presentation[7].

- Paying highway tolls, bus fair, or subway fees
- Transmitting health records to hospitals and doctors
- Connecting to wireless networks or pairing with Bluetooth devices
- Friending someone on Facebook or Google Plus with a "bump"
- Joining a multiplayer game with a friend
- Using as a hotel key
- Redeeming coupons and offers from merchants
- Using your phone as an ID or membership card

Security will be a concern for many people, but most supporters are confident that NFC will change the way we use our mobile devices. Especially since the same phones that are rolling into the market with NFC technology also have security features built in, like fingerprint and face recognition capabilities.

Look in the resource section of this chapter for additional reading suggestions and resources.

On Becoming Context-Aware

Context-aware is a blanket term that refers to applications and browsers that tap into a mobile device user's information to make the app or browsing experience more relevant and personal for the user. A context-aware app or browser may use information about a user's search history, interests, installed apps, geographic location, social media accounts, schedule, and more to anticipate the user's needs and suggest products, other apps, search terms, local businesses, or other relevant content depending on the function of the app.

Many of the tools we discuss in this book—location-based services, augmented reality, NFC, search apps—rely on context-aware algorithms to give users a more personalized experience. Even Google's mobile search algorithm, discussed on page 86, uses context-aware elements to make search result determinations. Context-aware apps are already here to stay; what we need to focus on is how context-aware search is going to affect search optimization in general.

Context-aware search trends will force us to make a paradigm shift in how we think about search optimization—especially as it applies to mobile devices. Part of this shift needs to be in understanding that mobile devices—smartphones in particular—are *not* personal computers. As we have learned throughout this book, smartphones are very personal devices that people use differently than desktop computers.

Mobile app developers can safely assume that only one person will be using a particular smartphone, and that the user has taken security precautions to keep others from accessing their device. This means that context-aware apps are more likely to appeal to smartphone users and work effectively on their devices since the app can hyper-focus on a single person's information, history, and habits. And what we know about the habits of mobile device users is that they prefer to be served local and relevant content and are more likely to act on it as a result.

It is easy to envision how mobile device usage and context-aware concepts apply to location-based marketing and tangible products. The challenge is figuring out how these trends affect search optimization for the rest of us. The best answer to this quandary is to apply organic search techniques to all of your content.

Gone are the days of convincing a search engine that your content is relevant just by placing keywords in your HTML—your content needs to be truly relevant and meaningful to place well in today's search engines. Organic search techniques can help you achieve this. Read more about organic search techniques on page 85, and look for the author's next book in this series, *The Bootstrapper's Guide to Organic Search*.

Here are some other ways you might leverage context-aware search apps and databases:

- Investigate the most popular search apps to see how your content is represented, and take measures to correct discrepancies.
- Determine where popular apps get their data and make certain your content is present and accurate in those data sources.
- Advertise in apps that are relevant to your target market.
- Investigate location-based services for opportunities to list your business, even if it does not have a physical address.
- Find creative ways to get your name or your business name attached to landmarks or other objects in AR and object recognition apps and databases.
- Keep abreast of the latest trends in context-aware apps and technologies.

Refer to the resource section of this chapter for a list of popular search apps, browsers, and organic search resources.

Endnotes

1. Gartner Newsroom. "Gartner Highlights Key Predictions for IT Organizatins and Users in 2010 and Beyond." http://www.gartner.com/it/page.jsp?id=1278413

2. QR Stuff.com. http://www.qrstuff.com

3. QRlicious. http://www.qrlicious.com

4. Craig Sullender. http://bitepress.com

5. ISO International Organization for Standardization. http://www.iso.org/iso/iso_catalogue/catalogue_tc/catalogue_detail.htm?csnumber=43655

6. Esponce. http://www.esponce.com

7. foursquare. https://foursquare.com

8. foursquare For Business. https://foursquare.com/business/merchants

9. Google places. http://www.google.com/places

10. Google places. "Connecting your business with local customers." https://www.google.com/local/add

11. Yelp. http://www.yelp.com

12. Yelp for Business Owners. https://biz.yelp.com/support

13. SCVNGR. http://www.scvngr.com

14. SCVNGR Small Business. http://www.scvngr.com/business

15. All Facebook. "The Unofficial Facebook Resource." http://www.allfacebook.com/facebook-places-business-2010-08

16. Telenav. Inc. "Survey Find One-Third of Americans More Willing to Give up Sex Than Their Mobile Phones." http://www.telenav.com/about/pr-summer-travel/report-20110803.html

17. Google Ad Words. http://adwords.google.com

18. Google Mobile Ads. http://www.google.com/ads/mobile/advertisers/build-your-brand.html

19. iAd Network. http://advertising.apple.com/brands

20. Google Mobile Ads Blog. "The power of search ads, now in mobile apps and sites." http://googlemobileads.blogspot.com/2011/10/power-of-search-ads-now-in-mobile-apps.html

21. Google Mobile Ads Blog. http://googlemobileads.blogspot.com

22. CSCA. Common Short Code Administration. http://usshortcodes.com

23. MMA Mobile Marketing Association. http://mmaglobal.com/policies/code-of-conduct

24. mobileStorm. http://www.mobilestorm.com

25. Texages. http://www.texages.com

26. TextMarks. http://www.textmarks.com

27. Flipboard. http://flipboard.com

28. wikitude. http://www.wikitude.com/en

29. Google Goggles. http://www.google.com/mobile/goggles/#text

30. Google product search beta. http://www.google.com/m/products

31. Google books. http://books.google.com

32. Urbanspoon. http://www.urbanspoon.com/choose

33. RedLaser. http://redlaser.com

34. Google wallet. http://www.google.com/wallet

35. Google wallet for Merchants. http://www.google.com/wallet/merchants.html

QR Code Notes

1. Custom QR Code Gallery. http://goo.by/wDSCmR/bgmw3-1

2. QR Code Marketing Campaign Worksheet. http://goo.by/w9Iqw5/bgmw3-2

3. Location-Based Marketing Campaign Worksheet. http://goo.by/w9Jo6K/bgmw3-3

4. Location-Based Marketing Presentation. http://goo.by/wWJz73/bgmw3-4

5. Creating a Mobile Landing Page Video. http://goo.by/w9cRkD/bgmw3-5

6. Augmented Reality Presentation. http://goo.by/w4WkQs/bgmw3-6

7. Near Field Communication Presentation. http://goo.by/wNYWKy/bgmw3-7

8. Chapter Three Resources. http://goo.by/w4wnqS/bgmw3-8

Additional Resources

Resources for the topics covered in this chapter can be found at TheBootstrappersGuide.com under the categories listed below. Additional resources and examples are added to the website on a regular basis.

Other Mobile Resources

- QR Code Scanning Apps
- QR Code Tools
- QR Code Services
- QR Code Tutorials
- QR Code Branding Tutorials
- QR Code Software
- Location-Based Services
- Location-Based Marketing Solutions
- Location-Based Books and Articles
- PPC Ad Campaign Books and Articles
- SMS Marketing Resources
- Rich Media Ad Services
- Landing Page Best Practices Articles
- Mobile Optimized Landing Page Services
- Augmented Reality Apps and Resources
- Object Recognition Apps and Resources
- Near Field Communication Resources
- Social Media Optimization Resources
- Mobile Search Apps
- Organic Search Optimization Resources

Other Mobile Tactics Worksheets

- QR Code Marketing Strategy
- Location-Based Marketing Strategy

Other Mobile Examples

- QR Code Examples
- QR Code Tool Examples

QR Code 3.8:
Chapter three resources[8].

Conclusion

Slow and Steady Wins the Race

We cannot predict where Internet technology will take us next. This makes it difficult to establish permanent optimization methods, but there are tried-and-true methods you can apply to your online endeavors, whether on traditional or mobile websites, or in social media or whatever is next year's model.

Bootstrappers know how efforts made today pay off in sales, leads, and customers tomorrow. Making efforts to have an optimized web presence are no different. If you select and use relevant key terms organically throughout your entire web presence today, that effort will yield positive results in the future.

But you must keep in mind that context is now an important element as we discussed on page 214. On page 86, we discussed how mobile search trends like Google Instant affect search results. The importance of *local* search is equally important. Your key term list should include local, personalized, and highly relevant terms that are as short as possible.

Once you have your key terms, apply them to your web presence by:

- Using them naturally in your meta titles, meta descriptions, and meta keywords on every one of your relevant web pages
- Using them in your social media profiles and other relevant places across your entire web presence
- Using them as tags in your relevant social media accounts and in online directories
- Using them in your outgoing link text and in the alt text of embedded images on every one of your relevant web pages and blog posts
- Using them within relevant titles, descriptions, and content body of every blog post

You want to include key terms only where they fall naturally into your web content. This should not be an issue if you choose highly relevant key terms. Such key terms do not need to be "planted." They will be a part of your natural, "organic" content—words that describe your business as it is.

So, I rest my case for consistency, relevancy, and the use of organic search optimization (until the next book, that is). And there was much rejoicing!

Here's to success in the mobile web...

Glossary of Terms

The following glossary of terms is not meant to be an exhaustive list of terms used in the book. They are terms that may not be defined within the text, or are used prior to being defined. Some of the definitions are taken from—or paraphrased from—the free encyclopedia, Wikipedia.org.

3G/4G: These represent the third and fourth generations of standards for mobile phones and mobile telecommunication services. Some of the standards include peak speed requirements, wireless voice telephone, mobile Internet access, video calls, and mobile TV.

Alt Text: Alternate (Alt) Text is text that is assigned to an image placed on a web page. The text appears in place of the image when the image cannot be displayed.

Analytics: Web analytics allows marketers to collect information about interactions on a website. Interactions provide the information to track the referrer, search keywords, IP address, and activities of the visitor.

API: An application programming interface (API) is an interface implemented by a software program which enables it to interact with other software.

Badge: Often used interchangeably with "widget," a badge is typically a graphical representation of a link that, when clicked on, takes the user to another site.

Cloud Service: Delivers software as a service over the Internet, eliminating the need to install and run the application on the customer's own computers and simplifying maintenance and support.

CMS: A content management system (CMS) is an application that is used to create, edit, manage, and publish content in an organized way. Web applications like WordPress do this by storing information in a database, and using scripting languages like PHP to access the information and place it on a website.

CNAME Record: A Canonical Name (CNAME) record is used to assign an alias to a subdomain for redirection purposes. You might assign a CNAME record to a subdomain like m.domain.com that directs visitors to the mobile version of your website.

CSS/CSS3: Cascading Style Sheets (CSS) is a style sheet language used to describe the look and formatting of a document written in a markup language like HTML. CSS3 is the latest version of the language.

Dashboard: A term used to describe the main control panel or home screen of a web-based service like a mobile web creation tool.

Desktop Browser: A web browser designed to work on a desktop computer or laptop. A desktop browser assumes a larger screen than a mobile browser does.

DNS: The Domain Name System (DNS) serves as the phone book for the Internet by translating human-friendly computer host names into IP addresses. For example, the domain name www.example.com translates to the addresses 192.0.32.10 (IPv4) and 2620:0:2d0:200::10 (Ipv6).

E-commerce: Electronic commerce (e-commerce) refers to the buying and selling of products or services over electronic systems such as the Internet.

Embed Code: Sometimes you want to pull information from outside sources onto your own website or blog—like a promotional widget for a web app. This is accomplished by copying code like HTML or Javascript from another site and pasting (or placing) it on your own site. This code is referred to as "embed code."

Feature Phone: A feature phone is similar to a smartphone, but has a less sophisticated operating system. Internet browsing, viewing video, and other high-end functionality is more difficult to accomplish with a feature phone.

Flash: Owned by Adobe, Flash is a multimedia platform used to add animation, video, and interactivity to web pages.

Framework: A web application framework is designed to support the development of dynamic websites, web applications and web services by providing libraries, databases, sample code, and templates.

Handheld: A small, hand-held computing device, typically having a display screen with touch input and/or a miniature keyboard. Used interchangeably with "mobile device."

Hosting: Short for web hosting, is a service that allows individuals and organizations to make their own websites accessible on the Internet. Web host companies provide space on their own servers for their clients to use.

HTML/HTML5: HyperText Markup Language (HTML) is the predominant markup language for web pages. HTML elements are the basic building blocks of web pages. HTML5 is the latest version of the language.

Icon: A small graphic image displayed on a computer screen that functions as a hyperlink or file shortcut to access a program on a computer system or mobile device.

JavaScript: A scripting language primarily used as part of a web browser for providing enhanced user interfaces and dynamic websites. JavaScript code is typically placed in or referenced from an HTML document.

Key Term: A term used to describe the meta keywords used in a web page, or the tags used to represent a website in directories, so that users can find the page easily in searches.

Landing Page: A landing page is the page on a website that a specific link returns to. So, if you place an ad on the Internet and include a link within the ad, the landing page for that link is where it sends the user to your site when they click on the link. It is common practice to create specific landing pages for tracking ads and other campaigns since page traffic is easily measured.

Legacy Browser: An older version of a web browser that is no longer in common use.

Meta Description: Part of the metadata of a web page, the meta description is placed in the header section of a web page, and is used by search robots to help categorize a web page. The meta description also serves as a way to let potential visitors know what is contained on a web page.

Meta Keyword: Part of the metadata of a web page, the meta keywords help search engines categorize a web page. Think of keywords as the terms that someone would enter into Google when searching for your site.

Meta Title: Part of the metadata of a web page, the meta title is placed in the header section of a web page, and is used by search robots to help categorize a web page. The meta title is the first thing a potential visitor sees in search results, so it is important that it accurately represents a web page.

Metadata: As it applies to search optimization, metadata is information about a web page that is used to help search engine robots properly categorize a web page in a search index. The most common metadata elements are meta title, meta description, and meta keywords.

Mobile Browser: A web browser designed to work on a mobile device. A mobile browser assumes a smaller screen than a desktop browser does.

Mobile Device: A small, hand-held computing device, typically having a display screen with touch input and/or a miniature keyboard. Used interchangeably with "handheld."

Multimedia: Used to describe a combination of text, audio, still images, animation, video, or interactivity content forms.

Open Source: Open-source software is software whose source code is published and made available to the public, enabling anyone to use, copy, modify, and redistribute the source code without paying royalties or fees.

Operating System: An operating system (OS) is a set of programs that manage computer hardware resources and provide common services for application software. A user cannot run an application program on the computer without an operating system.

Opt-In: A term that usually refers to how a user is added to mailing or subscription lists. Opt-in means that the user has chosen or "opted" to be added to a list.

Organic Search Optimization: Search optimization technique that relies on authenticity, relevancy, and consistency of web content. Modern search robots are better able to determine the relevancy of content without the need to rely on metadata, so producing relevant content is the key to optimization.

Permalink: A direct or "permanent" link to a blog post. Though originally used to define links to blog posts, it has evolved to refer to any permanent link to a web page or subdomain.

Placing Code: Sometimes you want to pull information from outside sources onto your own Website or blog—like a promotional widget for a web app. This is accomplished by copying code like HTML or Javascript from another site and pasting (or placing) it on your own site. This process is referred to as "placing code."

Proprietary Software: Software that is not open source software. The software may be free to use, but the code cannot be altered or distributed freely.

RSS Feed: RSS stands for Really Simple Syndication. An RSS feed is an XML file containing information—like blog posts, images, and video—that allows you to syndicate (share) that information across the Internet.

Script: Scripts are small programs written in a scripting language and run by a web browser to change the appearance or behavior of a web page, for example, to change the content to be specific to the current user.

Scripting Language: Scripting languages are special-purpose language used specifically to control the operation of web browsers and a user's interaction with a web page.

Scripting Library: A collection of pre-written scripts for scripting languages like JavaScript that allows for easier development of applications.

Sidebar: Similar to a column, a sidebar is the area on a web page that contains ads, widgets, links, and other elements separate from the main content area of the page.

Smartphone: A high-end mobile phone built on a mobile computing platform with more advanced computing ability and connectivity than a contemporary feature phone.

Social Media: A blanket term used to describe the interactive tools of Web 2.0, including blogs, social networking sites, media communities (like YouTube and Flickr), social bookmarking sites, wikis, etc.

Splash Screen: An image that appears while a game or program is loading that usually encompasses the entire screen.

Streaming: Streaming media is multimedia that is constantly received by and presented to an end-user while being delivered by a streaming provider. The term "streaming" refers to the delivery method of the medium rather than to the medium itself.

Tag: A keyword or term assigned to a piece of information (such as an Internet bookmark, digital image, or web page). This kind of metadata helps describe an item and allows it to be found again by browsing or searching.

Validation: Validation means that an HTML or XHTML document has been checked against established standards for well-formed markup. Markup validation is an important step towards ensuring the technical quality of web pages; however, it is not a complete measure of Web standards conformance.

WAP: Short for "Wireless Application Protocol," is a technical standard for accessing information over a mobile wireless network. A WAP browser is a web browser for mobile devices that use the protocol.

Web-Based: A service or software that can only be accessed via an Internet connection using a web browser.

Wi-Fi: A mechanism for wirelessly connecting electronic devices. A device enabled with Wi-Fi, such as a computer, video game console, or smartphone can connect to the Internet via a wireless network access point (or hot spot) using Wi-Fi.

Widget (also called a "badge"): A small snippet of code that performs some functionality like pulling information from another website, inviting users to subscribe to content, or promoting a website or web app.

WordPress: Though WordPress originated as a blogging platform, it has evolved into a content management system (CMS) capable of powering full-fledged websites.

XHTML: eXtensible HyperText Markup Language (XHTML) is a family of XML markup languages that extend HTML.

XML File: Extensible Markup Language (XML) is a set of rules for encoding documents in machine-readable form. XML is used for defining RSS feeds.

Zipped Folder: A folder containing compressed files.

Index

Symbols

51degrees 83
.apk file 133, 156
.mobi 23
.NET 131

A

AdMob 204
Ad networks. *See* Mobile app
Amazon Appstore 110, 131
  App assets 169–171
  Publishing to 132–133
Android 4, 109, 124, 175, 213
  AppMakr and 151, 156
  appMobi XDK and 143
  Developer account 133, 156, 166
  iBuildApp and 162, 165
  Mobile shortcuts and 147–148
  PhoneGap and 140
  PhoneGap Build and 141
  Push notifications 166
  Redirection and 172
  SDK 130–131
  Tiggzi and 139
  Widgetbox and 157, 161
Android Market 110, 120, 131, 175, 180
  App assets 169–171
  AppMakr and 156
  In-app purchases and 173
  Publishing to 132–133, 156
  Terms of use 174
Apple 146, 149
  Developer account 132, 141, 155, 166–167
  iAd Network 175, 204
  iTunes Connect 132, 173, 175
  Web app directory 116
Apple App Store 110, 120, 172, 175
  App assets 169–171
  AppMakr and 151, 155
  iBuildApp and 162
  Publishing to 131–133, 168

  Resources 184
  Terms of use 174
Apple iOS 4, 121, 173, 175, 179
  AppMakr and 151
  appMobi XDK and 143
  iBuildApp and 162
  PhoneGap and 140
  PhoneGap Build and 141
  Publishing native apps and 167
  Push notifications and 166
  Redirection and 172
  SDK 130–132
  Tiggzi and 139
AppMakr 151–156
  Customizing 153
  Monetizing 154
  Populating your app 152
  Publishing android apps 156
  Publishing Apple apps 155
  Push notifications and 154
  Settings and app assets 152, 154
  Setting up 151
  Testing 155
AppMatcher 176
appMobi XDK 141–142, 146
Appolicious 175, 176
appstorm 176
ASP 56, 82, 83
ASP.NET 56, 82, 83
Augmented reality 210–211
  Resources 218

B

Bills on Your Table 177
Binary file 112, 114, 131–133, 155, 168
Bing 84
Blackberry 92, 112, 121, 131, 133, 177
  Analytics and 179
  PhoneGap and 140–141
  SDK 130–131
Blackberry App World 110, 131
Blackberry Development Environment 131
bMobilized 56
Bootee Catcher 138–139

Brightkite 198
Build file. *See* Binary file

C

Cache-control 90
Certificate Signing Request 167
Click-to-call 18, 47, 53, 72, 73
CMS 2, 24, 27, 30, 31, 57, 63, 88, 101, 224
  Defined 220
  Mobile hosting solutions 62
  Mobile plugin solutions 57
Common Short Code Administration 208
Context-aware 214–215
Crunch4Free 22
CSR file. *See* Certificate Signing Request
CSS 25, 63, 85, 90, 117, 124
  AppMakr and 157
  Defined 220
  HTML5 template and 69–71
  Mobile website best practices and 21
  Responsive web design and 66–67
  Tiggzi and 139
  W3C validation and 93–96
  Web apps and 135
  Widgetbox and 159
CSS3 2, 17, 116, 128, 129, 145
  Defined 220
  JavaScript and 134
  Mobile websites and 70, 143
  Modernizr and 96
  PhoneGap and 140
  PhoneGap Build and 135
  Resources 106, 184
  Web apps and 115, 133, 144
  WebKit and 134
css3-mediaqueries 68
CUBIQ 150
Custom domain 23, 34
  Alias 79
  CNAME record 80
  Configuring 79–81
  DNS record 80
  goMobi and 39
  mobiSiteGalore and 44
  Mofuse and 55

Social media help for entrepreneurs from Internet marketing expert Deltina Hay

$24.95 ($27.95 Canada)

- Specific instructions for the best Social Media tools.

- Targeted strategies focus on the results YOU want.

- Step-by-step guides with hundreds of screenshots make it all easy!

The Social Media Media Survival Guide

Strategies, Tactics, and Tools for Succeeding in the Social Web

—by Deltina Hay, author of *The Bootstrapper's Guide to the Mobile Web*

Effective social media marketing for serious professionals like you! This is a book for the do-it-yourselfer: business owners, authors, publishers, marketers, PR professionals, students, and everyone else who needs to grow their business. *The Social Media Survival Guide* cuts through the clutter to focus on the proven tools that create results. Here are the specific strategies, tactics and tools that will help you reach a global audience, communicate with your customers more personally and effectively, learn what your customers really want, and deliver your message to people who are eager to hear what you have to say.

You'll get specific guidance on using the best Web 2.0 tools that have proven value, including RSS feeds, WordPress sites, podcasting, and social networking, and more important, you'll learn how to integrate these tools in a total Social Media marketing strategy built for your goals.

❝ The most authoritative, comprehensive, and technically accurate guide I have ever seen to social networking. ❞
—Bob Bly, author of over 70 classic business books.

Available from bookstores, online bookstores, and QuillDriverBooks.com, or by calling toll-free 1-800-345-4447.

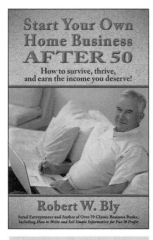

The next Bootstrapper's Guide ... from business technology authority Deltina Hay

The Bootstrapper's Guide to the New Search Optimization

Mastering the New Rules of Organic Search Using Relevancy, Context, and Semantics

—by Deltina Hay, author of *The Bootstrapper's Guide to the Mobile Web*

Optimizing for the Internet today is much more than just traditional search engine optimization (SEO). Social search, real-time search, semantic search, blog/RSS feed search, mobile engine and app search, and other types of search need to be considered for maximum exposure when optimizing for today's Internet.

The Bootstrapper's Guide to the New Search Optimization presents a practical framework that can help anyone achieve optimization in all of the relevant search channels using organic, semantic, and context-aware search techniques.

The Bootstrapper's Guide to The Search Optimization is a hands-on guide using real-world examples, avoiding a lot of technical jargon and cutting right to the heart of the matter—how to make sure your customers can find you.

Bootstrapper's Guides: Fast How-Tos for Jump-Starting Your Business

Available from bookstores, online bookstores, and QuillDriverBooks.com, or by calling toll-free 1-800-345-4447.

About The Author

Deltina Hay is a veteran web developer, publisher, and a pioneer of social media, Web 2.0, and Web 3.0, especially as it applies to small business and the publishing industry. She is an avid writer, presenter, educator, and blogger.

Hay's deep working knowledge of mobile web concepts, as well as how to apply them in the real world, make her writings and presentations some of the most exciting and accessible in the industry today. As the facilitator of many of Drury University's graduate digital marketing courses, she educates businesses and students on the strategies, technologies, and tools for creating a sustainable and optimized presence in the mobile web, the social web, and beyond.

As a publisher, small business owner, author, and bootstrapper in her own right, Hay knows firsthand the amount of traffic that proper online optimization and marketing can drive to a website, as well as the millions of potential customers and readers it can reach and influence. Her writings are filled with practical training in mobile web tactics due to her in-depth knowledge of the tools. She intuitively knows how to apply mobile web technologies because she can actually develop and adapt those technologies for business purposes.

A long-time advocate of open source technologies, Hay has been programming and/or developing for the web for over 25 years. Her graduate education includes computer science, applied mathematics, numerical analysis, fluid dynamics, nonlinear dynamics, and psychology. Hay joined the International Marketing Standards Board's Global Board of Advisors in 2010.

Already in its second edition, Hay's book, *The Social Media Survival Guide*, is used in countless colleges and universities as the basis of their social media and digital marketing courses.

Though a native Alaskan, Ms. Hay lives in Austin, Texas, with her two cats Wolfgang and Ludwig. When she is not in a wireless cafe contemplating the future of the Internet, she is hiking in a Texas State Park, contemplating silence.

More information can be found at http://www.deltina.com.